Shells to Satoshi:
The Story of Money
& The Rise of Bitcoin

Shells to Satoshi:
The Story of Money
& The Rise of Bitcoin

Deanna Heikkinen
with Joel Marquez

ISBN: 978-1-964944-00-5

Library of Congress Control Number: 2024911943

Published by Deanna Heikkinen

Book layout by Deanna Heikkinen
Cover design by Deanna Heikkinen

The information in this book is intended to be helpful and informative but is not a substitute for professional advice. The publisher and author are not responsible for any damages resulting from the use of information contained herein.

Visit the author's website at www.shellstosatoshi.com

For everyone who seeks to live a sovereign life.

Table of Contents

Preface

Throughout human history, few concepts are as universal and as evocative as money. Its story is as complex as the civilizations that have wielded it, a testament to human ingenuity, ambition, and, at times, avarice. As a college professor and private tutor teaching humanities, history, and anthropology, I have spent years exploring the profound narratives that have shaped our world. Yet it is my personal journey, marked by a deep-seated belief in the ideals of sovereignty and liberty and a resolute commitment to the revolutionary potential of Bitcoin, that has led me to write this book.

My academic career, centered on imparting the richness of the humanities, the pivotal moments of history, and the holistic study of humans, was driven by a love for the ideas, greatness, and human condition that came before our present time. In addition, the foundational ideals of the United States through the Declaration of Independence and the Constitution were embedded in me by both my father, who loved the principles that formed America, as well as my own curiosity. These documents represent the first instance in history where a nation was forged not on the whims of rulers or the accidents of geography but on the power of ideas, a bold experiment to ensure sovereignty for every individual. This profound respect for the intellectual underpinnings of freedom has always guided my teaching and research.

However, the journey of an educator is not without its challenges. In 2017, I found myself increasingly at odds with the prevailing winds in academia. Having also just completed a doctorate in education, ironically focusing on intellectual diversity in higher education for my dissertation, I knew I could not fight the broken system from within. The ideological corruption within the education system was just too far gone. That, along with the growing hostility toward the great minds of the Western canon by both students and colleagues, signaled a departure from the traditional academic pursuit of knowledge and critical thought that I held dear. It was this mindset that compelled me to walk away from my tenured post, a decision that, while difficult, was necessary for staying true to my principles. Thus, I started a new journey, creating a homeschool curriculum based on the greatest ideas, writing, and art of the West. I also became a private tutor for homeschool families and for motivated students who attended either private or public schools.

Although my love of teaching will always be part of me and my work, I wanted to make a bigger impact by writing something that could explain what happened to money over time. Through a lens of seeking a happy, sovereign life, I aim to provide a foundation to understand money, something neither myself nor my immediate family ever had growing up and even into adulthood.

Ultimately, this book emerges from a confluence of my experiences and convictions. It is an endeavor to provide context on how humans have continuously invented and reinvented the concept of money, shaping and being shaped by it in turn. Just as the United States, with its groundbreaking foundation, has not been immune to the forces of corruption and cronyism, particularly in the twentieth and twenty-first centuries, so too has the idea of money been manipulated and maligned.

At the heart of this narrative is the story of money. This is told through numerous narratives from history and indigenous societies around the globe. It ends with an explanation of how Bitcoin is the ultimate response to what has happened to money, a subject I have long championed as a "Bitcoin-only" person. Bitcoin represents more than just a technological marvel; it embodies the quest for financial sovereignty in the digital age. Through this book, I aim to inform a wider audience about what Bitcoin is, why it matters, and how it can serve as a bulwark against the excesses of centralized monetary policy. The economic resistance from the elites in positions of power is not merely an economic or technological challenge; it is an ideological battle over the future of individual sovereignty.

The hostility toward Bitcoin and its advocates mirrors the broader struggle against intellectual conformity and the defense of individual liberty. It is my hope that this book will serve as both a historical exploration and a clarion call for a sovereign life guided by the same principles that once inspired a nation to greatness.

As the story delves into the history of money, from ancient civilizations to the digital frontier, it uncovers not just the evolution of currency but also the story of human aspiration. It is a narrative that is ever-unfolding, challenging us to reimagine the possibilities of our future.

In writing this book, I seek not only to educate but also to inspire. May the story within its pages provide a deeper understanding of the forces that shape the world and bring forth the courage to forge a path toward greater sovereignty, both financial and personal, for individuals and their families.

With Gratitude,
Deanna Heikkinen
El Salvador, June 2024

Acknowledgements

As I reflect on the journey of writing this book, I am overwhelmed with gratitude for the network of friends and family who stood by me throughout this challenging yet rewarding process. First and foremost, I must extend my deepest thanks to my husband and co-author, Joel. Not only did he introduce me to Bitcoin in 2011, leading me down the rabbit hole with such patience over the years, but he has also been a fundamental contributor to this book. Joel has been my rock through leaving academia, starting and ending several businesses, and through our challenging but rewarding move to El Salvador. His insights have added profound clarity and depth to the philosophical discussions, Bitcoin explorations, and several of the later chapters. Although our journey together through the creation of this book was not always smooth, his steadfast support and expertise were indispensable. "Shells to Satoshi" simply would not exist without him, and I only wish I had asked him to collaborate earlier!

To my sister, Darci, my stalwart supporter first through college and graduate school then as an adjunct professor. Her support was crucial not only in those academic moments but also in her assistance with editing numerous chapters of this book. The backbone of this work, its historical and anthropological insights from my education and teaching, owes much to those years of academic toil and Darci's unwavering encouragement.

I am immensely grateful to my El Salvador Bitcoin "family." To Fran, Grace, Fabian, Belinda, and Annabella, your friendship has meant more to me than I can express. Despite my moodiness and introverted tendencies, you never ceased to believe in the importance of this work or in me. Thank you for the countless invitations to watch the sunset, which I too often declined. I promise we have many sunsets yet to enjoy together, and I look forward to each one. To Owen, Sandy, and Madis, your support and encouragement has kept me persevering and on course to finish this book, thank you. I look forward to more family dinners in our future!

This work was inspired by my involvement with Mi Primer Bitcoin. The team's dedication to changing the world, one Bitcoin lesson at a time, continues to make a profound impact on people across the globe. Furthermore, I am grateful to be able to write this book in my new home country of El Salvador. Under the leadership of Nayib Bukele, I have been able to live in a place where Bitcoin is accepted, where a president values freedom and education, and where there is optimism for a brighter future. To Mike Peterson and Roman Martinez, thank you for starting and creating Bitcoin Beach into what it is today. Your vision has led to more circular economies around the globe, which are making a positive impact on people's lives every day.

Lastly, to my fellow Bitcoiners, your daily efforts to educate and "orange pill" the world continues to inspire me. It is through your dedication to spreading the word about sound money that we pave the way toward a better future for all. This book is a tribute to all of you, a testament to the transformative journey we are on together. Thank you for sharing this path with me.

A Note on Citations and Sources

In preparing this book, I have drawn deeply from my experiences teaching history and anthropology over many years. The insights and narratives shared here are the culmination of the years spent in classrooms and libraries, wrestling with complex ideas and historical data to present them in the most engaging and enlightening ways possible to students. The unique approach to citations in this book reflects this extensive background.

Therefore, I have chosen to limit citations within the text to primary source material. This decision was made to anchor the discussion firmly in the original documents and firsthand accounts that have shaped our understanding of historical events. This focus on primary sources is intended to provide readers with a clear and direct connection to the past, unfiltered through the lens of subsequent interpretations or analyses.

The bibliography of this book is comprehensive; it includes not only the primary sources cited in the text but also a wide range of secondary materials that I have consulted throughout my teaching career. This compilation also incorporates more contemporary sources that I have reviewed to ensure the ongoing relevance and accuracy of the information presented. The goal is to offer readers a robust framework for understanding the topics discussed, supported by authoritative works in the field.

Furthermore, the appendices of this book are enriched with excerpts and documents from significant primary sources. These materials are included to offer you firsthand knowledge and the opportunity to engage directly with the historical sources that relate to the story of money. Whether you are a student, educator, or enthusiast, these resources are intended to enhance your understanding and stimulate further exploration of the topics discussed.

This book, therefore, is not just a reflection of past teaching experiences but an invitation to explore this history through the direct words of those who lived it. It is my hope that this approach will not only inform but also inspire a deeper appreciation of the complex tapestry of human history and the study of money's role within it.

You can find all the primary sources mentioned in the book on our website, https://www.shellstosatoshi.com/sources

List of Abbreviations

BIP	Bitcoin improvement proposals
BRICS	Brazil, Russia, India, China, South Africa
CBDC	central bank digital currency
DoS	Denial-of-Service
ECB	European Central Bank
ESG	environment, social, and governance
ETF	Exchange-Traded Funds
EU	European Union
FDIC	Federal Deposit Insurance Corporation
FED	The Federal Reserve
FEE	Foundation for Economic Education
FEMA	Federal Emergency Management Agency
IMF	International Monetary Fund
KYC	know your customer
NAFTA	North American Free Trade Agreement
NGO	Non-Governmental Organizations
PoW	proof of work
P2P	peer-to-peer
SEC	Securities and Exchange Commission
UAE	United Arab Emirates
U.S.	United States
USD	United States Dollar

Chapter 1: Introduction to Money

Those who cannot remember the past are condemned to repeat it.

– George Santayana

Money is at the foundation of virtually every aspect of modern life, from individual financial well-being to the stability and growth of the global economy. It not only facilitates daily transactions but also influences life choices, such as education, housing, and retirement planning. On a broader scale, it plays a central role in shaping economic policies, determining the health of markets, and influencing government decisions that affect national and international affairs. A solid grasp of how money evolved into how it functions today can empower individuals to make informed decisions about saving, investing, and spending, thereby enhancing their financial security and quality of life.

It is the history of money and systems built to support it that provides the information needed to understand it. In deciphering what money does for humanity it is vital to study how it evolved into its many and wildly varied forms. Furthermore, the answer to the question of what seashells, cacao beans, nutmeg, stamped metal disks, and electronic ledger entries all have in common can provide people with the knowledge of the sheer number of ways money impacts all people. This answer also provides the insight to understand the difference between the most and least optimal forms of money.

At its core, the need for money among humans transcends mere economic utility, touching on deep philosophical reasons that reflect our nature and the complexities of human society. Money, in its essence, is a manifestation of trust and a tool for facilitating the exchange of value, embodying a shared agreement on what worth means. This need arises from the fundamental human requirement to interact, trade, and cooperate with one another on a scale that goes beyond the limitations of barter systems, which ultimately proved inefficient and restrictive. Money enables individuals to go beyond immediate reciprocal exchanges, allowing for wealth accumulation, investment in future endeavors, and the expression of value across time and space.

In every era, money has been more than just a medium of exchange; it has been a symbol of power, a tool for social organization, and a driver of a civilization's expansion and innovation. Its influence extends beyond mere commerce, affecting art, culture, and governance, also embedding itself in the rituals and values of societies. The history of money is, in many ways, the history of humanity itself, reflecting our desires, ingenuity, and the endless pursuit of stability and prosperity. Through its constant presence, money has woven a thread that links disparate cultures and epochs, demonstrating its unparalleled capacity to adapt and endure, shaping not just economies but the very fabric of human life. Yet, as the story of money unfolds, so does the tale of how it can be used by those in power or those seeking power to hold dominion over others.

The story of money delves deeply into the essence, impact, and control of wealth, exploring its fundamental nature and the profound influence it exerts on individuals, societies, and nations. By examining the origins and evolution of money, an understanding of the underlying principles that have enabled it to become one of the most powerful forces in human history. In addition, the knowledge of this history can illuminate how and why people make financial decisions, impacting almost every aspect of life. Yet in today's world, financial education tends to focus on how to navigate the complexities of a broken system based on fiat loans, credit cards, and mortgages as opposed to understanding the fundamental aspects of money itself. It tells people how to make "informed choices" about saving for retirement, investing in the stock market, starting a business, and the ability to make sound financial decisions. However, what is not said is how modern "financial literacy" is based on a system in which people have little control over the money they earn and use.

The modern economy presents a complex web of financial products and services, along with potential pitfalls such as high-interest debt and fraudulent schemes. It does not teach people about the underlying principles of how the monetary system is broken on a global scale. In contrast, the financial literacy this book provides is one of historical context that encourages the reader to examine their relationship with the modern financial system while learning about a new form of money that makes individual financial sovereignty possible, Bitcoin.

Understanding what money truly is, how and why it came into being are crucial steps toward grasping the broader implications of what financial control means in one's own life. As a cornerstone of modern society, money not only facilitates daily transactions but also significantly influences personal freedom and societal autonomy. As humans, value is solely based on the time and energy expelled to create, produce, or offer something worthy of trade. This is how one earns money. Yet, if a person does not control the money he earns, he no longer controls his value or, for that matter, his own life. This is how people become slaves to the system of economic tyranny. Thus, the ability to control one's financial resources is a powerful determinant of one's ability to make choices, pursue opportunities, and navigate life's challenges. This control, or the lack thereof, can profoundly impact an individual's quality of life and freedom.

Consequently, delving into the history of money is not just an academic exercise; it is essential for understanding how the control and use of money have shaped societies and individual lives through time. By exploring how money has evolved, from ancient bartering systems to Bitcoin, mechanisms through which financial systems confer power and how that power affects freedom are uncovered. Understanding this history can not only prevent centralized authorities from relying on the ignorance of a population to justify their control of money, but more importantly, it empowers individuals to make informed decisions about their own finances. It ensures that they are not merely subjects of the economic forces that shape our world but active participants in deciding who can leverage money as a tool for their own personal freedom.

One unfortunate consequence of the increasingly complex evolution of social interactions in history is that money itself became an abstraction further removed from its source as a representation of the real value, stored in the form of some sort of currency. That very complexity drove control and decision-making power to be concentrated within centralized organizations that then had a vested interest in maintaining that control and power. These administrators of money discovered that it could become a tool to be manipulated and its underlying value distorted to suit their ends and deprive individuals of the personal sovereignty that the control of their own money provides them. Centralized control over money requires economic participants to be ignorant of the true nature of money, and from that ignorance, control is delegated to authorities entrusted to make "the right decisions."

Conversely, a decentralized monetary system, not controlled by a centralized authority but by the sovereign choices of a network of individuals, can lead to a society in which those individuals have greater freedom to shape their own destinies. In economies where access to financial resources and decision-making is widespread, there tends to be higher levels of social mobility and a greater capacity for individuals to pursue opportunities that enhance their well-being and happiness. This is not a coincidence, but rather, it is a causal outcome of decentralization and personal sovereignty.

Thus, the control of money is not just an economic issue but a fundamental concern of individuals seeking happiness and autonomy over their own lives. One way to start the process of understanding money is to ask what facts of human existence give rise to money. One can observe that humans, as the conceptual animal, have the ability to think, to reason, and to create. Human beings are producers, creators of valuable things, and given time, energy, and focus, they can create enough surplus that it can be traded for other valuable things made by other humans. Money, in its many and varied forms, is a human invention made to define, quantify, and ultimately communicate value itself for the purpose of immeasurably more efficient trade. Moreover, money incentivizes humans to think about their world beyond the satisfaction of immediate needs and in more of a conceptual manner, to look for opportunities to build, produce, create, and be rewarded.

Like any technology, whether the bow and arrow or silicon computer chip, humans created money to make their lives easier and serve a particular purpose. And, like any technology, it has evolved repeatedly through time, often becoming more complex, with greater utility, allowing for more efficiency in human interactions and trade. From the exponential scaling it makes possible, it further allows for the creation of previously unimaginable wealth. But progress and innovation in technology is neither linear nor inevitable. Monetary technology is no different.

Civilizations can sometimes get stuck at a certain point in their development and not be able to advance for lack of discovery, invention, or even will. Consider the history of the cowrie shell as a form of money that lasted nearly two millennia. It served as money because of its enduring utility and appeal across various societies from the third century BC to the nineteenth century AD. Originating primarily from the shallow waters of the Maldives and other tropical locales, these small, glossy shells were attractive because of their natural beauty, and became a cornerstone of trade and economy for numerous cultures, particularly those whose complexity of social structures did not demand a more sophisticated monetary system.

The introduction of cowrie shells likely began in regions such as China and India. It was in these areas where they were integrated into local economies that, while sophisticated in many respects, maintained forms of barter and commodity exchange that benefited from the simplicity of these shells. In ancient China, specifically during the Shang (1600–1046 BC) and Zhou (1046–771 BC) dynasties, cowries were used both as currency and as ritual offerings, illustrating their dual practical and symbolic value. Their use in China waned with the advent of cast metal coins, which offered greater divisibility and uniformity, traits desirable in the increasingly complex Chinese economy.

However, in other parts of the world, particularly in Africa and the Pacific Islands, the simplicity of the cowrie shell as a medium of exchange ensured its continued use well into the nineteenth century. African societies, for instance, found cowries especially useful due to their availability and the relative stability of their value. The shells were small, durable, and portable, making them ideal for use in the diverse and dispersed trading networks that characterized much of pre-colonial Africa. Here, the cowrie served not only as a tool for everyday transactions but also as a standard for measuring value in bride prices, social status payments, and even as fines in legal systems.

In these societies, the cowrie money system did not evolve significantly over the centuries, largely because it adequately met the needs of the communities that used it. These were generally smaller-scale economies with less emphasis on large-scale trade or complex financial instruments that might require more intricate monetary systems. The longevity of the cowrie shell as currency is clearly a reflection of the economic isolation and technological constraints of the societies in which it was used. Many of these communities were either geographically remote or had limited access to the broader trade networks that might necessitate a transition to more advanced monetary forms like metal coins or paper money. The cowrie system remained largely unchanged, continuing to facilitate trade and social transactions without the impetus for development seen in more interconnected economies.

The decline of cowrie shells used as money came only as the increased contact with European colonial powers and the global integration of trade networks emerged in the nineteenth century. The introduction of Western monetary systems, along with their associated economic structures and technologies, finally overcame the cowrie in places where it had circulated for centuries. These new monetary systems brought with them different values such as efficiency, standardization, and a tight control over money supply, resulting in qualities that the simple, organic cowrie system could not match. Throughout its history, those that accepted the shells held a belief that it could be used at a future point in time to facilitate a new trade. When the cowrie shell's time came to an end, it was because there were fewer and fewer who trusted that it would be accepted in the future.

These shells provide one example of how money has developed over time, and how it mirrors the evolution of human societies and their increasing complexity. In order to tell the story of money properly, it is crucial to study the earliest of human social interactions, how they grew in complexity and sophistication over time, and how they fulfilled the philosophical need to measure and communicate value. The science of anthropology provides a framework for just such a study.

Anthropology is the holistic study of humans, their biology, behavior, and societies in the past and present, encompassing the examination of material, cultural, social, biological, and linguistic aspects of humanity across time. By investigating the role of money from an anthropological perspective, one can uncover the deeper social meanings and functions of monetary systems, explore how they influence human behavior and societal organization, and understand the implications of economic interactions on cultural and social structures.

Turning to anthropology helps define the organization of human societies as they evolved from the primitive to the most complex, starting with the bands and tribes that represented foundational social structures (see table 1). Bands, or small, nomadic groups of foragers, relied on hunting and gathering with no formal leadership. They typically spent much of their time searching for food, raising children, and finding or making temporary shelters as they navigated the landscape. The need for further and more complex cooperation between bands drove the emergence of tribes, or larger social organizations that, while still nomadic, had enough population to support temporary encampments. With this semi-permanence, they maintained a loose organizational structure centered around kinship. These tribes often engaged in pastoralism, or raising domesticated animals and horticulture, focusing on smaller-scale multi-crop gardens.

The emergence of chiefdoms and states marked a significant shift in social organization. Chiefdoms introduced hereditary leadership and a more formal social hierarchy, laying the groundwork for the development of agriculture and permanent settlements. Chiefdoms also included a somewhat stratified society with chiefs, priests or shamans, and other official roles in the group. States further advanced this complexity with centralized governments, formal laws, and the monopoly on violence, leading to the development of cities, stratified societies, and the specialization of jobs and trades.

This progression from mobile bands to sophisticated states demonstrates humanity's adaptive strategies in managing resources, governing populations, and cultivating social and economic development. This development from human subsistence to complex political systems also mirrors how the technology of money evolves, going from simplistic forms of trade to an interrelated, international monetary structure.

In order to truly appreciate the role money has in one's life and in society, it is vital to understand its humble beginnings and what people did before the concept of money existed. The knowledge of how societies have used money in the past shows how humans dealt with this need and how this need evolved over time. The story of money begins with early humans, who had yet to invent money, and how they relied strictly on the barter system.

	Band	Tribe	Chiefdom	State
Population	• Small family or kinship groups from 12 to about 50 people • Mobile groups ª Temporary settlements • One language	• Groups of 50-100s of people, based on family and other alliances • Mobile groups • Temporary or very small, settlements • One language	•100s to 1000s of people based on kin, social rank, or residence • Fixed settlements or complex pastoralists • One language	• 10,000s+ based on class or residence • Fixed settlements involving cities and rural areas • One or more languages
Political Structure	• Headman (best hunter or patriarch but no real power) • Lead through consensus • No force used, just social mores and ostracized from group • Informal ad hoc conflict resolution • No hierarchy for settlement	• Big Man (can have some power, but not a lot) • Lead through consensus • No force used, just social mores and ostracized from group • Informal ad hoc conflict resolution • No hierarchy for settlement	• Chief, centralized leadership based on heredity • Sometimes one or two levels of bureaucracy • Can have some force to enforce rules or behavior • Conflict resolution is centralized, e.g. elder • Could have a central village among many for chief	• Centralized authority (democracy, monarchy, theocracy, oligarchy, etc.) • Many levels of bureaucracy • Force exists and is used • Formal laws and courts • Capital for bureaucracy

Table 1: Types of Political and Economic Organization

Society	• Not stratified by class • No slavery • No public spaces	• None to minimal class stratification • No slavery • No public spaces	• Kin based class or social stratification • Some slavery •Possibly some public spaces	• Class or social stratification • Some to large-scale slavery •Public spaces exist
Econo-mics	• Hunting and gathering • No domestication of plants or animals • No labor specialization, everyone contributes • Reciprocal exchanges (barter) • No formal currency • Band controls land • No formal money	• Hunting and gathering to minimal domestication of plants and animals • Minimal labor specialization • Reciprocal exchanges • Descent groups control land • No formal currency	• Horticulturalists and/or pastoralists • Some labor specialization • Redistributive exchange; tribute, religious practice • Chief controls land • Possible currency such as shells	• Intensive agriculture • Immense labor specialization • Redistributive (taxes) • State and individual people control land • Currency such as cacao, gold, or fiat

Source: Deanna Heikkinen

Chapter 2: Dawn of Trade and Barter

It is the necessary, though very slow and gradual, consequence of a certain propensity in human nature, which has in view no such extensive utility; the propensity to truck, barter, and exchange one thing for another.

–Adam Smith

The basic barter system is the oldest form of economic transaction. It involves the direct exchange of goods and services between two parties without use of the intermediary that is money. A barter transaction requires a "double coincidence of wants," so called because each side must come together for what both would consider to be an exact and equal exchange of value, otherwise the trade does not happen.

Finding trade partners with an exact double coincidence of wants can be difficult. Each party has to identify an individual need, i.e., something they want to exchange for and something else they need. Then, they must seek out a trading partner and agree to make a trade. This step requires that each party has what the other wants and is willing to part with it. For example, a farmer and a goat herder would need to meet and recognize that they can fulfill each other's needs. The farmer needs goat milk, and the goat herder needs grain. The exchange must not only satisfy the wants of each participant in terms of quality and quantity, but also time, since the value of many tradeable items can change rapidly as time passes. The goat milk will spoil if left alone for too long and the farmer's harvest might only occur once a year. Thus, timing and longevity also become a factor for barter.

Once someone finds a trading partner to fulfill their needs, they negotiate value. Yet, unlike modern transactions where prices are often set and standardized, in a barter system, the parties negotiate the value of the goods or services they are trading. This negotiation depends on the supply and demand of the items, their perceived value, and the urgency of the need. The farmer and goat herder might discuss how much grain is fair to trade for a certain amount of goat milk. Once an agreement is reached, the actual exchange takes place. This is a simultaneous or agreed-upon transfer of goods or services. The farmer hands over the grain, and the goat herder provides the milk in exchange. Thus, barter is a system focused on the present, satisfying the needs of the immediate and primal moment, without a deep regard for the future and the implications of planning, optimizing for efficiency, and scaling. An important aspect of the barter system is that there is no standardized pricing mechanism set by the totality of choices made by buyers and sellers in a sophisticated market. Instead, barter directly satisfies the needs of both parties in the transaction without intermediate processes similar to selling goods for money and then using that money to buy other goods. This often happens in smaller, less complex societies made up of kin groups.

Prior to the invention of money, when simple barter exchange was the norm, people lived in small, nomadic bands, often based on familial associations. They would be led by a head man who was usually the best hunter or patriarch of the family, living without a formal economic or political system. Because there were not that many people who needed to be fed, they could gather and hunt to sustain themselves while navigating their way through the natural landscape. Many of these small bands of foragers would live each day mainly working to find food and shelter to survive. They built temporary structures from available resources or would find natural shelters, such as caves, in which to live. There was very little accumulation of things outside of what was needed to survive, such as hunting tools, foraging needs, and clothing.

Eventually, these small bands developed into slightly larger tribes that would continue to be led by a head man but might also include several family groups and a shaman who would heal and lead any religious rituals. They may even have had semi-permanent settlements with a small area for small-scale farming and a few domesticated animals, such as a cow or goat, for milk. These tribes would have had their own territory for hunting and gathering, leading them to defend it from other groups. Over time, these groups began interacting with others, forming alliances and trading what they could find or make with things they needed or wanted from another small tribe of people. An example of this lifestyle could be seen in the nomadic band level !Kung San people of the Kalahari Desert in southern Africa. They subsisted on traditional hunting and gathering practices until the 1970s, engaging in a simple barter system to get what they needed.

The !Kung San people were deeply rooted in the immediate needs and personal relationships of a community rather than in any complex economic framework. Traditionally living as hunter-gatherers, the !Kung San's approach to exchange was straightforward and based on the principles of sharing and cooperation. This was essential for survival in the challenging environment of the Kalahari Desert. In this society, a common form of barter was not just about trading goods for other goods in a market sense but rather about sharing resources within the community. When someone succeeded in a hunt, the meat was distributed among the community members. This act of sharing was reciprocated by others when they had food or resources to share, creating a natural balance and ensuring that everyone's needs were met over time.

In addition, the !Kung San exchanged tools and handmade crafts. This form of trade was based on direct need. A person skilled in crafting bows might trade one for essential items like meat or other crafted goods like gathering baskets. This allowed for specialization and ensured that the skills of individuals benefited the entire community. Even services, such as those provided by shamans or healers, were part of this barter system. Their spiritual and healing services were compensated with support from the community, often in the form of food or labor. This system underscored the importance of each member's contributions to the well-being of the group, reinforcing social bonds and mutual support.

The !Kung San's economic interactions were thus characterized by an absence of accumulation of wealth as it was more focused on the well-being of the whole group. Their simple barter system highlights how human economies can operate based on trust, mutual aid, and the immediate needs of individuals within a close-knit group without the need for more complex economic structures.

In the simple barter system used by the !Kung San, goods and services were exchanged directly between individuals or groups without using money. Imagine a small, self-sufficient community where each group specializes in producing a certain type of good or offering a specific service. One person might be skilled in fishing, another in making pottery, while a third is adept at weaving cloth. When the fisherman's family needs new pots, they could offer fish to the pot-making family in exchange for a pot to cook the fish.

Similarly, if the weavers wanted fish, they might trade some of their fabric with the fisherman. This direct exchange system relies heavily on a personal and highly local understanding of the mutual needs of the participants and the value they assign to each other's goods and services. This system flourishes in close-knit communities where its people know each other well and have a strong sense of trust, validated by continual interaction and mutual support. If everyone knows each other intimately, no independent accounting system is required, and a "mental ledger" is sufficient to keep track of debts and credits in the event of barter trades that result in temporarily unequal value being exchanged.

However, as human interactions continued to become more complex and relationships between different tribes expanded, the small groups, or tribe-level societies, started connecting with each other during various parts of the year, creating alliances. These alliances developed into meeting patterns called seasonal rounds, allowing the smaller groups to come together a few times a year during seasons of abundance. These times enabled the sharing of resources and even the arranging of marriages and the building of ties between families. For many indigenous groups around the world, the seasonal round became an integral part of their economic and social structure, adding complexity to the human interaction between various groups.

An illustration of the seasonal round comes from the sharing of an unlikely food source, the bogong moth of Australia. The bogong moth is an insect that thrives in temperate regions, primarily flying at night. They have two long migration periods, which became a crucial time for native groups in southeastern Australia. The moth migration season marked a time when smaller communities would come together in the high country of the Australian Alps. As spring warmed into summer, the bogong moths, seeking refuge from the rising temperatures, migrated to the cooler mountain areas. These moths, dense in both protein and fat, became a vital food source for the indigenous people during this time.

To harvest the moths, tribes traveled to specific locations in the mountains where the moths were known to congregate, such as caves or under rock ledges. The traditional methods of gathering involved gently dislodging the moths from their resting places into containers or directly onto cloaks or skins. Once collected, the moths could be eaten raw, but they were often roasted to remove their fur. Roasting made them more palatable and easier to digest. The roasted moths could be ground into a paste and formed into cakes, dried, and then stored, providing a sustainable food source that could last for months. This practice would not only ensure food security during the resource sparse summer months, but it also allowed for the preservation of excess moths for use in the colder months when food was less available.

However, the bogong moth season was not solely used for food collection; it also facilitated significant social gatherings. As groups converged in the alpine regions, these seasonal gatherings were essential for maintaining social networks, exchanging knowledge, and reinforcing cultural traditions among the different indigenous communities. It provided a rare and valuable opportunity for social interaction, cultural exchange, and economic trade. People who lived isolated from each other for much of the year could reconnect, share stories, songs, and dances, exchange goods and knowledge, arrange marriages, and strengthen social bonds. Over time, the different tribes aligned themselves with other tribes during these times of abundance.

Ultimately, these types of seasonal rounds and interactions led to a more complex system of trade. What once were small bands of people making their own tools, shelter, and finding their own food evolved into a more sophisticated network of human interaction. Trading alliances were also formed, creating a system based on local resources the various bands or tribes had access to. The trade that occurred around these gatherings was based on barter, where goods and services were still exchanged directly without the use of a formal currency.

Items traded included not only the harvested bogong moths but also a variety of other goods such as ochre, used for ceremonial purposes and painting; stone tools and weapons; animal skins; and plant-based foods. These items were essential for the varying lifestyles and environments inhabited by the different indigenous groups. For example, coastal communities might trade fish or shells with inland groups for their tools or ochre, reflecting each group's knowledge and resource management.

With the example of the Australian indigenous groups, no single form of currency was used in their exchanges. Instead, the value of goods was determined by mutual agreement, with the importance of items varying between groups depending on their availability and cultural significance. The trade networks established through these gatherings were complex and extended well beyond the immediate regions, facilitating not only economic exchange but also social and cultural interactions among the indigenous peoples.

The bogong moth season highlights the seasonal round and how people skillfully managed their resources and social networks. By living apart, they ensured the sustainability of their resources and their survival. By coming together, they nurtured the social, cultural, and economic ties that bound them as a community, demonstrating a profound connection to both the land and each other. On a larger scale, these seasonal rounds allowed small groups, not only in Australia but also around the globe, to emerge into even more elaborate societies, eventually becoming more sedentary and developing a more stratified community.

As tribal trade alliances became even more complex in other regions, the use of shells as a measure of value for trade began. One such example comes from North American native groups living among the lush landscapes of what is now California. The story of how the Chumash and the Yokuts interacted and created their settlements, subsistence patterns, and trade network paints a vivid picture of adaptability, ingenuity, and how shells became a form of currency, adding more complexity to a barter system.

Nestled along the central California coastal regions and the Channel Islands, the Chumash people established around one hundred fifty communities supporting about twenty-five thousand people. Their settlements, often located near rich marine environments, included living quarters and acted as hubs of complex social and economic activity. The ocean provided abundance for the Chumash, who became skilled fishermen and gatherers. They crafted plank canoes, called tomols, which were feats of maritime engineering for that era. The tomols, which measured between eight and thirty feet long and held three to ten men, enabled them to forage and hunt for a variety of fish, shellfish, and sea mammals, such as seals and sea otters. These rugged canoes even allowed the Chumash to conduct whale hunts in the deeper waters.

The Chumash diet was not only rich in marine resources but was also supplemented by acorns gathered from the abundant oak trees in their region. Moreover, they hunted land animals and gathered various plant foods, demonstrating a deep understanding of their environment. The coastal and island landscapes provided materials like driftwood and tar used in tomol construction and unique shells that would become more and more valuable over time. Inland, the Yokuts tribes thrived in the fertile Central California Valley region, starkly contrasting with the coastal Chumash. The Yokuts consisted of sixty individual tribes with settlements spread across the valley's river systems and the foothills of the Sierra Nevada Mountain range. The eastern tribes lived in the foothills, while the western tribes lived on the valley floor. Estimates put their population as high as seventy thousand at its peak. Their subsistence patterns were primarily based on the abundant natural resources of the riverine and wetland ecosystems. They had access to various inland resources such as deer, elk, rabbits, and freshwater fish and waterfowl. The valley was also rich in plant resources, including acorns from the widespread oak trees, which were also a crucial part of their diet.

Additionally, the Yokuts had access to materials like obsidian used for arrowheads and tools from the mountainous regions. In fact, obsidian is such an impressive material for blade technology that surgeons still use it today for its remarkable sharpness and ability to make precise cuts. With the rivers and lakes, they also exploited different types of reeds and grasses, which were ideal for basketry. The Yokuts, along with the Chumash, conducted controlled burnings to manage and enhance plant and animal habitats, ensuring sustainable sources of food and materials.

What truly demonstrates the sophistication of these societies was their extensive trade network. With their seafaring prowess, the Chumash traded with inland tribes, exchanging their marine resources for items not available in their coastal and island environments. Their tomols facilitated not just fishing but also the transport of goods and ideas across considerable distances. The Yokuts, positioned in the vast Central Valley, became a central trading hub for tribes from different regions, extending to the coastal tribes, including the Chumash, and even reaching the more eastern tribes in the Great Basin that went beyond the Sierra Nevada mountains. Both overland and riverine routes were used in facilitating exchanges.

The trade between these two groups was driven by the desire to acquire resources unavailable in their own territories. The Chumash valued the inland resources of the Yokuts, particularly the obsidian for making tools and the high-quality basketry materials and finished baskets, which were prized for their intricate designs and utility.

Impressively, the baskets created by the Native American groups of California were so tightly woven and then lined with bitumen, or tar, that they were waterproof. The indigenous basket weavers used them to transport and hold liquids and could even cook in them using hot stones.

The Yokuts, in turn, were interested in the marine resources of the Chumash, including dried fish, the shells used for ornamentation or jewelry, and the tomols. In valuing these items for trade, both groups likely considered factors such as rarity, the skill and labor involved in production, and the utility or ceremonial significance of the items. For example, while common in the Yokuts territory, obsidian was rare and highly valued by the Chumash for its sharpness and effectiveness in tool making. Similarly, the Chumash's seashells, abundant in their region but rare inland, held significant value for the Yokuts.

The Chumash shells used to create shell beads formed a type of currency and, over time, held a value beyond their decorative or symbolic use. This evolution of shells beyond their original use reflects a sophisticated economic system among the Chumash and their trade partners, particularly the inland Yokuts. Initially valued for their beauty and rarity, being used as jewelry, ceremonial items, and status symbols, the skilled craftsmen of the Chumash began to produce these shells not just for personal or tribal use but also for trade as a form of money.

The most notable of these beads were the ones made from the purple olive snail (*Olivella biplicata*), which required considerable skill to manufacture, ensuring their scarcity. These beads, known as Olivella shell beads, were drilled, shaped, and polished to create standardized sizes and forms, making them ideal for use as a trade medium. As these shell beads became more integrated into the trade networks, their value as a currency solidified. They were traded for durable goods and services, and their acceptance across different tribes and regions illustrates their significance as a form of money. The standardization of bead types and sizes facilitated this process, allowing for a common understanding of value among those who traded them.

Using shell beads as currency also had implications for social and political structures within the Chumash community and their neighbors. Control over the production and distribution of these beads could lead to increased wealth and status for individuals or families, influencing social hierarchy and power dynamics. Over time, the Chumash shells tell the story of how a natural resource, through human ingenuity and social agreement, can transform into a valuable commodity, driving the development of complex trade systems and influencing the social and economic fabric of a society.

The barter system, even one that values shells beyond their utilitarian usefulness, can be effective in simple, small-scale economies. However, it has limitations in larger and more complex societies. As always, the requirement for a double coincidence of wants makes it difficult to find suitable trading partners. Additionally, bartering does not easily allow for storing value like money as it evolved later does. In addition, it can be challenging to divide goods or services for trade without losing value. Humans had to figure out more sophisticated barter systems that included trade for a valuable commodity like the shells used by the Chumash and Yokuts in order to overcome the limitations of barter.

With a more complex economic system that fosters intricate and more diverse trade, society becomes further stratified as more people start living in closer proximity. This progression can be seen where the first civilizations arose, particularly with the habitation and subsistence patterns transitioning from small bands and tribes primarily foraging and hunting to larger chiefdoms and states focusing on domesticating plants and animals. Consequently, more people began living in the same area, which started to look like small cities and led to more specialized jobs. With a more advanced social structure, larger sedentary societies developed the first cities and created a complex civilization in what is now the Middle East.

Chapter 3: Mesopotamia's Economic Revolution

If a merchant gives an agent corn, wool, oil, or any other goods to transport, the agent shall give a receipt for the amount, and compensate the merchant therefore. Then he shall obtain a receipt from the merchant for the money that he gives the merchant.

–Hammurabi

Located in modern-day Iraq, Syria, Jordan, and neighboring countries is a region collectively called Mesopotamia, meaning the land between two rivers, the earliest civilizations in the world developed and flourished for thousands of years. This area was also known as the Fertile Crescent, where these early peoples settled near fresh bodies of water, such as rivers or lakes, to ensure they had fresh water for drinking and farming. Encompassing several impressive empires, most notably the Sumerians, Babylonians, and Assyrians, these societies supported larger populations than earlier settlements, setting forth innovations like the wheel, writing, and a more complex barter system that would eventually impact the rest of the world.

The first of these states, the Sumerians (ca.4100–1750 BC)⬜, was characterized by a collection of independent city-states, e.g., Ur, Uruk, and Eridu, each with its own ruler and main deity. Although culturally aligned through language, writing, and religion, the political fragmentation of ancient Sumeria influenced their economic practices, with each city-state managing its own financial affairs. The complex economic system allowed the Sumerians to establish a standard value for the things they were trading between and within the cities.

The Sumerian economy was heavily based on agriculture, utilizing the fertile lands between the Tigris and Euphrates Rivers. They were pioneers in developing irrigation systems that allowed them to grow surplus crops, particularly barley, which served as a basic unit of the Sumerian economy and was used for trade. It also served as a standard for measuring value. Sumerians engaged in long-distance trade with regions such as the Indus Valley, Egypt, and Anatolia (modern-day Turkey), exchanging textiles, leather goods, metal wares, timber, and precious stones. Craftsmanship was highly developed, particularly in pottery, textiles, and metallurgy.

Just like today, these early people had specialized jobs, serving as kings, priests, farmers, ranchers, metal workers, textile workers, and much more. The Sumerians left behind art, writing, and artifacts that let archaeologists and historians know about their economics. For example, it is evident from a piece of art that has lasted for over 4,000 years, The Standard of Ur, that people had different jobs, such as farming, being a soldier, or a king. It can also be inferred from this beautiful artifact of the kinds of clothing, animals, and food they had.

In addition, it was in Sumer where the first writing occurred. Originally a more literal pictographic writing, the Sumerian written language became increasingly abstract into what is known as cuneiform. This ancient writing system was characterized by wedge-shaped marks inscribed on clay tablets, where specially trained scribes used the ends of sharpened reeds sourced from the rivers to document transactions, inventory, bills of sale, letters, and even literary works. These scribes could be hired or serve the king or priests. In fact, writing was so coveted that the scribes were seen as an elevated class within the stratified social structure of Mesopotamian civilizations.

For Sumerians, grain was the main commodity. Yet, because of its bulk, it was not always practical to serve as the unit of trade. Moreover, in Sumer, just as today, not everyone grew their own food to eat. In fact, they lived in a community where everyone had different skills or jobs. Some Sumerians worked at the temple, others worked in government, and some were craftsmen making pottery and leather items. Others farmed grain or raised animals for food. This complex social and economic system required the Sumerians to figure out something that could be used to pay people for the work they put in or to trade beyond the double coincidence of wants.

In other words, what people spent their time and energy on, the value an individual is paid for, had to be rewarded in something they could use and allowed for it to be redeemed at some point in the future. Since grain was the central part of their diet, they decided to use grain as the means to value anything being traded. Trading grain for skills or goods developed into its use as a kind of currency; basically, it became a standard unit of trade to value goods, services, labor, and even legal fines.

Ultimately, the Sumerians set the standard measurements for grain as a bushel, which weighed about sixty pounds (27.2 kilograms). As one might imagine, the Sumerians found this cumbersome to carry around when they needed to trade it. Therefore, finding something more portable became essential, and the idea of using bronze and silver as a unit of trade came into practice. They devised a standard system based on known weighted stones for a measurement of bronze called a sila and used the mina and shekel as standard units of silver. The numerous clay tablets left behind reveal the Sumerians developed a system that not only used grain to value other things but also introduced the idea of using melted-down metals, such as bronze and silver, to equal a certain amount of grain.

Despite their advanced economic system and the use of metals as a medium of exchange, the Sumerians did not develop coinage as it is understood today as a series of metal disk shapes of uniform weight. However, they did take the simpler barter systems described in Chapter 2 and altered them enough using highly coveted metal as a trade intermediary, allowing it to represent something that could be traded later for something else. Economic transactions were facilitated by using a determined weight of metals, primarily silver and bronze, to serve as a standard of value and medium of exchange. This method, while effective, was still more cumbersome than using coined money that would come later.

This early use of metal in a more complex barter system necessitated the presence of scales and weights at the point of transaction. It also relied on a mutual agreement on the standards of weight and the purity of the metal. In fact, the system was codified and written down in one of the first law codes on earth, The Law Code of Ur-Nummo. In this early set of laws, Sumerians both defined the value of things using commodities or raw materials that could be traded or sold, as well as bronze and silver that were melted down into bullion.

This system of using metals as trade objects helped the Sumerians trade large things like goats for smaller things like mud bricks. For instance, if someone needed a clay pot and only had a goat to trade, it would be difficult to divide the goat to equal one clay pot. By using metal as a unit of trade, one would no longer need to divide a goat into pieces to buy a clay pot from someone else. The Sumerian use of metals solved the problems of divisibility, having small enough things to trade for what one needed, and portability, being able to transport what someone needed for trade. These were two money innovations by the Sumerians that earlier hunter and gatherer peoples lacked.

Alongside the use of metals as currency, the Sumerians developed a banking system that further enhanced their economic capabilities. Their clay tablets reveal the first commercial writing in human history. These earliest writings demonstrate a need to keep track of commodities and exchanges. In fact, modern accountants could describe these clay tablets as a rudimentary ledger. These advances also revealed a need for a central location where people could go to conduct and record these transactions.

Temples and palaces were not only religious and administrative centers but also played an important role in this early economic system. They acted as depositories for wealth, including grain and precious metals. These religious centers also received offerings in the form of grain, livestock, and metals from the community, which they stored in large granaries and treasuries. Over time, these temple complexes began to act as banks, offering loans and credit to individuals and facilitating commercial transactions. These institutions accepted deposits, managed payments, and facilitated the exchange of goods, acting as central hubs in the Sumerian economy.

Priests and temple officials managed these resources and could issue receipts for deposits and loans, essentially creating a system of written financial records that serves as some of the earliest evidence of banking practices. This system allowed for the accumulation and creation of new wealth, by accommodating the allocation of surplus wealth to productive endeavors, financing everything from trade expeditions to agricultural improvements and construction projects. The primary commodities used for loans in Sumer included grain and silver. Loans were made for various purposes, including agrarian needs, trade ventures, and personal loans. Loans made by these early banks came with interest, indicating a sophisticated understanding of lending practices.

Texts from the period show that interest rates could be quite high, reflecting the risk taken by the lender. Transactions, including loans, were formalized with contracts. These contracts were written on clay tablets and included details of the loan terms, such as the amount, the interest rate, and the repayment schedule. These written contracts demonstrate the Sumerians' advanced approach to managing financial transactions. Loans often required collateral to secure the agreement, which could include land, crops, or other valuable goods. In case of default, the collateral would be forfeited to the lender, a practice that continues in various forms in modern banking. These practices were also codified into the laws.

The next great Mesopotamian civilization that arose was Babylon. Under leaders like Hammurabi (r. 1792–1750 BC), Babylon (1894–539 BC) emerged as a centralized state that unified much of Mesopotamia under its control. This centralization allowed for a more uniform economic policy and administrative efficiency across the empire. Hammurabi's code is one of the earliest and most comprehensive legal documents. It included laws regulating economic practices such as trade, loans, wages, and contracts, creating standardization across the empire.

Like the Sumerians, the Babylonians relied on agriculture, benefiting from the advancements in irrigation and farming techniques developed by the Sumerians. They also expanded trade networks, leveraging their political power to secure trade routes and resources, including trade in grains, wool, and crafted goods for raw materials unavailable in Mesopotamia. Temples and palaces continued to serve as financial centers by managing deposits and loans and even engaging in currency exchange. Also, silver as a standard of value for transactions became more systematized.

Silver continued to be used in transactions to purchase goods and services, facilitating trade by providing a universally accepted value standard. Silver's role as a unit of account allowed for prices and debts to be denominated in weights of silver. These units, called shekels, would become synonymous with money itself. This standardization allowed for the clear valuation of diverse goods and services, simplifying economic calculations and contracts.

As a precious metal, silver also served as a store of value, enabling the Babylonians to save and transport wealth. This was especially important in an economy where wealth was traditionally held in land or agricultural produce. The Code of Hammurabi also included numerous references to silver, such as specified fines, prices, interest rates, and wages in silver, indicating its role in both commercial and legal contexts. Temples and palatial complexes conducted lending activities, often with silver as the medium.

Contemporaneous with but located in the mountainous northern part of Mesopotamia were the Assyrians (1365–609 BC). As one of the ancient world's most formidable military powers, they had a complex economy that supported its expansionist ambitions and sophisticated state apparatus. This led to the extraction of tribute from conquered peoples in exchange for protection, a cornerstone of Assyrian economic policy. This tribute, paid in goods, livestock, and sometimes precious metals or labor, provided a significant source of wealth for the empire. In addition to tribute, Assyria engaged in extensive trade networks, exchanging goods like textiles, metals, and agricultural products with neighboring regions. The Assyrian military protected and controlled these trade networks, ensuring a steady flow of resources into the empire.

Like other Mesopotamian societies, Assyria relied heavily on agriculture. The empire's heartland in northern Mesopotamia, although less fertile than the southern regions, was made productive through irrigation and other agricultural innovations. The state organized and controlled large agricultural estates, which were worked by enslaved people resettled from conquered lands, contributing to the empire's food security and economic base.

The Assyrians were adept at managing and exploiting natural resources, including using forests from the mountains of Lebanon for timber, which was a scarce commodity in the desert region of Mesopotamia and essential for building projects and military purposes. The mountainous region in the north also allowed for massive stone structures, such as the library and palace of Ashurbanipal (r. 669–ca.631 BC). The central government, often directly involving the king, oversaw these activities, indicating a highly organized approach to resource management.

While the concept of banking in the modern sense did not exist, the Assyrians had sophisticated mechanisms for managing wealth, credit, and financial transactions, which can be seen as early forms of banking activities. Like the Sumerians and Babylonians, temples and palaces played a central role in the Assyrian economy, acting as depositories for wealth and venues for large-scale economic transactions. They received, stored, and distributed grain, precious metals, and other goods, functioning much like modern banks. These institutions also provided loans, often in the form of grain, to farmers and traders, with interest rates documented in contracts.

Documents from the Assyrian period show that commercial loans were common, with interest rates explicitly stated. These loans could be made in silver or even in grain. The terms varied depending on the agreement between the parties. The existence of promissory notes and detailed records of transactions indicates a sophisticated level of financial literacy and practice. Assyrian merchants, often operating with the backing of the state or temple institutions, engaged in long-distance trade that required financing. They would receive goods or capital upfront, with the expectation of returning with profits from their ventures. This practice helped facilitate Assyria's extensive trade networks and contributed to the empire's economic prosperity.

The Mesopotamian approach to economics, with its use of metal currency and banking practices, laid the groundwork for the civilizations that followed. Their innovations in creating a standardized medium of exchange and developing a banking system that could support commercial and governmental activities demonstrate a high level of sophistication in managing and expanding their economy. This system enabled these early societies to not only facilitate trade and commerce within their own society but also to engage in international trade with neighboring regions, spreading their influence and integrating their economy with those of other ancient civilizations.

Yet the absence of coinage in their civilizations can be attributed to several factors, including the technological and conceptual developments of the time. The idea of stamping metal to indicate a standardized value and authority, two key aspects of coinage, requires a certain level of administrative control and technological capability for minting. While they all had a complex bureaucracy capable of managing grain distributions, temple offerings, and land allocations, the leap to minting coins was a step only later civilizations would take.

The Sumerian system of using weighted metals laid important groundwork for financial transactions, emphasizing the value of metals as a medium of exchange and the need for standardization in economic practices. However, the transition to coinage awaited further developments in political, economic, and technological realms that would come to fruition in subsequent civilizations. Despite these limitations, bartering has been a fundamental aspect of human trade and interaction throughout history and remains in use in various forms, even in modern economies, especially in localized or informal settings.

These Mesopotamian practices also set the foundation for developing more complex barter systems. These ultimately played a significant role in shaping economic practices in the ancient world, influencing other early civilizations through trade, cultural exchange, and the spread of monetary concepts. Mesopotamia, often hailed as the cradle of civilization, was a hub of innovation and development, particularly in writing, law, and economics. The introduction of silver as a medium of exchange represented a critical step away from purely goods-based trade to a more flexible and scalable system of commerce.

The Indus Valley, Egypt, and Anatolia civilizations interacted with Mesopotamian traders, adopting and adapting the concept of using precious metals as a standard of value in their own economic systems. In Egypt, for example, gold and silver became significant in financial transactions, both in internal trade and in dealings with foreign lands. Using metal as money facilitated the development of more complex economic systems, including the ability to accumulate wealth, invest in large projects, and support the administration of state activities.

Moreover, the concept of using silver as a medium of exchange likely influenced the development of weighted money and, eventually, the creation of coined money, which first appeared in Lydia in what is now Turkey around the seventh century BC. This evolution marked a further step in the abstraction of money from physical goods to symbols of value, a principle that underlies modern monetary systems.

Chapter 4: The Advent of Coinage

The ascent of money has been essential to the ascent of man.

– Niall Ferguson

The next phase in the history of money began with the fashioning of coins from gold and silver. A revolutionary development, these coins were stamped with marks to signify their weight and purity and often bore symbols of the ruling authority. The use of coins made trade easier and more efficient. Unlike barter goods like grain, coins were portable and non-perishable and had a universally recognized value. This helped facilitate local trade and opened doors for long-distance commerce, allowing for the movement of goods across regions and cultures.

The innovation of coinage began when precious metals were shaped into standardized units and stamped by an authority, such as a king or city-state. This was done to certify their weight and purity. In what is now western Turkey, the Lydians (1180–547 BC) developed electrum coins stamped with official symbols, which represented a significant evolution in monetary systems. It combined the Mesopotamian practice of using precious metals as a medium of exchange with the concept of standardization and official validation.

While Mesopotamia did not invent coinage, its economic practices provided essential precursors to this invention. The Mesopotamian system of weights and measures, using precious metals for trade, and complex economic infrastructure influenced the regions around it, including the Greeks and Lydians. Mesopotamian banking and financial practices also indirectly influenced Anatolian and Greek civilizations. Traders, explorers, and colonists ventured far beyond their city-states and established connections across the Mediterranean and into the Black Sea. There, an extensive network of trade routes facilitated not only the exchange of goods but also the sharing of ideas and practices.

While Lydia was geographically close to the Greek city-states of the Aegean coast, and there were significant interactions between the Lydians and the Greeks, the Lydians were not Greek. They were an Anatolian people with their own distinct language and culture. Culturally and politically, Lydia had interactions with the Greek city-states, including trade, warfare, and alliances. The Lydian kings, particularly Croesus (r. ca. 560–546), were known for their wealth and patronage of the arts, and their capital, Sardis, was a major center of commerce and culture that attracted Greek artisans and traders. Despite these interactions, the Lydians maintained their distinct identity.

Like the Mesopotamian societies, Lydian history includes a line of dynasties or generations of ruling families who would conquer and then get conquered by another dynasty. However, the king of one of these ruling families, Ardys (r. ca. 644–637 BC), imagined the next revolutionary innovation for money: a standardized, stamped coin. It is believed that Ardys used the first metal coins to pay his soldiers, and in doing so, he stamped a lion on one side to represent the symbol of his dynasty. The stamp was there to guarantee the weight and value of the metal. This saved the users of the coins, primarily the merchants and bankers, the time-consuming process of weighing and verifying its contents. The standardized weight of the metal was a crucial part of using it as money and minting or creating coins. The weight of the coin was based on regulated stone weights. Although not widely distributed, these Lydian coins did mark the beginning of coinage instead of just using bullion or ingots.

Two generations later, Ardys's grandson, Alyattes (r. ca. 610–560 BC), took his grandfather's idea of a stamped coin and became the first person in human history to distribute stamped coins to his people on a large scale. The importance of this cannot be overstated. While the uniformity, malleability, and scarcity of metals like gold and silver allowed them to be used as a trade intermediary, it was the innovation of the stamp that provided validation and trust, saving time, and allowing for much faster transactions.

The widespread introduction of coinage revolutionized economic transactions. It significantly enhanced trade by providing a portable, durable, and divisible medium of exchange that was readily accepted and recognized across various regions. Traders and merchants no longer needed to weigh and assess the purity of metal at every transaction, thus simplifying and speeding up commerce. The use of coins also facilitated the accumulation and storage of wealth in a more compact and secure form than ever before. Moreover, the stamp on the coin, signifying its authenticity and value, represented an early form of government assurance. This not only bolstered trust in economic transactions but also established a precedent for the role of governments in regulating and backing their currency.

In addition, Lydia was well-suited for the first metal coin creation as it had an abundant source of electrum, a naturally occurring alloy of gold and silver. Electrum was found in the river sands and gravel in the Pactolus River, which originated in Mount Tmolus and ran through the capital of Sardis. Initially, the alloy metal was used as bullion and ingots, just as the Mesopotamians used metals. However, with the variability of how much gold was in each amount of electrum, it became cumbersome for users to verify the value of each small piece they had in their possession. The blend of gold and silver required a difficult and time-consuming process of separating them, thus encouraging the use of electrum in its original form. Because of its abundance locally, electrum remained the metal of choice for trade in this region.

So, over time, the Lydians found a way to standardize the value of the electrum by adding in silver, leading to its fungibility, or an ability to interchange one coin for another, since ensuring each had equal value. Naturally occurring electrum sourced from the river usually had between 65% and 85% gold content. However, with the added silver, the gold was stabilized at 55%. This was intentional, and in addition to standardizing the value, it also likely prevented counterfeiting. Initially, the coins were minted by individuals around the region in numerous denominations or weights for Ardys. Deciding to take control of the minting process, Alyattes and the next king, his son Croesus, subsidized coin-making to allow more people in their kingdom to use it. During Croesus's reign, he valued the electrum coins based on the natural, higher gold content, even though it had been lowered. Croesus made a profit from the coins, but his dishonest practice ultimately caught up to him when people realized the inflated value of the coins and refused to take them. As a result, Croesus was essentially forced to create the first gold coins to build back trust. The gold coins were more sophisticated, stamped on both sides, and denominated in different weights. These were also the first gold coins minted by the state and put into circulation for use by its citizens.

However, Croesus's coins never really caught on, nor did they become widespread outside of his region. Even so, the idea of the state minting pure gold and silver coins transferred to neighboring areas. Yet, the introduction of coinage also brought with it certain shortcomings. The very success of the gold coins in facilitating trade and wealth accumulation led to new challenges for those who produced and used the coins, including counterfeiting and debasement. As coins became a preferred medium for economic transactions, the temptation to create counterfeit coins or to shave the precious metal content in official coins to profit from the difference became a persistent issue. This required governments and authorities to take measures to protect the integrity of their currency, adding a layer of complexity to economic management that the Greeks would adopt next.

While the Lydian civilization was not part of the ancient Greek world in terms of ethnicity and language, its geographical proximity and interactions with Greek city-states meant that it had a significant influence on, and was influenced by, the cultures of the Greek world.

The Greeks were among the next to embrace and further develop coinage, significantly expanding its use and influence throughout their city-states and colonies. This diffusion of coinage by the Greeks marked a pivotal evolution in its use and significance. Greek city-states, recognizing the benefits of a standardized medium of exchange, began minting their own coins with distinctive symbols and designs that reflected their identity, values, and sovereignty. For example, Athens minted coins featuring the owl of Athena, while Corinth used the image of Pegasus, the winged horse.

The spread of coinage among the Greeks facilitated not only local and regional trade but also helped in the accumulation of wealth and the economy's expansion. It also played a crucial role in the dissemination of Greek culture, as coins carried Greek imagery and ideas far beyond the borders of the city-states. The Athenians, recognizing the value and utility of the coinage system, adopted this innovative concept but made several key improvements that reflected their own needs and ambitions.

First, the Athenians moved from electrum to pure silver for their coinage. The Athenians capitalized on their rich silver mines, particularly those in Laurion, to bolster their coinage system. A it was more abundant in the region, it allowed for greater control over the purity and weight of the coins. The production of coins in larger quantities facilitated the expansion of their trade networks and boosted their economy. Using their own silver resources also meant that Athens was less dependent on external sources for the precious metals required for coinage, giving them a significant economic advantage.

Another improvement made by the Athenians was the introduction of a more refined system of weights and measures for their coins. While the Lydians had borrowed the practice of standardizing stones to measure the weight of coins from Mesopotamia, the Athenians developed a more precise system using a casting method in their creation. This change ensured that each coin had a consistent weight and value. This precision in measurement fostered greater trust in Athenian coins both domestically and in international trade. The most famous Athenian coin, the silver tetradrachm, became widely recognized for its reliability in terms of weight and silver content. This standardization made Athenian coins a preferred medium of international trade. The Athenian state took an active role in the minting of coins, implementing strict controls on the production to ensure consistency and trust in their currency.

Beyond technical advancements, the Athenians established a legal and economic framework that supported the use of coinage, including laws related to counterfeiting and the standardization of measures and weights. This legal backing further enhanced the reliability and precision of Athenian coinage. Another significant Athenian advancement was the development of higher-quality coin designs. The Athenians emphasized the aesthetic and symbolic aspects of their coins, introducing intricate designs that often-featured images of gods and goddesses, symbols of the city, or other iconography that reflected Athenian identity and values. For example, the silver tetradrachm bore the image of Athena, the patron goddess of Athens, on one side and the owl, a symbol of wisdom and Athena's sacred bird, on the other. These designs not only served as a mark of authenticity but also as a tool for propaganda, promoting Athenian culture and political power across the Mediterranean.

The early rulers adopted the idea of coins when Athens was just establishing itself and had a rudimentary system of trade. They used the coins to replace the traditional yet cumbersome *obeloi*, or metal rods, previously used for trade. These metal rods varied in weight and size, but some were as long as one and a half meters. Even so, they were traded widely during the Archaic period (800–480 BC). To ensure the drachma could replace this traditional currency, the Athenian coins included numerous denominations, from the obol, worth one-sixth of a drachma, to the tetradrachm, worth four drachmas.

What also differed between Greece and other civilizations that had come across the Lydian coins was the structure of the Greek states. Athens and Corinth were on a journey to create a new form of government: the polis or city-state. Ancient Greece consisted of a collection of autonomous, or self-governed, cities that set their own trading system and had their own specific cultures. For instance, Athens was a democracy, a type of government where every citizen had a vote and was ruled by an archon or chief magistrate and the Areopagus, a governing body made up of past archons. Athenians valued art, architecture, and literature, and this is where the three great Greek philosophers, Socrates, Plato, and Aristotle, all taught.

Over time, Athens aligned with other city-states, forming the Delian League for military purposes. The Delian League adopted the Athenian currency, increasing its acceptability by giving it a wider reach. Like previous societies regulating bullion and ingots with weights, the Athenian drachma and its denominations were minted and guaranteed by the state. Athens gained trust, or confidence in the composition and value of the money, of the Delian League. Athenians had built an alliance, not just for military support, but in the trust that the currency had value.

No longer was the coin a rare item used in only a few circumstances. Athenians used coinage as a unit of account or common standard that allowed for measuring the economic value of goods and services. Ultimately, it set a new standard for commerce and employment; for example, two *obol* equaled a day's wage. In addition, using coinage verified by the state streamlined both public and private enterprise, allowing Athens and other areas to flourish. In fact, with their successful widespread adoption, and corresponding portability, and trust, state-sponsored coinage became part of the function of money for future civilizations. After the Greek Classical Age (ca. 510–323 BC), Greek coinage use became more widespread when Alexander the Great (356–323 BC) established his vast empire, with coins that featured his portrait and were distributed from Macedonia to Egypt to India.

Following the Greeks, the concept of coinage spread to other civilizations, including the Achaemenid Empire (559–330 BC), who adopted coinage after coming into contact with Greek and Lydian cultures during their expansion. The use of coinage by the Persians under Darius I (r. 522–486 BC), for example, signified its adoption by one of the largest empires of the time, further integrating the practice into the economic systems of the ancient Near East. From there, coinage continued to spread, reaching regions and civilizations interacting with the Greeks and Persians, including the Romans. They would eventually adopt and adapt coinage for their own needs, creating a monetary system that supported their vast empire.

In addition to revolutionizing coinage, the Athenians developed a banking system that played a significant role in their economy, especially as Athens became a major trade and naval power in the ancient world. While different in structure and function from modern banking, this system provided various financial services facilitating commerce, trade, and personal finance. These bankers were known as *trapezitai*, a term derived from the Greek word for the tables *(trapeza)* they used in their trade. These bankers operated in the agora, the central marketplace of Athens, and offered services that included money changing, deposits, loans, and even letters of credit for merchants and traders. The Athenian banking system was primarily private, with wealthy individuals providing the capital to run these banking operations.

A primary function of the Athenian bankers was to exchange foreign currency for the local Athenian currency. Athens's significant trade networks meant merchants and sailors across the Mediterranean would bring various currencies into the city. Bankers facilitated commerce by converting these currencies into Athenian silver drachmas. Bankers also accepted deposits, providing a safe place for citizens and foreigners to store their wealth. Depositors could withdraw their money on demand or use it to make payments. In addition, the bankers lent money, charging interest on these loans. Loans were made to individuals, merchants, and even the state for various purposes, including commercial ventures, personal needs, or public projects.

The Athenian banking system was sophisticated for its time, with bankers keeping detailed records of deposits, withdrawals, and loans. While there was no central bank or formal regulatory body as commonly understood today, the importance of reputation and social standing helped ensure that bankers operated with a degree of integrity. Legal frameworks also existed to regulate financial transactions and protect depositors and borrowers to some extent.

Despite the absence of paper money or electronic transactions, the Athenian banking system provided essential financial services that supported the city's economy. It facilitated the growth of Athens as a commercial hub, enabling it to engage in extensive trade networks throughout the ancient world. The system also allowed for the accumulation and investment of capital, contributing to the economic dynamism and prosperity of Athens during its golden age. Athens's innovation in coinage and banking would spread throughout the Mediterranean, eventually reaching Rome.

Chapter 5: Roman Banking and Economic Power

A good reputation is more valuable than money.

–Publilius Syrus

As Roman territories expanded into Greek areas in the third century BC, particularly during the Punic Wars, Romans came into increasing contact with societies that used coinage and established banking practices. However, in the evolution of banking, the Roman system's complexity surpassed that of the earlier Greeks and Mesopotamians. This was due to several key developments reflecting the vastness encompassing the Roman world and its economy. As Rome expanded, it incorporated a wide array of peoples and territories, necessitating a more sophisticated financial infrastructure to manage the new economic demands. Compared to the banking practices of the Greeks and Mesopotamians that focused on loans, deposits, and offered currency exchange, the Roman system developed a more integrated, legally sophisticated network capable of supporting a larger scale of economic activity. This structure would ultimately grow to support the massive Roman Empire economy, facilitating its trade networks and contributing to the administrative cohesion that helped maintain its dominance for centuries.

The ancient Roman civilization began as a small, agrarian society that eventually conquered neighboring groups. Over time, Rome unified these groups during the Roman Kingdom (625–510 BC) and into the expansion of the Roman Republic (510–31 BC). Rome connected these tribes through shared language, governance, and culture. The money system also aided in consolidating the region, with the first Roman coins being minted after the Republic was established.

During the early Republic, Rome was relatively small and initially used bullion and ingots of bronze for trade. These eventually became large, easily counterfeited bronze coins divided into different denominations, such as the Roman pound and ounce. During this era of rudimentary metal money, they were measured in a unit called as, which equaled twelve Roman ounces. Thanks to neighboring groups like the Etruscans and the Punic Wars, the Romans learned about Greek coinage. Over time, Roman coinage became more refined, being issued by the state and stamped with the images of Roman gods and leaders.

The Roman Republic's banking system also went from being a simpler model of a business that held commodities in exchange for redeemable receipts to offering more complex services. In the early days of the Republic, banking was an essential service for commerce, especially given Rome's expanding trade networks. Bankers accepted deposits, made loans, exchanged foreign currencies, and facilitated money transfers, functions crucial for both domestic and international trade. However, these activities were not regulated by the state. The system depended on the trustworthiness of individuals serving as bankers to provide liquidity.

As Rome transitioned from the Republic to the Empire (31 BC–AD 476), the banking system underwent significant changes, reflecting broader political and economic power shifts. During the Roman Republic, the banking system was characterized by its private nature, with individuals known as *argentarii* playing a central role. These bankers conducted their operations from shops in the Forum, the market area in the city of Rome. The *argentarii* engaged in money changing, deposit banking, and lending. The system was largely informal, relying heavily on personal networks and the bankers' reputations. Under the Empire, the state played a more prominent role in financial affairs, influencing banking practices. Even so, as banking in the Roman Empire became a more complex system regulated by the state it also continued to involve private, often wealthy citizens as its bankers.

With the establishment and growth of the Roman Empire, the scale and complexity of economic activities increased. The expansion of the Empire brought about a greater need for financial services, and in response, the state increased its role in the economy, including the regulation of financial transactions and the oversight of banking practices. One significant change during this period was the increased involvement of the state in major financial operations, such as the funding of public works and military campaigns, which required large-scale financial management capabilities beyond what private bankers could provide. This period also saw the emergence of more sophisticated financial instruments and practices, including a greater reliance on written contracts and legal documentation for financial transactions.

Additionally, the Imperial government occasionally intervened directly in the banking sector, such as providing bailouts to stabilize the financial system during crises. The emperor Augustus, for example, is known to have used his personal wealth to offer interest-free loans to banks to alleviate liquidity crises or the need to have access to cash, demonstrating a form of state intervention in the banking system. Despite these changes, private banking continued to thrive during the Empire, with wealthy individuals and families financing a wide range of public and private ventures. The social and political elite, including the two very high-ranking offices of senators and equestrians, often engaged in lending as a means of increasing their wealth and influence.

One of the primary ways in which Roman banking changed was its extensive reach across the empire. Roman bankers established branches and conducted transactions throughout the Mediterranean and beyond, facilitating trade and the movement of money across vast distances. This network enabled the efficient transfer of funds from one region to another, supporting both local and long-distance trade on a scale previously unseen. Moreover, the Romans introduced more advanced financial instruments and practices. They extensively used letters of credit, reducing the need to transport large amounts of cash over long distances, which was risky and impractical. This practice not only made trade safer and more efficient but also laid the groundwork for more intricate banking operations, such as more complex currency exchange and investment financing.

The legal framework in Rome also contributed further to the growing complexity of its banking system. Roman law provided sophisticated regulations concerning loans, debts, and property rights, offering a level of legal protection for transactions that was advanced for its time. This legal environment enabled the development of diverse financial services, including savings accounts, loans with interest, real estate financing, and government bond markets.

Banks served as places where individuals could hold their money or seek out loans. However, even in these early days of banking, the private bank owners would often lend out more money than they had on deposit, allowing them to issue more loans at greater profit. However, this also ran the risk of not being able to satisfy depositors who wanted their money back unexpectedly. For example, in 88 BC, depositors wanted more of their money back than the bankers had available, so the bankers had to liquidate their own assets to make good on the demands of their customers. This caused many bankers to close their doors. In turn, Roman citizens lost their trust in bankers, causing the number of bankers to further decline. With this, the ability to take out loans on credit for individuals and businesses also declined, leading to an economic downturn.

Additionally, during this time, the Roman economy saw the emergence of public or government-owned banks involved in managing state finances, including tax collection and the funding of public works. This was tied to the Roman institution of the census, which was conducted to levy taxes on its citizens. These institutions worked alongside private banks, creating a dual system that could mobilize financial resources for both public and private needs.

The intricacy of the Roman banking system was also evident in its adaptability to economic crises and changes. For example, during times of financial instability, the Roman state could intervene in the banking sector to stabilize the economy by guaranteeing certain debts or providing liquidity to banks in distress. Banks could also offer transactions solely on paper without exchanging money for their clients. In some cases, the client did not even have the money to cover it. This was a system of credit that was sometimes backed by capital or valuable items used as collateral, but at times credit was issued without anything to back it up. This new use of money allowed banks and even the state to profit from money that individuals did not actually have.

Throughout Roman history, but particularly during the Empire, rulers and senators exerted influence over banking policies and used financial strategies for personal gain, to garner support, or to achieve political objectives. The intertwining of political power and financial activities was a hallmark of the Roman elite, with several specific examples illustrating how this dynamic played out. One of the most notable instances of an emperor taking direct action in the financial sector was during the reign of Emperor Tiberius (r. AD 14–37). In AD 33, Rome faced a financial crisis due to a combination of factors, including a tightening of credit and a lack of liquidity in the banking system. The Roman historian Suetonius noted:

> XLVIII. He displayed only two instances of public munificence. One was an offer to lend gratis, for three years, a hundred millions of sesterces to those who wanted to borrow; and the other, when, some large houses being burnt down upon Mount Caelius, he indemnified the owners. To the former of these he was compelled by the clamours of the people, in a great scarcity of money, when he had ratified a decree of the senate obliging all money-lenders to advance two-thirds of their capital on land, and the debtors to pay off at once the same proportion of their debts, and it was found insufficient to remedy the grievance. The other he did to alleviate in some degree the pressure of the times.[1]

---

[1] Suetonius, "Tiberius Nero Caesar, Book XLVIII," *The Complete Works of Suetonius,* trans. Alexander Thomson (East Sussex, England: Delphi Classics,

To alleviate the situation, Tiberius implemented a bailout plan, using the imperial treasury to lend money to banks and individuals at a low-interest rate.

Prior to this though, it was Emperor Augustus (r. 27 BC–AD 14) who played a part in shaping the economic landscape of Rome. He initiated numerous public works projects, which were funded through his personal wealth and contributions from wealthy allies. Suetonius documented these projects:

> XXIX. The city, which was not built in a manner suitable to the grandeur of the empire, and was liable to inundations of the Tiber, as well as to fires, was so much improved under his administration, that he boasted, not without reason, that he "found it of brick, but left it of marble."...A great number of public buildings were erected by him, the most considerable of which were a forum, containing the temple of Mars the Avenger, the temple of Apollo on the Palatine hill, and the temple of Jupiter Tonans in the Capitol. The reason of his building a new forum was the vast increase in the population, and the number of causes to be tried in the courts, for which, the two already existing not affording sufficient space, it was thought necessary to have a third. It was therefore opened for public use before the temple of Mars was completely finished; and a law was passed, that causes should be tried, and judges chosen by lot, in that place...He erected the temple of Apollo in that part of his house on the Palatine hill which had been struck with lightning, and which, on that account, the soothsayers declared the God to have chosen. He added porticos to it, with a library of Latin and Greek authors; and when advanced in years, used frequently there to hold the senate, and examine the rolls of the judges.
>
> He dedicated the temple to Apollo Tonans, in acknowledgment of his escape from a great danger in his

Cantabrian expedition; when, as he was travelling in the night, his litter was struck by lightning, which killed the slave who carried a torch before him. He likewise constructed some public buildings in the name of others; for instance, his grandsons, his wife, and sister. Thus he built the portico and basilica of Lucius and Caius, and the porticos of Livia and Octavia, and the theatre of Marcellus. He also often exhorted other persons of rank to embellish the city by new buildings, or repairing and improving the old, according to their means. In consequence of this recommendation, many were raised; such as the temple of Hercules and the Muses, by Marcius Philippus; a temple of Diana by Lucius Cornificius; the Court of Freedom by Asinius Pollio; a temple of Saturn by Munatius Plancus; a theatre by Cornelius Balbus; an amphitheatre by Statilius Taurus; and several other noble edifices by Marcus Agrippa.[2]

Augustus's financial policies aimed to stabilize the currency, increase public revenues, and control inflation. By doing so, he not only strengthened the Roman economy but also used these measures to bolster his political standing and secure the loyalty of the populace and the elite. This intervention helped stabilize the economy, but it also set a precedent for the emperor to engage in private banking.

Following Augustus's lead, senators and other members of the Roman elite also frequently engaged in financial activities to increase their wealth and influence. Many senators were involved in money lending to cities, provinces, and individuals across the Empire, often at high interest rates. They frequently used these loans as a tool for political leverage, allowing politicians to exert influence over debtor cities or provinces. The practice, which was not just a problem during the Empire but had also been rampant during the Republic, was so widespread and potentially exploitative that several laws were enacted to regulate the interest rates and terms of these loans. The Roman historian Tacitus wrote about this in his Annals, stating that during the Roman Republic, the Law of the Twelve Tables forbade the charge of interest.

---

[2] Suetonius, "The Life of Augustus, Book XXIX." 1607.

Moreover, wealthy Romans, including senators, invested in land and commercial ventures throughout the Empire, using their financial resources to further their political careers. Patronage was an essential aspect of Roman society, with the elite providing financial support to clients and lower-class plebeians who, in return, offered political support. This system was underpinned by the wealth accumulated through banking, lending, and other economic activities. The economic and political spheres were deeply intertwined in ancient Rome, with emperors, senators, and other members of the elite using financial strategies to support their political objectives, consolidate power, and maintain the loyalty of the populace and other influential groups.

By the end of the third century AD, due to immense territorial expanses and increasing administrative challenges, Emperor Diocletian (r. AD 284–304) established two distinct seats of power within the Roman Empire. This division was solidified under Emperor Constantine the Great (r. AD 307–331), who founded Constantinople (modern-day Istanbul) in AD 330 as a "New Rome" and the eastern capital of the Roman Empire. During the fourth-century reigns of Constantine the Great (r. AD 306–337) and Theodosius I (r. AD 379–395), the banking system continued to evolve in response to the changing economic, social, and political landscape. This period was marked by significant transformations, including the establishment of Constantinople and the legalization and eventual adoption of Christianity as the state religion with the Edict of Milan. With these changes came extensive administrative and monetary reforms.

As the Empire grew and evolved culturally and politically, so did the regulatory attempts over the money and banking industry. Constantine's monetary reforms influenced banking and financial practices in this era, which included the introduction of the solidus, a gold coin that became the standard for Byzantine and European currencies for more than a millennium. The solidus helped stabilize the economy and facilitated trade and financial transactions across the empire and with other regions. The stability and reliability of the solidus as a currency was crucial for bankers and moneylenders who dealt with exchanges, deposits, and loans.

In addition to the problems with banking, the Roman Empire also faced problems with currency debasement, or the reduction of the valuable metal, usually gold or silver, within the composition of a coin. This was a process that evolved over centuries, often reflecting the financial pressures of the times. One of the earliest instances occurred under Nero (r. AD 54–68) who reduced the silver content of the denarius from around 84 percent to 79 percent. Although this might seem minor, it set a precedent for future emperors to manipulate coinage as a source of state revenue.

The situation with currency debasement escalated during the Crisis of the Third Century, a period marked by political instability and economic decline. Emperors during this time frequently debased the currency to pay for growing military expenses and to support the Roman bureaucracy. By the time of Emperor Severus Alexander (AD 222–235), the silver content of the denarius had fallen to just over 40 percent. His successors pushed this even further; by the reign of Gallienus (AD 253–268), the silver content in the *antoninianus*, a coin introduced to seemingly double the value of the denarius, dipped below five percent. This drastic reduction led to rampant inflation, as the public lost faith in the value of the coins.

One of the most striking examples of the impact of debasement was during the reign of Claudius II Gothicus (AD 268 –270), where the *antoninianus* coins contained almost no silver, being primarily made of base metals with a thin silver wash. The coins circulated far below their intended value, leading to widespread economic distress. During these years of crisis, the chronic debasement of Roman currency not only fueled inflation but also eroded economic stability and trust in the financial system of the Empire. Local populations began to reject imperial coinage, turning instead to bartered goods or localized currency systems that they deemed more reliable.

Yet, the Roman monetary system was able to recover under Emperor Diocletian's (r. 284–305) reforms at the end of the third century AD. Recognizing the dire economic situation, Diocletian introduced a series of comprehensive measures aimed at stabilizing the economy. One of his most significant actions was the overhaul of the Roman currency system. In 301 AD, Diocletian issued the Edict on Maximum Prices which attempted to curb inflation by setting price controls on thousands of goods and services, although this was difficult to enforce and had mixed results. More effectively, he reintroduced coins with higher precious metal content. Diocletian also attempted to reform the taxation system to be more equitable and efficient, linking taxes more closely to the resources and populations of the regions, thereby stabilizing the state's revenues and providing a more consistent basis for government spending.

Following Diocletian, Emperor Constantine continued these reforms. He further stabilized the currency by continuing the issuance of the solidus and reducing the number of old, debased coin types. Constantine's economic policies helped restore faith in the Roman monetary system and provided a foundation of economic stability that supported the empire for several more centuries, particularly in the Eastern regions, which later became the Byzantine Empire. Ultimately, the recovery from the currency debasement crisis was a gradual process, facilitated by significant monetary and fiscal reforms that took decades to fully stabilize the Roman economy.

In the later Empire, banking activities also underwent changes although they were not yet centralized in a modern sense. Instead, they were carried out by private individuals who provided a variety of services, including changing money, keeping deposits, making loans, and facilitating the transfer of funds, especially for commercial and governmental transactions. The presence of a strong, stable currency like the solidus made these activities more straightforward and reliable.

Constantine's and Theodosius's eras also saw the continuation and expansion of the state's involvement in the economy, including regulating financial practices and supervising markets and trade. Laws from this period, including those codified in the Theodosian Code, contain several that deal with financial and economic matters. While the Code covers a broad range of subjects, from civil and criminal law to administrative regulations, it includes specific provisions related to taxation, state finances, commerce, and property rights that reveal the Roman state's approach to economic regulation. Specifically, it addressed issues related to usury or the charging of excessive interest, the duties and responsibilities of bankers, and the protection of depositors and borrowers. These regulations reflected the government's interest in ensuring economic stability and fairness in financial dealings.

The Code also includes various laws concerning the levying and collection of taxes. These laws regulated how taxes were assessed on individuals and land, stipulated tax exemptions for certain classes or professions, and outlined penalties for tax evasion. In addition, it outlined the laws related to the management of state finances, including the funding of public works, the maintenance of the army, and the administration of state-owned lands. These laws aimed to ensure the efficient use of public resources and the financial stability of the state. Furthermore, the laws that governed commercial activities, such as regulations on the sale of goods, trade practices, and the protection of merchants, sought to facilitate commerce while protecting both buyers and sellers from fraud and other malpractices.

Laws related to property rights, including the transfer of property, inheritance, and the management of estates, also had significant financial implications. These regulations ensured the legal transfer of wealth and the protection of property rights within the Roman legal system. Theodosius's Code addressed issues related to debt, lending practices, and the resolution of financial disputes. This included regulations on the charging of interest, the rights of creditors and debtors, and procedures for debt recovery. Moreover, the expansion of the Christian Church and its increasing role in society also impacted banking and financial transactions. The Church's teachings on usury influenced legal and moral attitudes toward lending and interest. In some cases, the Church itself became involved in financial activities by receiving donations, holding property, and making loans, thus playing a role in the broader economic landscape.

Similar to the Theodosian Code, the laws of the Byzantine Emperor, Justinian (AD 527–565), included reforms and new laws concerning money. In his Digest of Justinian, part of the larger Corpus Juris Civilis, he offers a comprehensive overview of Roman law, including regulating financial matters. Like the Theodosian Code, these regulations covered a wide array of financial activities, such as the terms of loans and interest, the responsibilities of debtors and creditors, the handling of deposits, and the execution of fiduciary transactions. The legal texts within the Digest provide detailed guidance on resolving financial disputes, the legality of various financial practices, and the protection of parties involved in financial transactions.

In addition, the Digest serves as a compilation of Roman legal principles and writings. In terms of loans, the Digest outlines the obligations of borrowers to repay the principal amount and, under certain conditions, interest. This section clarifies the legal stance on lending money and the protections afforded to lenders, including recourse in cases of non-repayment. It emphasized the importance of mutual consent in loan agreements and detailed the consequences of default, underscoring the legal framework within which lending and borrowing occurred.

The Digest examines the duty of depositaries to safeguard deposited goods and return them upon the depositor's request, reflecting a trust-based nature of deposits. This concept, central to banking, outlined the responsibilities of parties involved in deposit agreements and the legal remedies available in case of loss or damage to deposited property. Interest rates and their regulation are also a significant focus, with a discussion of the legality of charging interest on loans, permissible interest rates, and the penalties for usury. This sophisticated legal approach to managing lending practices and protecting against exploitative interest charges had been dealt with repeatedly since the early Roman Republic. This legal discourse on interest reflects concerns over fairness and economic stability, themes that are still relevant in modern banking regulation.

Fiduciary transactions covered in the Digest also involve situations of transferring property with certain conditions, resembling modern secured loans or trusts. These sections detail the rights and duties of parties in such transactions, including the conditions under which property can be used, profits shared, and the eventual return of property to its owner. Overall, the Digest of Justinian's discussions on money, loans, deposits, and interest rates illuminate the legal foundations of financial transactions in ancient Rome, showcasing a complex legal system that addressed the challenges of managing money and credit. These ancient legal principles laid the groundwork for many concepts central to contemporary banking, highlighting the enduring influence of Roman law on the financial world.

Both the Digest of Justinian and the Theodosian Code demonstrate the Roman state's interest in regulating financial matters, albeit from different legal and historical perspectives. The Digest, with its detailed legal discussions, offers insight into the private law aspects of financial transactions, emphasizing contractual obligations, property rights, and personal liability. Meanwhile, the Theodosian Code provides a view of the public aspects of financial regulation, such as taxation and state oversight of economic activities, highlighting the role of imperial authority in managing the economy.

Over time, diverging cultural, religious, and political paths led to the formalization of the split. The Western Roman Empire, with its capital in Rome, faced decline due to various internal and external pressures, ultimately falling in AD 476. The Eastern Roman Empire, known as the Byzantine Empire, with its capital in Constantinople, continued to thrive, preserving Roman law, Greek culture, and Christian faith, until it fell to the Ottoman Turks in 1453. Even though these civilizations ceased to exist, their influence on banking and money continued into the modern world.

Chapter 6: The Silk Road
and Chinese Paper

It is worthy of observation that every case of failure in finances, since the system of paper began, has produced a revolution in governments, either total or partial.

–Thomas Paine

The next significant leap in the evolution of money occurred because of a vast and successful overland trade system. This route, known as the Silk Road, was a network of trade routes that connected the East and West. It originated around the second century BC, primarily facilitating the exchange of silk from China to countries in Central Asia, the Middle East, Africa, and Europe. Yet the purpose of the Silk Road was not only to trade silk but also to exchange other goods, such as spices, textiles, precious metals, and jewels, along with ideas, cultures, religions, and technologies between the civilizations on its path. This extensive network of routes played a pivotal role in shaping the cultures and economies of the regions it connected, fostering a unique blend of cultural exchange that had lasting impacts on the world.

The origins of the Silk Road can be traced back to the Han Dynasty (206 BC–AD 220) when Emperor Wu (r. 141–87 BC) became interested in developing commercial relationships with the Western regions. The initial motive was to establish alliances and trade relations to secure allies against the nomadic Xiongnu tribes, who posed a significant threat to the empire. Zhang Qian (195–114 BC), a Chinese envoy, was sent on a diplomatic mission to the West. Although he was captured by the Xiongnu, he later returned to China with valuable information about the regions beyond China's western borders. His journey marked the beginning of the Silk Road as a major conduit for the exchange of goods and knowledge between East and West.

Early challenges faced by traders and travelers on the Silk Road were significant, including the difficult landscape they had to travel through, and the threats from thieving gangs. The route crossed some of the most inhospitable terrains, including vast deserts and imposing mountain ranges, which were compounded by the harsh weather conditions. These conditions made travel and transport of goods perilous. Moreover, the threat of banditry and political instability along the route posed constant risks to caravans. Various sections of the Silk Road were controlled by different political entities and shifts in power could disrupt trade or lead to increased taxes and tolls. Traders had to navigate these political complexities and sometimes pay protection money to local rulers or warlords to ensure safe passage.

Despite these challenges, the Silk Road flourished as a vital commercial highway. The exchange of goods was often conducted through a system of relay trade, with merchants covering only a portion of the route and goods being passed down the line from one trader to another. This system and the establishment of roadside inns that provided safe havens for travelers and their goods helped mitigate some of the risks and difficulties associated with long-distance trade.

The Silk Road reached its golden age during the Tang Dynasty (618–907). The Tang emperors expanded and secured the trade routes, making significant efforts to directly control large parts of the network. The Tang Dynasty's openness to foreign trade and cultural exchanges enabled a vibrant era of prosperity and intellectual exchange, with Chinese silk, porcelain, and tea being highly sought after in distant markets. After the Tang Dynasty collapse, the Song Dynasty (960–1279) brought a return to prosperity and stability, albeit with changes in the patterns of trade and commerce.

During the Song Dynasty, maritime trade routes began to gain importance alongside the traditional overland Silk Road. The Song government invested in navy and shipbuilding, enhancing its control over the sea routes connecting China to Southeast Asia, India, the Middle East, and even East Africa. This shift marked the beginning of a gradual decline in the overland Silk Road's prominence, as sea routes offered more direct and safer passages for goods.

However, during the age of the Mongol Empire (1162–1271), led by Genghis Khan (r. 1206–1227) and his successors, the Silk Road underwent a significant revival and experienced one of its most flourishing periods. The Mongol Empire brought about the *Pax Mongolica*, or Mongol Peace, which allowed for unprecedented stability and safety across the Silk Road. Merchants, traders, and travelers could cross vast distances with reduced risk of conflict, thanks to the protection and order imposed by the Mongols. The Mongol era saw increased trade and prosperity along the Silk Road. The security provided by the Mongols and their encouragement of trade resulted in a higher volume and diversity of goods being traded. Luxury items such as silk, spices, precious metals, gems, porcelain, and glassware traveled from East to West, while Europe and the Middle East supplied wool, silver, gold, ivory, and various glass products.

With the success of the trade route during the Tang and Song Dynasties, merchants were subject to theft and the cumbersome task of carrying large amounts of heavy coins. This inspired a new physical form of money: paper currency. This represented a groundbreaking shift away from the metal-based currencies that had dominated for millennia. This innovation, driven by the need to manage wealth and transactions safely in a rapidly growing economy, was transformative. By introducing paper money, China not only addressed the practical issues of weight and the difficulty of transporting metal coins over long distances but also laid the foundation for a new concept of money, one that was based on the trust of the issuing authority. This shift from metal to paper opened new avenues for economic development, allowing for greater flexibility in managing economies and expanding the scope of trade.

The initial emergence of paper money can be traced back to the Tang Dynasty era and the emergence of "flying money," a system of paper receipts from deposit warehouses that stored metal coins for safekeeping. Depositors would store their coins, receiving a receipt that proved ownership in return. The receipts themselves would then be used by merchants who called them "flying money" because they could easily fly away in the wind. These paper notes were created as a solution to the inconvenience of the weight of metal coins and the risk of theft and loss from merchants transporting large amounts over long distances.

Later, during the Tang Dynasty, merchants selected by the government of emperor Xianzong (r. 806–820) created a more organized system. This practice allowed people to deposit goods or coins in exchange for a paper receipt, which would then become a form of money. The paper money, issued to merchants from Xianzong's government in the capital city of Chang'an, could be exchanged for its value at any time. However, since it was transferable, merchants and traders often just exchanged it among themselves instead of turning it in for what it was worth, enabling the paper money to serve as currency without having to exchange it for its value first.

As these deposit house institutions grew, they expanded their services to include currency exchange. Crucial for facilitating trade along the Silk Road, it helped standardize transactions across regions that used different currencies, including various forms of paper money and coins. Moreover, these banks developed sophisticated remittance services, enabling merchants and individuals to transfer money across vast distances. This system of paper money allowed for the deposit of money in one location and its withdrawal in another, similar to the system that Rome established, which would become an essential part of later banking empires.

Over time, these deposit houses became corrupted through fraud and mismanagement. Instead of providing a secure location to hold one's valuables, the owners would take the deposits to try and make more money for themselves through speculative investments. In the event of failure, the deposit houses would lose their client's money, and in the event of large-scale failure, widespread economic instability would be the result. As a consequence of the corruption, the deposit houses were eventually shut down by the Tang Dynasty rulers.

After the fall of the Tang Dynasty, the Song Dynasty rose to power and advanced the idea of using paper as a form of money even further. In the early eleventh century, the Song government officially recognized the potential of paper money and began to issue state-backed currency, initially as a supplement to coins that were difficult to produce because of the scarcity of the copper required to mint them. This government-issued paper money was known as jiaozi and was produced in a sophisticated process that included features to prevent counterfeiting, such as special paper, seals, and serial numbers. The government established several offices to manage the issuance and redemption of paper money, creating a rudimentary form of central banking. The standardization and security features provided by the government to create a trusted form of money backed ostensibly by real assets like gold, silver, and even silk, were intended to solve many of the problems inherent in the "flying money" of the Tang era, while also creating new problems.

One problem is that despite the government's best efforts, counterfeiters were usually able to invent methods to easily replicate paper money. Metal coins, by contrast, not only required metallurgical knowledge to cast and stamp coins, but the metal itself had a value that would make counterfeiting efforts expensive and self-defeating. But paper was much cheaper and easier to produce, and if the value of the paper notes exceeded the cost of the paper and ink, it made counterfeiting a much more enticing proposition. Another issue that arose with the Song paper money was regionalism. Even though the government took over the production and control of money, rulers in the north region would not accept the money from the south, and vice versa. Thus, the currency was not valid throughout the empire, limiting its acceptability and causing a breakdown of trust, defeating the purpose of a ruling currency under centralized control.

Ultimately, the most significant problem created by the Song paper money system was the tendency for the government to over-issue it, causing inflation and an erosion of public trust. Government officials, tempted by the prestige of military campaigns and public works projects, would sometimes print more paper money than it could back with tangible assets, creating a true separation between money and the value the money is supposed to represent. As more paper money entered the economy without a corresponding increase of goods, services, production, and real value, the worth of each unit of paper notes declined, which the public experienced as the mysterious rising of prices.

Counterfeiters created this separation of real stored value and money in an unofficial capacity, as they printed copies of paper notes intended to deceive the public into believing the notes represent real value created and stored at some prior point in time. The notes did not actually represent real value, only a fraudulent doppelganger of value. However, when the state gained the power to issue paper notes, they gained the power to over-issue paper notes. Thus, they accomplished the same result as the counterfeiter, only on a larger scale, with greater public consequence, but under official auspices.

Even so, the use of paper money continued in some places during the Song Dynasty; however, it was in the thirteenth century that a new paper currency was created. Led by the Mongolian ruler who had conquered China, Kublai Khan (r. 1260–1294), the Yuan Dynasty Mongols unified the administration of their empire. By standardizing weights and measures, issuing paper money, and ensuring the security of the trade routes, they established a network of relay stations that provided essential services for messengers and merchants, greatly enhancing the efficiency and safety of overland trade. This period also witnessed a remarkable exchange of goods, ideas, technologies, and cultures among Europe, Asia, and the

Middle East. The Mongols' interest in the arts and sciences of the lands they conquered led to the active promotion of knowledge transfer across their empire. Technologies like papermaking and printing spread westward from China, while gunpowder was introduced to Europe, and medical knowledge was exchanged between the East and West.

Kublai Khan also developed a new paper currency to fix one of the big issues experienced in the Song Dynasty: acceptability. After Khan instituted the new currency, it replaced all the local currencies so that only one could be used in all of China. Khan even allowed the holders of Song money a few years to convert the old money into Yuan money. Under Yuan rule, coinage was also controlled more closely, which led to a wider use of the Yuan paper currency throughout a more unified empire in the East. Under the Mongols, the state took a more active role in issuing and regulating paper money, attempting to centralize the monetary system with the government engaging directly in the banking system to ensure the stability and trustworthiness of paper money.

It was also during the Yuan Dynasty when a European merchant explorer, Marco Polo (1254–1324), journeyed east to discover the trading network of Asia. Marco Polo wrote extensively about his journey along the Silk Road trading route. He brought back goods and ideas, including gunpowder, a postal system, using coal as fuel, and cartography techniques. Yet it was the diffusion of how people in China used paper money, as well as some of the more innovative banking practices, that he brought back which impacted the West the most. It changed how they dealt with money in perpetuity. In his journal, Polo wrote:

> Now you should know that he has money made for him in the following way. He has the bark stripped from trees- to be precise, from the mulberry trees whose leaves are eaten by silkworms. Then the thin layer of bast between the bark and the wood of the tree is removed. After being ground and pounded it is pressed with the aid of glue into sheets like those of cotton paper, which are completely black. And when these sheets are ready, they are cut up into pieces of

different sizes, rectangular in shape and of greater length than breadth. The smallest one is worth half a small tornesel; the next, one small tornesel; the next, half a silver groat; the next, a whole silver groat equal in value to a silver groat of Venice; the next, two groats; the next, five groats; the next, ten groats; the next, one gold bezant; the next, three gold bezants; and so on up to ten bezants. All these sheets of paper are stamped with the emperor's seal. And they are made with as much authority and solemnity as if they were cast from pure gold or silver; for several specially appointed officials write their names on each piece of money, each setting his own stamp, and when everything has been done correctly the chief of the officials deputed by the emperor dips the seal entrusted to him in cinnabar and stamps it on the piece of money, so that the imprint of the seal dipped in the cinnabar remains impressed upon it; and then the money is legal tender. And if anyone were to counterfeit it, he would be punished with the ultimate penalty.

The Great Khan has such a huge quantity of this money made that with it he could buy all the treasure in the world. And when these sheets of paper have been finished in the way I have described to you, he has all his payments made with them and has them distributed through all the provinces and kingdoms and lands where his rule holds; no one dares refuse them on pain of losing his life...

The emperor then summons twelve experts who are appointed to head up this task and are highly proficient at it, and orders them to examine the things the merchants have brought and see to it that what they judge to be fair value is paid for them. So these twelve experts cast their eyes over the goods and see to it that what they deem fair value is paid in the form of these sheets of paper I have told you about. And the merchants accept them willingly, because afterwards they spend them on all the things they buy throughout the emperor's lands. Moreover, I can tell you without a shadow of a doubt that the merchants bring so many things so often during the year that they are easily worth 400,000 bezants, and the emperor has them all paid with these sheets.

Let me further tell you that several times a year a proclamation is issued across the city to the effect that all those who have gems and pearls and gold and silver must bring them to the emperor's mint. And they do so, bringing them in such huge quantities that it is past all reckoning; and they are all paid with these sheets of paper. In this way the emperor accumulates all the gold and the silver and the pearls and the precious stones from all his lands.

I will tell you another thing worth repeating. When these sheets have been so long in circulation that they are torn and defaced, they are brought to the mint and exchanged for fresh new ones in return for surrendering three out of every hundred. And let me tell you a curious fact well worth recording in our book: if a man wants to buy gold or silver to make his service of plate or his belts or other finery, he goes to the emperor's mint with some of those sheets and pays with them for the gold and silver he buys from the master of the mint. All the armies are likewise paid with this kind of money.[3]

Marco Polo's detailed descriptions of this currency system fascinated Europeans and laid the groundwork for the eventual adoption of paper-based currency and how it could be used in banking that greatly transformed the West. Eventually, as paper money began to circulate widely in China, especially during the Song Dynasty and continuing through the Yuan and Ming dynasties, the Chinese banking system underwent significant evolution to manage this new form of currency. This initial innovation of paper money in China set the foundation for modern currency systems. It represented a major shift in economic thought and practice, showing that money could be based on government authority and trust. This early form of fiat money, or money established by the dictates of a centralized

---

[3] Polo, Marco. *Marco Polo: The Travels*, trans. Nigel Cliff (London: Penguin, 1974):151-152. https://archive.org/details/thetravelsbymarcopolo

authority such as a government, would eventually spread across the world, ultimately transforming global economies.

Furthermore, the evolution of the Chinese banking system in response to the introduction of paper money was marked by significant adaptability and innovation. Despite facing various challenges, the Chinese banking system's response to paper money showcased remarkable innovation that would influence financial practices for centuries to come. Ultimately, with Marco Polo's exploration and journal entries, these Chinese contributions to the history of money would eventually influence the world.

Chapter 7: Exploring Money's Essential Traits

Money is only a tool. It will take you wherever you wish, but it will not replace you as the driver.

–Ayn Rand

After exploring the evolution of human trade relationships from simple barter to intermediaries like beads and bits of metal, to stamped coins and paper money, it is easy to see how each of these historical examples demonstrates by what means forms of money can emerge and flourish, only to develop a limitation or impediment that made its population stop using it. As a society gets more complex, money becomes more complex, and new forms of money emerge that allow old limitations to be overcome. Before moving on to look at some of those complex monetary systems, it is important to ask what the common denominators are that are seen in money itself, and examine why this cycle of flourishing, abandonment, and advancement keeps happening.

Barter's requirement for a double coincidence of wants was sufficient for band level societies with the trust that comes from the intimate knowledge of all trade participants so that insufficiently resolved trades could be settled at a later time. Beads and unrefined metal allowed trade to occur within more complex tribal societies by providing a material intermediary that could be substituted for the goods being traded, solving the problem of trust. While the future promises of trade settlement might not be trustworthy, the pretty beads or useful metal had a value that could be trusted on its own. As state-level societies became so complex, more sophisticated money systems had to be developed. As a result, these became more and more removed from the underlying value they represented, from paper deposit house receipts to paper currency issued by the government. Through it all, money continued to evolve, and as the monetary history of the past is examined, they all have some things in common.

Philosophers, economists, and scholars have debated this issue for thousands of years, with the outcome still unresolved among various schools of thought, as will be explored in a later chapter. However, the history of money reveals three primary functions it needs to fulfill in order to work as a facilitator of trade.

» Medium of Exchange: Money expedites trade transactions by acting as an intermediary, or a substitute, in the exchange of goods and services. This function allows trade partners to overcome the limitations and inefficiencies of barter by not requiring a double coincidence of wants and allowing trade to function immediately.

» Store of Value: Money that retains its worth as a trade intermediary that will continue to be accepted over time allows its owners to save it for future use instead of spending it immediately. This lets economic participants consider deferring short term gratification for future benefit, opening the door for the kind of complex projects that can only occur with an orientation toward long term planning.

» Unit of Account: This function provides the means and the standard by which goods and services can be measured and priced. Money can be considered as a unit of account when it is so widely used that it becomes synonymous with value itself. It then becomes the standard by which other things are priced by, ultimately even being used to denominate debt, as well as profits and losses, providing a mechanism for long term planning. The very question

"How much does this cost?" provides the unit of account if the answer is a currency such as shekels, ducats, pounds, or dollars.

Each of these functions can fluctuate in their efficiency, depending on a variety of external factors. Money used as a medium of exchange might be accepted in one region, but not another. The price of a good may be denominated in a particular currency being used as a unit of account, but in the event of inflation and a loss of trust, the currency can no longer fulfill its role because of the changing value of the currency. In the same way, a diluted currency makes its monetary role as a store of value impossible to achieve because its value declines in the future. If the current money falls short in any of these functions relative to the available alternatives, it will be rejected and the economic participants will find something else, even if those alternatives might take a while to gain acceptance.

Over time, in order to properly judge whether money fulfills its functions efficiently, participants in an economy generally considered the following six characteristics and asked whether they are present in the money they are using.

» Acceptability: Money must be universally accepted within a particular economy to be chosen and used in trade. For thousands of years, cowrie shells were accepted until trade interactions became so complex that their limitations caused them to be rejected.

» Divisibility: Money must be able to be divided into smaller and smaller units without losing its relative value. The choice of metal allows for coins of various sizes while a bead cut in half would destroy its value.

» Durability: Money must be able to stand up to physical handling without losing its value to circulate through an economy. Metal coins are more likely to survive rough handling than shell beads.

» Fungibility: Money must be uniform and must be interchangeable with another unit of money to allow for quick verification of authenticity in transactions without confusion. A stamped coin of a particular denomination is easily verified as equal to another stamped coin of the same denomination, while two equal amounts of metal ingots are decidedly different and not uniform, making them difficult to facilitate efficient transactions.

» Portability: Money must be easy to carry and transport. Metal coins may be more durable, but they are also heavy. This can make paper money more attractive for long distance transport.

» Scarcity: Money must be of limited supply so that its value remains consistent, difficult to dilute, and therefore trustworthy. Scarce metals like gold and silver have been chosen as money over plentiful metals like iron for this reason.

Different cultures in history regarded some of these properties of money as more important than others, and the degree to which they are prioritized depends on the context of their needs and the period of history in which they lived. In fact, circumstances both internal and external to the manner in which the money is used can affect how well it is regarded. Change happens all the time, as the following cases will show.

As an example of a widely accepted form of money embodying the first characteristic on this list, the Roman denarii represent a significant advancement and its introduction and widespread acceptance expedited economic activities by providing a standardized and convenient method of transaction, which greatly enhanced trade and commerce in their respective civilizations.

The Roman denarii, introduced in the third century BC, became the backbone of the Roman economy, circulating not only within the vast boundaries of the Empire but also in regions beyond its control. As a durable and portable silver coin, divisible by being minted into smaller denominations, the denarius allowed for the easy valuation of goods and services. Furthermore, its uniformity in weight and purity, guaranteed by the state, instilled a high level of trust among users. This simplified transactions by providing a common currency that was accepted across the diverse regions of the Roman Empire. This trust and standardization helped expand trade networks, both internally and through external trading partners, allowing for it to function as a medium of exchange, a unit of account, and for a period of time, a store of value.

Yet, as illustrated in Chapter 5, while it contributed to the economic prosperity and stability of the Empire, the denarii were also issued and controlled by the Roman government and eventually subject to the temptation of debasement by its rulers. Roman emperors such as Nero (54–68 AD) would begin to extract a small amount of silver from the coinage slowly, while later emperors would extract larger and larger amounts, alloying the coinage with cheaper base metals and rendering it nearly worthless. Trust in the currency was destroyed and Roman citizens rejected it in trade, demonstrating that, over the course of history, the acceptability of a particular form of money is a product of countless individual decisions in a society that continuously judges whether the money is worth accepting.

As an example of portability in money, trade beads used by European merchants to conduct commerce in Africa and Asia from the late Middle Ages until the nineteenth century were a good example. The aggry, or glass trade beads, were introduced by European explorers and became widely used by peoples in Africa. These beads, created and crafted by European artisans, allowed those using them to widen their trade network, demonstrating how portability became a crucial factor for money. Originating in various parts of Europe such as Venice and the Netherlands, these beads were a cornerstone of trade, especially between European traders and Indigenous peoples in Africa and North America from the sixteenth through the nineteenth centuries.

Trade beads were small, made from decorative glass beads, and came in a variety of colors, sizes, and designs. They were beautiful but also served as a practical and effective form of currency in different parts of the world, most notably in Africa. Their physical characteristics, small size, and lightweight nature made trade beads an ideal medium for economic transactions, especially in contexts where portability was essential, such as for long-distance trade by ship. European traders widely used these beads in their dealings with African communities, exchanging them for gold, ivory, and palm oil. Though man-made, they required skill and craftsmanship to create, making them relatively scarce, as their rarity and decorative appeal of the beads in Africa added to their desirability and value as a trade item.

Beyond their function as a tool of commerce, trade beads also held significant cultural and social value, just like the Olivella shells in California. They were used not only as a form of currency but also as adornments and symbols of status. This further solidified their value in the societies that used them. The versatility and widespread acceptance of trade beads across various regions and cultures showed their effectiveness as a portable form of money. Here too, anyone can see the decline of this form of money, particularly in African communities, as the European traders flooded the market with beads, which diminished their scarcity value and made them less desirable.

Another characteristic of money, divisibility, can be shown in a form of money popular in feudal Japan during the Edo period (1603–1868). In this rice-based economic system, rice was measured in units called koku, or an amount sufficient to feed one person for one year (approximately 150 kg./330 lbs.). The use of rice as a currency was deeply rooted in Japan's agrarian society, where rice was not only a staple food but also a symbol of wealth and power. In fact, using rice as a form of money dates back to the seventh century. However, due to previous political instability and infighting, it was not until the early Edo period that the Tokugawa shogunate would bring peace, stability, and a more widespread use of koku.

As a tangible and consumable commodity, a koku could be measured and divided into smaller units, making it adaptable for a wide range of transactions. This flexibility was crucial in a predominantly agricultural economy, where varying amounts of rice needed to be allocated for different purposes, from paying samurai stipends to settling tax obligations. The koku system's adaptability facilitated both large-scale transactions, such as trade and payment of taxes to the feudal lords, and smaller, more routine exchanges at the local level. The standardization of the koku across feudal Japan also provided a consistent basis for these economic activities, fostering stability and predictability in the market.

Furthermore, the koku system intertwined Japan's economic and social structures. As the primary form of payment for samurai and a measure of a domain's wealth, it played a central role in the hierarchy of feudal Japan. Lords would distribute rice to their samurai as a means of sustenance and loyalty, and the amount of rice produced by a domain, or rice farm, determined its economic power and status. However, the system's reliance on agricultural output also meant that it was vulnerable to fluctuations in rice production, which could be affected by factors such as weather and natural disasters.

The Edo period witnessed significant urbanization and commercialization. Cities like Edo (modern-day Tokyo) and Osaka grew rapidly. The increased demand for goods and services led to the diversification of the economy, with rice playing a central role as both a food staple and a form of currency. However, similar to the physical limitations of grain in Mesopotamia, as the economy grew, carrying large amounts of rice became impractical for large transactions. This led to the development of rice certificates, which represented a certain quantity of rice and could be traded as a form of currency. Although this served as an early form of paper money in Japan, the koku system remained a fundamental part of the Japanese feudal economy and governance until the late nineteenth century.

Another required characteristic of money is scarcity. Fundamentally, if a particular kind of money cannot be replicated easily, it becomes more valuable because it cannot be diluted. An example of this comes from the early international trade network known as the spice trade. In the Banda Islands, now part of Indonesia, nutmeg and other spices native to the island proved valuable because of their limited availability. At the height of the European spice trade during the sixteenth century, these rare spices became highly coveted as an elite commodity.

Nutmeg, along with other spices like cloves and mace, were highly valued in Europe for their culinary, preservative, and medicinal properties. Being native only to the geographically isolated Banda Islands, European powers recognized the immense value of nutmeg. Thus, they engaged in fierce competition to control the spice trade routes and the islands where it was produced. This competition was driven by the desire to control a rare and valuable resource in order to achieve economic dominance.

Through the Dutch East India Company, the Dutch were particularly successful in gaining control over the Banda Islands, establishing a monopoly over the nutmeg trade in the early seventeenth century. Their approach to maintaining strict control over the production and distribution of nutmeg focused on ensuring that its supply remained limited to the Banda Islands. This strategic control allowed the Dutch to dictate the supply of nutmeg and, consequently, its price in European markets. The scarcity of nutmeg, artfully maintained by the Dutch, ensured that it remained a high-value commodity central to the lucrative spice trade that significantly influenced the economies of Europe and the East Indies.

Due to this scarcity, nutmeg functioned as more than just a spice; it became a form of money in the trading ports of the East Indies and Europe. Due to its limited availability, the high value meant that even small amounts of nutmeg could facilitate substantial transactions, making it a powerful medium of exchange. Back in Europe, nutmeg's status as a luxury item, affordable only to the wealthy, demonstrated its significance as a symbol of status and wealth. The spice trade, driven by the scarcity of commodities like nutmeg, was one of the most profitable enterprises of its time, illustrating the profound economic impact that a single, scarce commodity can have.

The next characteristic that plays an important role in defining money is fungibility. The state-level civilization of the Maya (ca.1500 BC–AD 900) flourished for centuries from Mexico to El Salvador in Central America. Cacao, a product from local trees and used to make chocolate, was highly valued by the Mayans, who integrated it into many aspects of their culture, including religion, where they also believed it was an ingredient in the creation of humans. Requiring a labor-intensive effort to turn into a usable product, the Mayan civilization used cacao as a form of money, extracting it from large pods full of individual cacao beans harvested from the native tree. As each bean was fairly uniform, they had a roughly equivalent value, making them highly fungible. This allowed for a standard of currency where one bean could be easily exchanged for another since there was little variation in individual size.

Cacao beans were used for a variety of transactions in Mayan society. They were often used in markets to purchase everyday items and for larger transactions, such as trading commodities between different regions or cities. The beans could buy food, clothes, and other goods. Historical records suggest that there were established exchange rates, allowing them to be used as a unit of account, with a specific number of cacao beans equating to various items, such as a small rabbit or a large piece of cloth. The use of cacao beans as currency continued until the nineteenth century but declined prior to that for a variety of reasons, including the arrival of Spanish who introduced their own currency system, displacing the indigenous forms.

Strangely, even though demand for chocolate grew wildly in Europe, increasing the value of cacao beans as a trade commodity, its value as a currency declined. This was because it was used for small and mundane transactions in the indigenous population, while large and sophisticated transactions were conducted with colonial Spanish currency. Thus, holders of cacao beans found it more valuable to export their beans to Europe rather than transact with it in Central America.

Each of these examples tells the story of some kind of material substance imbued with certain qualities that allowed it to eventually be accepted as money. They were able to fulfill important trade functions within an economy, perhaps initially accepted due to some non-monetary value but ultimately achieving a monetary value on its own because of its usefulness as an intermediary for trade. These examples embodied each of the historically accepted properties of money as a manifestation of physical characteristics. But not all forms of money fulfill their monetary characteristics this way.

One of the most unusual forms of money to ever exist had both physical characteristics and immaterial monetary qualities. Likely used for centuries before contact with Western explorers, Rai stones emerged as a currency among the population of Yap Island. Part of a remote group of islands in the South Pacific known today as Micronesia, Yap Island is less than one hundred square kilometers in size. The Rai stones, also known as Yap stones, were massive stones carved from limestone into disks of variable sizes from one foot in diameter all the way up to twelve feet across. The stones were not native to Yap Island, but were quarried from islands such as Palau, over two hundred and fifty miles away. The earliest Yap Stones date back as early as the sixteenth century. Therefore, bringing the stone back to Yap Island took enormous effort, particularly without the technological advancements of shipbuilding from Europe or the Americas.

The value of Rai stones was not based on the limestone material itself but on a combination of factors including their size, history, and the effort taken to quarry and transport them. They were not divisible, fungible, or portable, due to the uniqueness, lack of uniformity, and sheer weight of the stones. However, they were durable, and the difficulty in procuring them made them scarce. The great effort required to extract, transport, and shape them made them a symbolic proxy for work itself. The stones were not used for daily exchanges but were accepted for larger socially significant transactions like marriage dowries, inheritance, political deals, or to signify social status. And the most unusual aspect of how the Rai stones were used within the Yapese culture was how they changed ownership. As many of the stones were too heavy to move, a transfer of ownership simply required an announcement to the Yapese community. No modifications needed to be made for the stones themselves, no additional carving, engraving, or branding. A public declaration sufficed, the community established a social consensus over the ownership, and the multi-ton stones would never need to move.

It is clear that this form of money could only exist in a culture with a high degree of social cohesion and trust reinforced by centuries of tradition. It is difficult to imagine this kind of trust in a culture of any larger size and without a well-accepted system for adjudicating disputes. But it also demonstrates that it is possible to have a kind of money whose value does not lie exclusively with the possession and custody of a physical object. In the case of the Rai stones, their value was rooted as much in the stories told about them, the enormous effort expended for them, and the social consensus that determined ownership, as in the physical stones themselves.

Though the system of the Rai stones worked well for centuries, changes in technology and culture changed how the Rai stones would be accepted among the Yapese people. In approximately 1871, the Irish American sailor, David O'Keefe, arrived on the Yap Islands. He became a prominent figure in the local economy, facilitating the trade of dried coconut meat, known as copra. While on the islands, he learned about the Rai stones and their economic value. He also knew that in order to get enough copra for trade, he needed to hire local workers who had no particular interest in working for him, as he had nothing of value to trade with them.

After observing how the Yapese people used the Rai stones for trade, O'Keefe attempted to create monetary value to pay the islanders by traveling to one of the original quarries on Palau and creating new stones. He realized he could do this relatively inexpensively with better tools and boats than what the Yapese had used when the original stones were created. Many of the island tribesmen were opposed to his plan because part of the value of the initial Yap stones was the history of how they arrived, the stories of the great effort made to bring them to Yap Island, and the social consensus agreement of ownership over time. However, O'Keefe still brought new stones to the island as a way to pay locals to farm coconuts for his business enterprise.

Consequently, with the introduction of new stones, the value of the initial stones drastically declined as the islanders realized the new stones could easily be brought into the monetary system. Not only did that diminish the scarcity of the stones, but it also destroyed the importance of the history behind them. After all, if the original stones were significant because of the effort expended to retrieve them, then the demonstration of the new and easily quarried stones made the history of the older stones far less significant.

The Rai stones tell a story about a unique form of money with great physical limitations, such as a lack of divisibility, fungibility, and portability. But it nevertheless achieved acceptance within the Yapese culture because of intangible features such as social consensus that established ownership through community agreement, which made those limiting issues less important. The next chapter will examine other forms of money that also carry non-material features that not only solve certain physical limitations such as portability, but also greatly enhance the complexity of trade, and make new forms of monetary relationships possible through the issuance of credit.

Chapter 8: Renaissance to Riksbank

I sincerely believe that banking establishments are more dangerous than standing armies, and that the principle of spending money to be paid by posterity, under the name of funding, is but swindling futurity on a large scale.

–Thomas Jefferson

Although more intricate than its Mesopotamian and Greek predecessors, the Roman and Chinese banking systems still lacked many aspects of the banking system of today. Yet it was the Italians during the Renaissance that brought banking closer to its modern form. This was done by an Italian family, the Medici, who advantageously capitalized on the wealth and connections they had developed through their wool trading business. The Medici established their first bank in Florence, aptly named the Medici Bank, quickly recognizing the potential for expansion by serving the financial needs of the Catholic Church and other powerful entities of the era. This banking empire marked the emergence of modern banking concepts, including double-entry bookkeeping and the creation of banking institutions that not only facilitated commercial transactions but also began accumulating and lending capital in ways that would be recognized today. Among these innovations, the Medici Bank stands out for its pioneering role in creating a network spanning major European trade centers, laying the groundwork for international banking.

The Medici bank was founded by Giovanni di Bicci de' Medici (ca.1360–1429), and in 1397, he moved his bank from Rome to Florence, where he was from. This move sparked the beginning of a banking empire that would span much of Europe and last for over nine decades. One innovation that expanded the Medici Bank was the creation of branches throughout Italy and, eventually, other major European cities. Although owned by the Medici, these branches acted independently from one another, having their individual balance sheets and relationships with the other branches. They even had their own names and governance structures. The Medici's choice of locations for their bank branches was strategic, focusing on major commercial and political centers of Europe, including Rome, Venice, Milan, and Geneva, and branches in major trading hubs such as Bruges, London, and Avignon. These locations were selected for their vibrant commercial activities, which offered ample opportunities for financial services such as currency exchange, trade financing, and handling of remittances for the Church and other large clients.

To operate these branches effectively across the diverse and geographically dispersed regions of Europe, the Medici relied on a network of trusted family members, loyal employees, and agents. They often sent younger family members or trusted managers to oversee the operations of these branches, ensuring that the bank's interests were closely aligned with those of the family, while still giving enough autonomy to deal with local issues. This network allowed for efficient communication and the transfer of funds between branches, facilitating their larger European operations, and enabling the Medici to engage in lucrative currency exchange transactions across their network of branches.

Furthermore, the Medici Bank was adept at cultivating relationships with powerful clients, including the Catholic Church and various European monarchs. These relationships were key to the bank's success, as they provided a steady stream of business and helped to mitigate the risks associated with lending and other banking activities. This network enabled the Medici to spread their financial risk and take advantage of local variations in interest rates, exchange rates, and the demand for money. By operating in multiple jurisdictions, they could shift resources and capital to where they were most needed or where they could earn the highest return, all while maintaining adherence to the Church's teachings in a nominal sense.

Thus, as the Medici conducted its banking business in many places, it helped them avoid local and religious-based laws against usury. The Medici family cleverly navigated the religious and ethical constraints of their time. Since charging interest was essential for the profitability of lending money, the Church's stance against it threatened to limit the scope of financial activities that banks could engage in without falling afoul of religious doctrines. To circumvent these restrictions, the Medici developed innovative financial instruments and practices that effectively allowed them to profit from lending money without overtly violating restrictions on charging interest.

One such practice was the use of a financial instrument they developed called a bill of exchange. This involved providing merchants with a document in one city that could be redeemed for cash in another, thus facilitating trade across long distances. The difference in exchange rates between different cities allowed the Medici to earn a profit akin to charging interest, but it was not classified as such, thus skirting laws that prohibited the activity. The Medici also engaged in creative accounting and using nominal partnerships to disguise interest as a share of profits, which was not prohibited by the Church. By making their clients and borrowers so-called partners in their ventures, the profits shared could include what would traditionally be considered interest payments. This provided a return on the Medici's investments without explicitly charging interest.

Through these methods, the Medici not only expanded their banking empire across Europe but also laid the groundwork for modern financial practices. Their ability to navigate the complex landscape of religious laws, combined with their innovation in financial instruments, set a precedent for future banks to operate on a large scale, contributing significantly to the development of the global financial system. This blend of financial acumen, geographic expansion, and regulatory navigation allowed the Medici to amass unparalleled wealth and influence, marking them as pioneers in the history of banking.

Yet possibly more impactful than the branch structure of the Medici Banks was their bookkeeping systems. Although the Medici were not the first to create a double-entry method of accounting, which had different columns for debits and credits, they used it to their own advantage. The double-entry ledger system was designed by merchants in the fourteenth century and was first written down by a monk named Luca Pacioli in his work *Summa de arithmetica* (1494). Pacioli described:

> For each one of all the entries that you have made in the Journal you will have to make two in the Ledger.
>
> That is, one in the debit {in dare) and one in the credit (in havere). In the Journal the debtor is indicated by per, -the creditor by a, as we have said. In the Ledger you must have an entry for each of them.
>
> The debitor entry must be at the left, the creditor one at the right ; and in the debitor entry you must indicate the number of the page of the respective creditor. In this way all the entries of the Ledger are chained together and you must never make a credit entry without making the same entry with its respective amount in the debit. Upon this depends the obtaining of a trial balance (bilancio) of the Ledger.[4]

This more advanced accounting process allowed bankers, merchants, and even individuals to assess how much money was coming in versus how much money was going out within an account. Using this accounting system as a base, the Medici established a set of "secret books." These documented not only the money coming and going but also who owned it. This allowed them to see risk or

---

[4] Pacioli, Luca. *Ancient Double-Entry Bookkeeping: Lucas Pacioli's treatise (A.D. 1494 - The Earliest Known Writer on Bookkeeping* (Denver: John Geijsbeek, 1914):46. https://archive.org/details/ancientdoubleent00geijuoft.

evaluate the possibility of losing money on a person or entity they loaned to or invested money in. The Medici were able to systematically evaluate who their customers were in terms of who was paying back their debts versus those who did not.

The Medici continued to influence banking with their innovations and practices with what was likely the most significant influence in monetary systems, which came when the Medici and their wealth were used to help control politics and culture in Florence. From their early involvement in the Florentine Republic, the Medici family steadily climbed the ranks of political influence, paralleling their ascent in the financial sector. An early family member, Ardingo de' Medici, served on the prestigious signoria council in the late thirteenth century, setting a precedent for the family's political entanglements. Over the next fifty years, the Medici's presence in the signoria was a frequent occurrence, marking the start of their extended political influence in Florence.

The family's political control reached its height under Cosimo de' Medici (1389–1464), who discreetly manipulated the political scene of the Florentine Republic by capitalizing on the prosperity of the Medici bank. Avoiding an official royal title to outwardly respect the republic's values, Cosimo instead employed strategic negotiation and bribery to influence political affairs and elections. After the Medici family was expelled from Florence in 1494, leading to the closure of the Medici Bank, the family eventually returned to power in Florence. However, they did not reopen the Medici Bank in its previous form or scale. While the Medici continued to be involved in financial operations and maintained their influence in European financial matters, the original banking enterprise that had propelled them to the height of economic and political power in the Renaissance did not make a comeback.

The Medici family shifted their focus toward governance, patronage of the arts, and the accumulation of political power. They produced several popes, including Leo X (served 1513–1521) and Clement VII (served 1523–1534), and married into European royalty when Marie de' Medici (1575–1642) married Henry IV of France (r. 1589–1610). These prestigious roles by the Medici family members further solidified their status as one of the most influential families in Europe. Their legacy lived on through their contributions to art, architecture, and the political landscape of Italy rather than through banking.

However, despite the eventual decline of the Medici Bank in the late fifteenth century due to a combination of poor management, political upheavals, and competition, their innovative banking practices and the international network of branches they established had a lasting impact on the banking industry, setting the stage for modern financial systems. The Medici family's intertwining of banking, politics, and culture during the Italian Renaissance also set a powerful precedent for how financial institutions could wield their influence far beyond the realm of commerce, shaping the very fabric of society.

Moreover, with their relationships with powerful merchants and politicians, their currency exchanges providing enormous liquidity, their status as elite citizens and patrons of the arts, and their navigation of the Florentine regulatory environment, the Medici gained the ability to issue credit at a scale unprecedented in human history. Their bills of exchange were essentially "I owe you" debts that served as a cash-like financial instrument, sometimes trading multiple times before being settled. Their network of branches across Europe and their double-entry bookkeeping system that gave them the ability to better judge credit risk enabled them to extend credit across a broader geographical area than any other state or institution had before.

From examples of the forms of money in previous chapters, it can be seen that each new advancement in the technology of money solved a problem that kept a particular society from advancing because of the limitations in its money system, while also creating a new problem with new limitations. Melted down bits of metal served as a good intermediary for bulky bushels of grain but had to be examined and weighed against a standard to prove their authenticity and quantity. Stamped coins offered uniformity and trust, solving the problem of meticulous authentication, but proved to be heavy in large quantities when used in long distance trade. Paper money solved the problem of weight but reintroduced the problem of authenticity and trust with easily counterfeited and inflatable paper currency. And ultimately, though each new advancement solves a pressing economic issue, the money becomes more abstract and distant from the value it is supposed to represent.

The Medici, while not the first to issue credit, did so on such a scale and quantity that it became a form of money itself, backed by their social prestige as well as their proven ability to assess risk. They solved multiple economic problems such as reducing the risk of transporting large amounts of physical money, facilitating international trade by operating in multiple regions, increasing liquidity and providing more capital for investment, and managing risk through sophisticated bookkeeping methods. But at the same time, just as prior monetary advancements had done, the very idea of credit as money became an even more abstract concept, distant as ever from the value that it represented.

The Medici legacy of credit creation backed by banking innovations, political ties, and cultural patronage by banking dynasties set the stage for the next significant evolution in the world of finance: the emergence of central banking. In this continuum of financial history, the establishment of the Riksens Ständers Bank or the Estates of the Realm Bank in Sweden during the seventeenth century stands as a pivotal moment. This name reflects the bank's foundation in the political structure of Sweden at the time, as the Riksdag of the Estates was the legislative body in Sweden. It consisted of four levels: the nobility, the clergy, the burghers (merchants and townspeople), and the peasantry. These estates represented the different classes of Swedish society and were involved in the governance of the country, including fiscal and monetary policies.

Founded in 1668, the Riksens Ständers Bank, which changed its name in 1867 to Sveriges Riksbank, was among the first institutions to function as a central bank. It introduced concepts that would redefine banking on a global scale. The Sveriges Riksbank continues to be the oldest central bank and is now referred to simply as the Riksbank. Unlike the Medici bank, which was a private entity deeply involved in political machinations and throughout much of Europe, the Riksbank represented a move toward institutionalized financial governance. It was tasked with managing the nation's currency and overseeing monetary policy, functions that have become synonymous with the role of central banks today.

This transition from private banking dynasties like the Medici to state-regulated central banking systems marked a significant evolution in financial history. It highlighted a new way of thinking about banking, driven by the belief that political actors could bring on a more structured and regulated approach to managing the economic and financial aspects of a nation. By being closely linked to the Riksdag of the Estates, the bank's operations and policies were inherently connected to the interests and governance of the Swedish state, reflecting an even more overt connection between the government and the bank in managing the country's financial issues.

One of the key functions of the Riksbank that underscored its role as a precursor to modern central banks was its authority to issue currency. As with China and the development of paper money by the Song Dynasty and the Mongols, this shifted the control of the money supply from private hands into a centralized public authority. A more coordinated management of the nation's economy enabled it to issue currency and provide the government with a mechanism to finance its activities without relying on private loans. This ultimately reduced the state's dependency on private bankers such as the Medici, who imposed limits on the credit they created through dedicated risk analysis and the need to not exceed the boundaries of their prestige. The Riksbank, backed by the power and prestige of the state, could now arbitrarily separate money from the underlying value it represented. With prior monetary advancements, this separation was an unintentional consequence. For the Riksbank, it was their purpose and reason for being.

Furthermore, the Riksbank played a larger role in Sweden's economy by managing credit and interest rates, another hallmark of modern central banking. By regulating the amount of money in circulation and setting key interest rates, the Riksbank could influence economic conditions within the country. Although claiming to prevent the kind of financial crises that were common when banking was dominated by private interests, the establishment of the Riksbank represented a fundamental rethinking of the role of banks within the state. It was designed to serve the financial needs of the political few to manage the economic welfare of the many, laying the foundation for the development of central banks worldwide. This transition was not just revolutionary in Swedish banking but also set a precedent for the evolution of financial institutions globally, moving toward models that emphasize public trust, and the facilitation of state policy.

The Sveriges Riksbank was a significant change from an earlier attempt at creating a national bank, Stockholm Banco, which collapsed in 1664. The Stockholm Banco was established in 1656 under the auspices of the Swedish crown and is often considered the precursor to the Riksbank. Founded by Johan Palmstruch, it was the first bank in Europe to issue paper currency on a regular basis, a step meant to facilitate transactions and stimulate the Swedish economy. This initiative marked a significant departure from the sole reliance on metal coins as currency throughout Europe and was aimed at overcoming the shortages of coinage that hampered trade and economic activity.

However, the ambitious project of the Stockholm Banco was not without its flaws, which ultimately led to its collapse. The bank issued more paper money than it could back with silver and gold, which led to inflation and a loss of confidence in the currency. Initially, these banknotes were a convenience, allowing for easier transactions and reducing the need for cumbersome coinage. Yet, as the bank continued to issue more notes without sufficient metal reserves to redeem them, the value of the notes began to plummet. The situation worsened due to the bank lending heavily to the Swedish government, which further strained its reserves. The government's financial demands, driven by military campaigns and the ambition to expand Swedish territorial control, meant that the bank's resources were increasingly tied up in loans that could not be easily liquidated. This made it difficult for the bank to respond to depositors' demands for their money.

The crisis came to a head when depositors, losing faith in the bank's notes, began demanding redemption of their paper money for metal coins. The bank's inability to fulfill these requests eroded public trust even further, leading to a run on the bank. In 1664, the situation became untenable, forcing the Swedish government to intervene. Johan Palmstruch was held personally responsible for the bank's failure and was initially sentenced to death. His sentence was later commuted to life imprisonment. The government took over the bank's operations, attempting to stabilize the situation by withdrawing the devalued notes and trying to restore confidence in the currency. With Stockholm Banco shut down, there came a need for a new bank.

The Riksbank varied from its predecessor, as it was created by the government instead of a private individual. In addition, it was designed to make sure that the king could not just take away people's money from the bank. This was important because people needed to trust that their money was safe after what happened with Stockholm Banco. The Riksbank was also important to the government because it helped manage its own money and debts. These tasks spurred discussions while the bank was being formed on improving the government's way of borrowing money. Unlike earlier central bank models, the Riksbank involved the people of Sweden, albeit through a government advisory assembly called the Estates. This was an attempt to balance the power between the government and the citizens.

Since the Riksbank was also tasked with managing the nation's money supply, regulating credit, acting as a lender of last resort to other banks, and setting the foundation for modern central banking practices, it used the lessons learned from the Stockholm Banco's failure. This greatly influenced the operations and policies of the Riksbank as it adopted a more conservative approach to issuing paper currency, ensuring it had sufficient reserves to back the notes it issued. This aimed to maintain public confidence in the paper currency and prevent the kind of crisis that led to the Stockholm Banco's downfall.

The creation of the Riksbank as the first central bank was a major step in the history of money. It influenced not just Sweden but also how banks and governments worked together in other parts of

Europe, helping to shape the modern banking system that exists today. In this way, the collapse of the Stockholm Banco directly led to the creation of the Riksbank, as it underscored the need for a banking institution that could provide stability and confidence in the monetary system. The establishment of the Riksbank marked the beginning of a new era in banking, with the central bank model eventually becoming a standard feature of national economies worldwide. With complexity in banking connecting more regions, global trade took on a larger role throughout Europe, Africa, Asia, and the Americas.

Chapter 9: Spices and Global Trade

With the sinews of war, money in abundance.

– Cicero

While the international banking system was pioneered by the Medici family, trade on a global scale originated in India during the mid-1600s with one of the world's largest private companies in the history of the world, the East India Company and the larger network of trade demanded a shift in monetary practices. Not only had banking become more complex, with a global trade system emerging, funding trade ventures and settling payments between different currencies became pivotal in the story of money.

Wanting to profit from the lucrative spice trade in Southeast Asia that the Dutch and Portuguese had been developing, Queen Elizabeth I of England granted a royal charter to form the East India Company in 1600. This charter was unique in allowing for a joint-stock company, a company where there was a group of private investors that created limited liability for the individual investors. This ultimately allowed investors to put money into the company to reduce the risk so they would not lose everything if the venture failed. Allowing for the parties who put up money, whether government, individuals, or banks, to share the liability if the venture failed, this also raised needed funds for the East India Company's activities.

By the eighteenth century, trading companies in Britain, Spain, Portugal, France, and the Netherlands had established trade routes across the Americas, Africa, and Asia. This era of exploration opened new markets, leading to the flow of goods such as spices, sugar, tobacco, tea, and coffee. The use of these resources and the development of trade networks were instrumental in accumulating wealth in these European countries. This emerging international trade caused gold and silver to become universally recognized as a store of value and a medium of exchange as it was easily divisible, relatively portable, scarce, and immutable. Originally using both metals as currency, these commercial networks eventually led nations to adopt a more stable way of dealing with money by only using gold, which had more scarcity and value. This allowed for bills of sale to be used with only one way of valuing them and without the need to value individual currencies against each other. The use of both gold and silver for commerce, or bimetallism, was a complicated system that required a way to consistently value merchandise using a ratio of the value between silver and gold in order to transact trade in either currency.

With a shift to using just gold for trade, it allowed for a single value to back currency. From this monetary approach, Britain adopted the gold standard, or tying currencies to a fixed quantity of gold, with the Gold Standard Act of 1819. However, this was not the first time Britain had tied their money to gold. In fact, in 1717, Sir Isaac Newton (1642–1727), the Master of the Mint in Britain, set the official silver price against the gold guinea at twenty-one shillings, "…I humbly represent, that a pound weight of Gold Eleven Ounces fine, and 1 ounce Allay is cut into 44½ Guineas, and 1 Pound weight of Silver 11 Ounces…"[5] This created a consistent value to measure the silver against gold regardless of outside price influences. This decision established a non-binding gold standard in Britain. This policy undervalued gold relative to silver though, which led to the prevalence of gold over silver in circulation. Following this about one hundred years later, the 1819 act legally fixed the value of the

---

[5] Newton, Isaac. Isaac Newton to the Lords Commissioners of the Treasury, October 22, 1718. The Newton Project. https://www.newtonproject. ox.ac.uk/view/texts/normalized/NATP00282

British Pound Sterling to a specified amount of gold, which then established a stable basis for international trade.

After its success in Britain, the gold standard began to have widespread adoption in the nineteenth century. Between the years 1871–1873, Germany adopted a gold standard while the United States (U.S.) came up with their official policy in 1875 with the Specie Resumption Act. The beginning of the Act states:

> "An act to provide for the resumption of specie payments." This act provided for the redemption of paper currency in gold or silver and a reduction in the amount of outstanding paper bills, the so called "Greenbacks", beginning in 1879. Restoring convertibility was a necessary step in the re-establishment of the gold standard.

> Be it enacted by the Senate and House of Representatives of the United States of America in Congress assembled, That the Secretary of the Treasury is hereby authorized and required, as rapidly as practicable, to cause to be coined at the mints of the United States, silver coins of the denominations of ten, twenty-five, and fifty cents, of standard value, and to issue them in redemption of an equal number and amount of fractional currency of similar denominations, or, at his discretion, he may issue such silver coins through the mints, the sub treasuries, public depositaries, and post-offices of the United States; and, upon such issue, he is hereby authorized and required to redeem an equal amount of such fractional currency, until the whole amount of such fractional currency outstanding shall be redeemed.[6]

Similarly, Japan implemented their gold policy in 1897. One thing to note about the Japanese gold standard act is that the denominations by type of metal as well as the metal content listed in the legislation, "The composition of the coins shall be as follows: Gold coins 900

---

6 United States Congress. "Specie Resumption Act." The Statutes at Large and Proclamations of the United States of America, vol. XVIII, part 3, (1873-1875): 296.

parts of pure gold to 100 parts of copper. Silver coins. 800 parts of pure silver to 200 parts of cop)per. Nickel coins. 250 parts of nickel to 750 parts of copper. Copper coins. 950 parts of copper; 40 parts of tin, and 10 parts of zinc."[7] The Japanese act also specified how much each metal could be worth, "Gold coins shall be legal tender to any amount. Silver coins shall be legal tender to the amount of ten yen. Nickel and copper coins shall be legal tender to the amount of one yen."[8] Many other nations also embraced this standard, marking this a period often referred to as the "classical gold standard." Ultimately, the gold standard provided a common measure for international transactions. Leading that standard was the British pound sterling, a currency so trusted and widely accepted in the powerful British Empire that, at its height, became the world's reserve currency.

The global reserve currency established a guideline where all countries who wanted to participate in international trade needed to accumulate and hold British Pounds in reserve. For example, if a merchant sent a ship loaded with sugar and tobacco from the Americas to Portugal, they would very likely take British pound sterling as payment. But the local banks in Portugal also needed to acquire and hold British pounds because they knew that is what these traders would demand in return. This worldwide demand for the British pound was created by the power and might of the British Empire, while at the same time, the demand for the British pound gave strength and prestige to the empire. This reserve currency cycle would cause Britain to emerge as a world's most powerful nation in terms of economic and political influence.

As the emerging global trade network became more and more lucrative, both trading companies and the nations that granted charters to them fought to protect their interests abroad. The trading companies used their growing financial might to project political influence within government. As this led to corruption and cronyism, governments took more control over trade and made poor

---

[7] Laughlin, J. Laurence. "The Gold Standard in Japan. " Journal of Political Economy, 5, No. 3, (1897): 380.
[8] Laughlin, J. Laurence. "The Gold Standard in Japan." 381.

economic decisions that impacted the international commercial network. For example, in nineteenth century London, private banks formed a network, and not only did they take deposits and issue bank notes, but they also started loaning more money to commercial interests and to governments beyond their deposits, essentially extending more and more credit. This is not unique as in general as banks make money by taking the currency in reserve, loaning it out, and then charging interest on the loan banks. Yet, when banks loan too much money it artificially creates more money in the economy, causing inflation, while also causing potential economic instability with the likelihood of making risky loans that could go bad.

Initially, during the time of the East India Company and the flourishing spice trade from the seventeenth century onwards, trade was conducted using precious metals like gold and silver, which were universally accepted as a medium of exchange. This period was characterized by mercantilism, an economic theory that advocated for widespread government action to impose regulations on trade under the belief that state power would be enhanced by a positive balance of trade. This required that the net amount of exported goods is higher than imported goods. The goal of mercantilist policies, therefore, is for a country to export more than they import, and accumulate foreign currency to make up the difference, which in this period of time meant precious metals.

Companies like the East India Company were granted monopolies by their governments to trade in specific regions, and their activities were closely tied to national interests. However, as international trade expanded, the limitations of relying on precious metals became apparent, particularly with the need to add more precious metals to the coffers as well as the physical movement of them. This was both risky and inefficient for settling international transactions. These challenges, along with the need to finance increasingly expensive wars in Europe, prompted the development of more sophisticated financial instruments and institutions.

The concept of central banking emerged as a proposed solution to these challenges, offering a way to manage the money supply more effectively and provide stability to the financial system. The Bank of

England, established in 1694, is often cited as the first modern central bank. It was initially created to raise money for King William III's war against France, but it quickly assumed broader responsibilities, including managing the government's debts, issuing banknotes as a more efficient medium of exchange, and later, regulating the money supply and acting as a lender of last resort to other banks during financial crises.

Over time, other countries established their central banks, drawing on the Bank of England's model. These institutions were tasked with issuing national currencies, managing inflation through monetary policy, overseeing the banking system, and ensuring financial stability. The shift towards central banking reflected a move away from mercantilist policies that drove colonial and economic expansion through state-chartered companies towards a centralized governmental control of monetary policy. This was seen as essential for supporting economic growth, facilitating international trade, and responding to financial crises. Along with the Riksbank, the Bank of England set the precedent for modern central banks as it managed state finances and commercial banks, as well as issued currency and set economic policies. As time went on, the central banks became an ad hoc government institution with these roles but to also lend money to the government and serve as the bankers' banks.

These new central banks institutionalized and normalized a lending practice known since the ancient world, which today is called the fractional reserve system. In simple terms, it means that banks keep only a fraction of the money people deposit with them as reserves or money they have available to pay out. They then lend out the rest to earn interest and make a profit. For example, if someone deposited $100 in a bank, the bank might keep only $20 as a reserve and loan out the remaining $80 to borrowers. The idea behind this system is that not everyone would ask for their money back at the same time, so banks could use the money they had lent out to earn more and pay interest to depositors. However, it also meant that if too many people wanted their money back at once, the bank might not have enough reserves to cover all the withdrawals. The resulting collapse of banks on a small scale would often only hurt those who had deposited their funds and the private owner of the bank.

In the past, banks knew that if they engaged in too much risk, depositors would withdraw their funds, which would make the bank go out of business. For banks to attract depositors in the first place, they needed to project safety and caution through their actions over time in order to engender trust. But when central banks began to assume the role of regulatory oversight; they gained the power to certify private banks and grant to them a veneer of approval and trust driven by political considerations instead of economic ones. The approval of fractional reserve lending by central banks introduced a new kind of undisciplined carelessness to the risk management of banks. Without the need to protect sacred customer deposits, banks could now engage in much more ambitious and risky loan issuance. Consequences that would ordinarily be limited to the local level led to the potential for larger bank collapses and the systematic uncertainty of national and even global boom and bust cycles.

These cycles were characterized by periods of rapid economic expansion often driven by malinvestment, followed by severe contractions or crises from the collapse of said malinvestment. For example, this is what happened with the first big modern economic crisis that occurred in Britain, aptly named the Panic of 1825. This financial catastrophe was triggered by over speculation, or investing a large amount of money in hopes the gain would outweigh the risk. This over speculation occurred when private banks in Britain had issued a large number of notes to finance Latin American mining companies. When these mining ventures failed, it led to a string of bank failures. This crisis highlighted the dangers of unregulated note issuance by private banks as well as the potentially costly issue of speculation driven by risky credit issued by banks unencumbered by the need to have sufficient reserves.

As the private banking sector became larger and more integrated into global trade, governments sought the power to regulate the money supply and oversee the banking system even more, ignoring their own role in the approval and spread of fractional reserve banking.

Private banks in the eighteenth and nineteenth centuries were instrumental in developing many aspects of modern banking, including the issuing of currency, providing credit, facilitating trade, and becoming more and more profitable. As such, they attracted officials of government and their powerful cronies who used the ongoing issues of the boom-and-bust cycles and their devastating economic instability to justify more government action to regulate financial systems. What resulted led to the development and evolution of central banks as key financial institutions in the economy.

One key factor for the increased power of central banking was the increasing occurrence of financial crises and the perceived need for a lender of last resort, or a lender that would help failing banks, to prevent banking panics. Whether a lender of last resort could actually prevent these panics or cause them in the first place by providing a bailout guarantee and essentially removing the need for responsible lending practices, was a question that was never taken seriously. Government action frequently leads to destructive consequences, which frequently then leads to more government action. Similarly, the dictates of central banks often cause economic dislocations resulting in the creation of more damaging policies, ultimately granting them more power. The role of central banks became more tied to the government via the politicians who enacted legislation as they were tasked with regulating the issuance of bank notes, managing national reserves, overseeing commercial banks, and, in some cases, setting monetary policy to counter inflation, deflation, and other economic issues a nation was facing.

The influence of the central banks reached its height in a country that was one of the last of the major world powers to implement one. In the early twentieth century, following a banking crisis where banking cartels, or groups of private banks, joined together, along with the government, to create a central bank in the United States, one that would become the most powerful and influential central bank ever.

Chapter 10: From Gold to Wars

The first panacea for a mismanaged nation is inflation of the currency; the second is war. Both bring a temporary prosperity; both bring a permanent ruin. But both are the refuge of political and economic opportunists.

–Ernest Hemingway

In the later nineteenth and early twentieth centuries, the central banking institutions played an even bigger role in the attempt to manage their respective national currencies and oversee the banking sector. The increasing size of the central banks allowed them to help finance government actions that would normally not occur, such as wars. Ultimately, these institutions gained the power to regulate the supply of money, issue credit to fight against inflation and deflation, and come up with a system that would give governments enough money to carry out their policies, whether they were at home or abroad, peaceful or at war. Yet, even though there was more government intervention and crony practices between politicians and bankers, the central banks continued to operate using gold or silver as a way to back up the currency they printed, as their notes were generally still redeemable for the underlying precious metals.

The period from 1900 to 1913 was a pivotal era for monetary policies across the globe. It was characterized by the widespread adherence to the gold standard and significant developments in the establishment and evolution of central banking. This era, right before the outbreak of World War I, was marked by economic growth, increasing international trade, and financial globalization, but also by the challenges of maintaining monetary stability amidst rapid industrialization and expansion.

It was here, during this age of exponential growth, that central banking could demonstrate their advantages over a pure gold standard. Gold, while fulfilling monetary characteristics such as acceptability and immutability, failed as a portable form of money in the world of industrialization. In fact, its virtue as a physical commodity impervious to counterfeiting, was the very quality that made it fail at portability, in exactly the same way that made the Song Dynasty in China adopt paper currency as money.

Central banks not only had the power to use paper currency and give it legitimacy with the backing of gold reserves, but they could also, with the advent of the telegraph and radio, communicate changes to their ledgers and allow the money to be portable through space instantly. It is important to note, however, that this newfound capability came at the cost of verifiability and trust. A gold bar could be authenticated by a chemical assay, and a gold coin could be authenticated by its weight and the stamp on its surface. Confidence in changes made to a ledger, by contrast, was based on the faith that a customer had in the institution maintaining the ledger. Without a mechanism for authentication beyond a cumbersome audit, only the institution's track record, and a certain amount of suspension of disbelief, made transactions possible.

During these years, the gold standard played a crucial role in guiding monetary policies, as it still retained a historical and cultural authenticity that no other form of money could match. Countries pegged their currencies to a specific quantity of gold, facilitating a stable international exchange rate system that encouraged trade and investment across borders. Central banks were primarily tasked with maintaining gold reserves to defend the currency peg, which often involved adjusting domestic interest rates to influence the flow of gold and stabilize the currency. High interest rates would attract gold inflows by offering higher returns to investors, while lower rates would discourage outflows.

The era also saw significant steps towards the acceleration of central bank power and influence. In Europe, central banks such as the Bank of England and the Reichsbank in Germany were already playing central roles in their economies, managing gold reserves and setting discount rates to influence economic activity. These institutions were also engaged in what might now be recognized as open market operations, or the large-scale buying and selling of government bonds. This allowed for the manipulation of the market through interest rates as a whole with the purpose of controlling the amount of money circulating in the economy, albeit on a more limited scale than would be seen in later years. This period was also notable for international cooperation among central banks, particularly in times of crisis, which allowed them to engage in collaborative efforts to maintain the gold standard and address liquidity crises. With a global economy, central banks recognized that financial instability in one country could quickly spread through the interconnected global economy.

However, the reliance on the gold standard and the mechanisms central banks used to defend it made it difficult for them to manipulate their economies and attempt to create economic activity during downturns, or control inflation during high periods of activity. Efforts to attract gold inflows by raising interest rates. For example, they could lead to reduced investment and economic decline if the cost of the capital for new economic ventures, expressed by interest rates on loans, was too high.

Still, gold remained as the universally accepted expression of real value, unlike the increasingly complex credit creation tools of the central banks. Gold had no counterparty risk, no debtor that could fail in a risky venture and lose their ability to pay a loan, and no creditor like a bank customer who might suddenly want their deposit back. Though heavy and difficult to transport in large quantities, gold was still considered pristine, true, and immutable. As long as the currency being used was pegged to a certain amount of gold that could be redeemed on demand, the central banks would always be limited in their ability to manipulate the economy and finance government expenses. Thus, the advocates of central banking and its ability to manipulate the market and provide for unlimited government spending would always find themselves at odds with the limitations that the gold standard placed on their powers.

In the U.S., the concept of a central bank had always been contentious, going back to the founding of the nation. In fact, James Madison and Thomas Jefferson who penned the Constitution and the Declaration of Independence, respectively, both argued against the idea of a central, or national bank. They were concerned that a central bank would favor the interests of the wealthy and the industrial North at the expense of farmers and the agrarian South. Jefferson and Madison both argued that the Constitution did not explicitly grant the federal government the power to create a bank, making the institution unconstitutional in their view. They feared that a central bank represented an overreach of federal power and threatened the rights of states.

Despite that, in 1790, Alexander Hamilton, first Secretary of the Treasury advocated for the central bank. He believed that a national bank was essential for stabilizing and improving the nation's credit, managing the national debt, and creating a common currency. Hamilton's vision led to the creation of the First Bank of the United States in 1791, which was modeled after the Bank of England and was intended to serve as a depository for federal funds, issue banknotes that could serve as a national currency, and provide loans to the government and businesses. The debate over the First Bank of the United States encapsulates the broader philosophical divide among the founding fathers concerning the role of government in the economy and the centralization of financial power. The bank's charter was not renewed in 1811, partly due to these ongoing debates.

The War of 1812 and its financial aftermath demonstrated the problems the young country had in managing its postwar debt, which central bank advocates used as justification for the establishment of the Second Bank of the United States in 1816. With as need to fund the military, the argument for a national currency and bank tool hold. Under Madison's advice, the short-lived Second Bank was created. In an address to Congress in 1814, Madison stated:

> ...The arrangement of the finances, with a view to the receipts and expenditures of a permanent peace establishment, will necessarily enter into the deliberations of Congress, during the present Session. It is true, that the improved condition of the public revenue will not only afford, the means of maintaining the faith of Government with its Creditors inviolate, and of prosecuting successfully the measures of the most liberal policy, but will, also, justify an immediate alleviation of the burthens imposed by the necessities of the war. It is, however, essential to every modification of the finances, that the benefits of a uniform national currency should be restored to the community.

> The absence of the precious metals will, it is believed, be a temporary evil; but until they can again be rendered the general medium of Exchange, it devolves on the Wisdom of Congress, to provide a substitute, which shall equally engage the confidence, and accommodate the wants, of the Citizens throughout the Union. If the operation of the State Banks, cannot produce this result, the probable operation of a National Bank will merit consideration;9 and if neither of these expedients be deemed effectual, it may become necessary to ascertain the terms, upon which the notes of the Government (no longer required as an instrument of Credit) shall be issued, upon motives of general policy, as a common medium of circulation...[9]

The Second Bank of the United States ceased to operate as a national institution after its federal charter expired in 1836. Following a bitter political struggle, President Andrew Jackson vetoed the recharter bill in 1832, arguing that the bank was

---

[9] Madison, James. "Annual Message to Congress Washington December 5, 1815. Fellow Citizens of the Senate and of the House of Representatives." https://www.loc.gov/static/js/lib/pdf-2.6-es5/web/viewer.html?file=https://tile.loc.gov/storage-services/service/rbc/rbpe/rbpe22/rbpe228/22803100/22803100.pdf

unconstitutional, monopolistic, and favored the interests of the wealthy over the common people. In the opening, Jackson argued,

> A bank of the United States is in many respects convenient for the Government and useful to the people. Entertaining this opinion, and deeply impressed with the belief that some of the powers and privileges possessed by the existing bank are unauthorized by the Constitution, subversive of the rights of the States, and dangerous to the liberties of the people, I felt it my duty at an early period of my Administration to call the attention of Congress to the practicability of organizing an institution combining all its advantages and obviating these objections. I sincerely regret that in the act before me I can perceive none of those modifications of the bank charter which are necessary, in my opinion, to make it compatible with justice, with sound policy, or with the Constitution of our country.[10]

Despite the veto, the bank continued to operate until the end of its charter using its state charter, which it had obtained in Pennsylvania in 1816. After 1836, without a national charter, the Second Bank of the United States was reorganized as a state bank under the name The Bank of the United States of Pennsylvania. This state-chartered bank faced financial difficulties and eventually closed in 1841.

After the Second Bank of the United States was not rechartered in 1841, the U.S. entered the "Free Banking Era" which lasted until 1863. During this time, banks were chartered by state governments without federal oversight, leading to a proliferation of state-chartered banks issuing their own currencies, which were often unstable. This lack of uniformity and stability led to the National Banking Acts of 1863 and 1864, which established a system of nationally chartered banks and introduced a uniform national currency. Some scholars have argued that the subsequent banking panics of 1873 and 1893

---

[10] Jackson, Andrew. President Jackson's Veto Message Regarding the Bank of the United States, July 10, 1832. https://avalon.law.yale.edu/19th_century/ajveto01.asp.

were caused by the rigid and inelastic currency supply imposed by the centralization of control and regulatory framework brought about by the National Banking Acts, and support for the cause of central banking in America continued to fall short.

With the contentious history of a national bank and due to the controversy, that would ensue from public discussion for a central bank, in 1910 a secret meeting to create a U.S. central bank convened on Jekyll Island. Located off the coast of the state of Georgia in the southeastern U.S., in attendance were seven very wealthy and influential men. The meeting was initiated by U.S. senator Nelson Aldrich of Rhode Island with a goal to "fix" the banking system. He invited six others to join him on this remote hideaway, including Abraham Piatt Andrew, Assistant Secretary of the U.S. Treasury; Henry P. Davison, senior partner of the J.P. Morgan Company; Charles D. Norton, president of J.P. Morgan's First National Bank of New York; Benjamin Strong, head of J.P. Morgan's Bankers Trust Company; Frank A. Vanderlip, president of the National City Bank of New York and representative of the Rockefeller interests; and Paul M. Warburg, a partner in Kuhn, Loeb, & Company with ties to the Rothschilds and other European banking families. Knowing that secrecy was imperative, the men met in a secret train car under the cloak of night to make their journey from New York. An early account of this meeting was published in 1916 by B. C. Forbes, who would later find the magazine named after him. Of what many believed for decades to be hearsay Forbes described:

> Picture a party of the nation's greatest bankers stealing out of New York on a private railroad car under cover of darkness, stealthily hiring hundreds of miles South, embarking on a mysterious launch, sneaking on to an island deserted by all but a few servants, living there a full week under such rigid secrecy that the names of not one of them was once mentioned lest the servants learn the identity and disclose to the world this strangest, most secret expedition in the history of American finance. I am not romancing. I am giving to the world, for the first time, the real story of how the famous

Aldrich currency report, the foundation of our new currency system, was written.

> The utmost secrecy was enjoined upon all. The public must not glean a hint of what was to be done. Senator Aldrich notified each one to go quietly into a private car of which the railroad had received orders to draw up on an unfrequented platform. Off the party set. New York's ubiquitous reporters had been foiled . . . Nelson (Aldrich) had confided to Henry, Frank, Paul and Piatt that he was to keep them locked up at Jekyll Island, out of the rest of the world, until they had evolved and compiled a scientific currency system for the United States, the real birth of the present Federal Reserve System, the plan done on Jekyll Island in the conference with Paul, Frank and Henry . . . Warburg is the link that binds the Aldrich system and the present system together. He more than any one man has made the system possible as a working reality. [11]

Although the meeting was not verified for a long time, it was believed that Warburg had leaked the details even before he alluded to it in his 1930 book, The Federal Reserve System, Its Origin and Growth.

Even though the goal of the secret meeting was to create a way to stop the cycles of booms and busts, or the over lending of credit and the crashing of banks due to loans that could not be paid back, their means for accomplishing this was to create a central bank. The Jekyll Island group preferred this approach rather than letting the market operate as it will. With those in attendance primarily coming from large banks, it is not surprising that they would not want the banks bearing the full weight of the consequences of their actions while depositors chose their banks accordingly. The members of the Jekyll Island meeting believed that with a bank that combined all their resources, they could keep smaller banks from failing, ensuring trust by the public and businesses in banks. If a bank began to fail, it

---

[11] Forbes, BC "Men Who Are Making America." *Leslie's Weekly*, Oct. 19, 1916.

could simply borrow from the central bank and be solvent once again while also escaping from the responsibility of their risky decisions. Yet, the six men who were invited to attend all had interest in maintaining the solvency and power of their own interests, very large banks.

The secretive gathering on Jekyll Island marked a pivotal moment in American financial history. By setting the stage for the creation of the Federal Reserve System, these financiers believed that they could mitigate the harsh cycles of economic booms and busts that had plagued the nation, just by using their power and influence. Their solution, establishing a central bank, although designed to provide a safety net for smaller banks and maintain public and business confidence in the banking system, ended up giving more power to themselves and less to a free market, while also setting the conditions for a "moral hazard" in which parties are incentivized to take excessive risks because they do not bear the full consequences of those risks. The outcome of their clandestine strategy session ultimately led to the Federal Reserve Act of 1913, signed into law by President Woodrow Wilson. This action reshaped the American financial landscape by centralizing monetary control and creating mechanisms for crisis management. The structure of the newly formed central bank included twelve regional Federal Reserve Banks overseen by a Board of Governors in order to have regional representation and local input. Even so, there were and remain ongoing debates about the concentration of financial power and the transparency of such influential decisions.

While the U.S. was just establishing their central bank, European nations had their own central banking issues with the onset of World War I in 1914. The central banks around Europe, including the United Kingdom, France, Germany, Austria-Hungary, Russia, and Italy were greatly disrupted by the conflict. Many of these countries suspended the gold standard to print more money to finance military expenditures. To manage the economic demands of the war, these banks also used newly printed money to buy government bonds or to directly lend funds to governments. All of these actions led to a substantial increase in the money supply.

Ultimately, this period saw significant government spending of currency they printed but did not have anything to back it up, which resulted in a widespread use of fiat currencies. As one would imagine, following the economic policies of WWI, there was global economic upheaval, mainly because the attempts of countries to return to the gold standard between the end of WWI and the beginning of WWII failed. Yet, the role of central banks continued to evolve between the two world wars especially during the Great Depression of the 1930s.

This era was another turning point in the history of money, and many took it as a need for a more active management of the economy by the government and the central bank. The Great Depression, a global economic crisis, began in 1929 and is most famously marked by the U.S. stock market crash on October 29, 1929, known as Black Tuesday. This event, however, was not the sole cause but a symptom of a series of underlying economic weaknesses and imbalances that had developed during the preceding years. The crisis was driven by the nation's banks and their ability to engage in risky behavior because they knew that they could be saved by the lender of last resort, the Federal Reserve.

In the U.S., the roaring twenties had fostered an era of optimism and financial speculation. The stock market experienced rapid growth, fueled by easy credit and excessive investments in the financial markets that led to inflated stock prices. When the bubble burst, it initiated a chain reaction. Banks had heavily invested in the stock market, and the crash led to a crisis of confidence, widespread bank failures, and a contraction in the money supply, severely impacting the broader economy. Unemployment rates soared, businesses failed, and a downward economic spiral began.

The impact of the Great Depression spread globally through several channels. First, the U.S. was a significant lender to Europe post-World War I (WWI), and as American banks collapsed or sought to recover funds to cover domestic losses, they withdrew investments from Europe. This led to banking crises and economic contractions abroad. Furthermore, Germany experienced a devastating impact due to its reliance on American loans to pay reparations imposed by the Treaty of Versailles. This Treaty, signed in 1919, marked the official end of World War I and imposed a series of penalties, territorial adjustments, and restrictions on the defeated Central Powers, notably Germany. Economically, the treaty had profound and lasting impacts, particularly through its reparations clause, which required Germany to make substantial financial payments to the Allied Powers as compensation for war damages. These reparations placed a significant strain on the German economy, leading to hyperinflation and economic instability in the early 1920s. The burden of these payments and the loss of valuable industrial territories under the treaty's terms hindered Germany's economic recovery and contributed to the economic hardships faced by its population.

Beyond Germany, the treaty's economic impact extended to the global stage. The redistribution of colonies and territories affected trade routes and access to resources, altering the economic balance among European powers and in their colonial holdings. The economic provisions of the treaty, combined with the establishment of new nation-states in Eastern Europe, reshaped international trade and economic relations in the post-war period. The treaty also had indirect effects on the global economy by contributing to political instability in Germany and other parts of Europe. This ultimately undermined confidence in the international financial system. This instability, coupled with the uneven economic recovery of European countries, set the stage for the economic turmoil of the 1920s and 1930s, culminating in the Great Depression.

Britain was less affected initially, due to its cautious approach to the stock market speculation that characterized the American economy in the 1920s. However, as international trade plummeted, Britain's export-oriented industries suffered greatly, leading to high unemployment and economic stagnation. The British government responded by abandoning the gold standard in 1931, guided by the belief that by allowing the pound to depreciate they could make British exports more competitive. In France, they held onto the gold standard longer than Britain, but in the end, the economy contracted even further than Britain. French political instability and reliance on agricultural exports, which suffered from declining prices, compounded the country's economic woes.

Countries outside of Europe and North America were also impacted by the Great Depression. In Asia, Japan faced declining silk exports, a major economic sector, leading to rural distress and urban unemployment. However, Japan tried to combat this with its military expansion into Manchuria in 1931 as a way to secure resources and markets for its goods. In Latin America, which was heavily dependent on the export of raw materials, commodity prices collapsed. Countries like Brazil, which relied on coffee exports, and Argentina, dependent on beef and wheat, entered severe recessions. Many Latin American countries responded by moving towards import substitution policies, aiming to reduce dependency on volatile international markets.

The global nature of the Great Depression underscored the interconnectedness of the world's economies at the time. International trade collapsed, and protectionist policies, such as the U.S. Smoot-Hawley Tariff Act of 1930, which raised tariffs on thousands of imported goods, exacerbated the downturn. The recovery from the Great Depression was slow and uneven, as significant government interventions over the next decade only made the problem worse, followed by World War II (WWII) which brought previously unseen levels of devastation, as the countries of the world mobilized their economic production in the service of war.

In the nations engaged in WWII, their economies were redirected towards wartime production, with industries converting to manufacture military equipment, vehicles, and supplies at unprecedented scale. This shift not only boosted industrial capacities in countries like the U.S., which emerged from the war with a significantly expanded manufacturing base, but also led to technological advancements and innovations, such as the creation of nylon, acrylic paint, plexiglass, and radar. However, for many European countries, the war resulted in extensive destruction of infrastructure, factories, and cities, leading to a long and difficult recovery process post-war. Financially, the war led to enormous expenditures by governments, financed through a combination of taxation, borrowing, and in some cases, printing money. This resulted in high levels of national debt and, in many cases, inflation. The U.S., lending extensively to Allies through programs like Lend-Lease, emerged as a creditor nation and saw the United States Dollar (USD) strengthen its position in the global economy.

Internationally, the war disrupted trade routes and patterns. The destruction and reallocation of resources towards the war effort led to shortages of goods, food, and raw materials, prompting rationing in many countries. For instance, people created victory gardens in the U.S. to grow their own food so commercial farming could feed the troops. In addition, the U.S. created other financial incentives to fund the war such as war bonds, which deferred present day consumption for the future. The war also accelerated decolonization and the shift towards independence in many parts of Asia and Africa, as colonial powers were weakened economically and politically. This led to the emergence of new nations and new challenges in economic development and integration into the global economy.

In the United States, the war effort also catalyzed a massive economic boom, pulling the country fully out of the Great Depression. The U.S. government's investment in military production led to a significant expansion of the industrial base. For instance, the production of aircraft increased from about three thousand planes in 1939 to over 300,000 by the end of the war. The war also led to the establishment of the so-called "Arsenal of Democracy," the name given by the American wartime president Franklin D. Roosevelt to describe how the productive power of the United States was mobilized to become the principal supplier of war material to the Allies with factories and workers across the country producing a vast array of military equipment. Post-war, the U.S. emerged as the world's leading economic power, with a strengthened industrial sector and a dominant position in global finance.

In contrast, Germany's economy was devastated by the end of WWII. The Allied bombing campaign had destroyed significant portions of Germany's industrial infrastructure, leading to a massive loss of productive capacity. The war also left Germany divided between a communist East and economically freer West. Furthermore, the Marshall Plan, which provided U.S. financial aid for European reconstruction, was used to rebuild West Germany's economy in the following years. Similar to East Germany, Japan faced ruin at the war's end, with many of its cities and industrial facilities in ruins due to bombing raids, including atomic bombings in Hiroshima and Nagasaki. However, with the post-war American occupation, Japan benefited from significant economic reforms and investments. This laid the groundwork for Japan's rapid economic growth in the subsequent decades, transforming it into a major global economic power.

Meanwhile in Europe, the United Kingdom emerged from the war victorious but financially drained, having spent vast sums on the war effort, borrowing heavily from the U.S. and Canada. The British economy was exhausted, leading to the slow dismantling of the British Empire and the loss of its status as a premier industrial nation. Rationing in Britain, which began during the war, continued into the 1950s, highlighting the prolonged impact of the conflict on domestic resources.

As a result of the extensive impact of WWII, global leaders knew something had to be done to help fix the global financial system. In July of 1944, a mere month after the successful D-Day invasion, a meeting that would impact international economics occurred in Bretton Woods, New Hampshire. As a way to figure out how to help the global economy, seven hundred thirty delegates from forty-four countries came together at the Mount Washington Hotel in rural New Hampshire. They were there to attend the United Nations Monetary and Financial Conference, which had specific goals, including the need for stable money. This stability was designed to also help nations form their own monetary policies, in other words to retain their economic independence.

Among the delegates were two men who each put forth a plan to fix the global money issues. Economist John Maynard Keynes (1883–1946) and the chief international economist at the U.S. Treasury Department, Harry Dexter White (1892–1948) each presented a plan, which would lead to some compromises and ultimately change the face of the global economy. The influential Keynes, whose ideas will be explored in more detail in a subsequent chapter, wanted to create a global central bank called the Clearing Union while White preferred a solution with more restricted powers. Keynes's vision for the Clearing Union was essentially a plan to establish a global central bank aimed at facilitating international trade and achieving post-war economic stability. This institution was intended to manage international payments, enabling countries to balance their accounts without resorting to restrictive economic measures that could hinder global trade and economic recovery.

Furthermore, Keynes's idea proposed the use of a new international currency, which he called Bancor, to be used in transactions between central banks participating in the Union. The Bancor was to be anchored in a fixed value of gold but was not intended for circulation outside of central bank transactions. The Clearing Union would allow countries with trade surpluses to accumulate Bancors, while those with deficits could temporarily overdraw. The aim was to encourage global economic balance by penalizing both surplus and deficit extremes, thereby promoting economic stability and preventing the kind of competitive devaluations or protectionist policies that he believed exacerbated the Great Depression.

In contrast, the American proposal, led by Harry Dexter White, favored the creation of what would become the International Monetary Fund (IMF) and the World Bank. White's plan was more conservative regarding the powers and scope of the new international financial institutions. It envisioned a fund to which member countries would contribute and from which they could borrow to address balance of payments issues, but it did not involve a new global currency or as extensive a mechanism for managing trade imbalances as Keynes had proposed.

Ultimately, the negotiations led to a compromise that established the IMF and the World Bank. The IMF was tasked with overseeing the international monetary system, providing temporary financial assistance to countries to help stabilize their currencies and maintain balanced trade, but it did not adopt the more ambitious features of

Keynes's Clearing Union concept. The delegates came to an agreement on different aspects within the two plans, which ultimately created a new international monetary system. The agreement also created the World Bank Group, which was tasked with assisting the reconstruction efforts of nations impacted by WWII as well as developing countries.

This system, set forth in the Bretton Woods Agreement, was a groundbreaking international monetary framework designed to create global economic stability and cooperation. In addition to the IMF and World Bank, the Bretton Woods Agreement fixed the price of gold against the USD. This exchange rate plan pinned world currencies against the USD, which in turn was converted to gold at a fixed rate, of $35 dollars per ounce. Fixing this rate of gold meant that the value of gold would remain at $35, in the attempt to make it immune to the forces of supply and demand, though in reality it was controlled artificially through monetary policies influenced by Keynes. These were then imposed by the U.S. Just as what happened with Newton's linking the price of silver to gold in the eighteenth century, linking the price of gold to the USD also led to disparities between the market value of gold and its fixed price. This would ultimately cause a whole new set of problems a few decades later.

Because of the policies established with Bretton Woods, the U.S. would come out on top. At the time, the U.S. industrial power and economy was thriving because of their wartime industriousness and the gold reserves that were left comparatively intact after WWII. This allowed the U.S. to hold more economic strength as the other great powers of the world, such as England and Germany, had theirs destroyed during the war. This fundamentally shifted the world reserve currency from the British pound to the USD. Although this system was designed to provide stability to the post-war global economy, America grew richer and richer as the demand for its currency increased from the need to settle debt and trade transactions in its USD. In fact, American businesses and economy grew at a rate never before seen in human history. But just as with previous empires, the U.S. would not make smart economic decisions. Even though they took advantage of their powerful status, they continually implemented monetary policies modeled after the economic ideas of Keynes, funding expensive wars and implementing costly social programs.

The U.S. spent much of the second half of the twentieth century expanding its money supply to fund various domestic and international commitments, including the Vietnam and domestic welfare programs. This along with the fact that more USD were also held by foreign banks led to a higher demand of the currency. With the growing imbalance between the amount of gold the U.S. held and the USD in circulation, foreign governments increasingly sought to convert their USD reserves into gold, leading to a reduction of the U.S. gold reserves. The disparity between the amount of USD in circulation and the gold available to back those dollars led to a crisis of confidence in the American monetary system. As a result, many foreign holders of USD began to lose faith in their ability to redeem their currency for gold at the agreed upon fixed rate. Like what has been seen during the Great Depression with a run on banks, by the late 1960s, the U.S. was experiencing economic pressures, including high inflation and a growing deficit.

This era of economic history demonstrates the complex interplay between monetary policy, global trade, industrialization, and geopolitical events. But the policy decisions made during this period were not made in a vacuum. Every choice was made by a belief, whether correct or incorrect, of what money is. Every action was advanced by an argument that justified those actions based on a particular reading of economic history and a theoretical conception of the nature of money.

History is said to be a battle of ideas and it becomes clear that political and economic choices made in the twentieth century were deeply rooted in underlying economic theories and philosophies. These theories, often polarized, provided the frameworks within which policymakers operated. The next chapter delves into the intellectual battleground that shaped these decisions, and understanding this intellectual clash is crucial to comprehending how these economic doctrines influenced policy, shaped financial systems, and ultimately determined the course of history.

Chapter 11: Battle of Economic Ideas

There are two and only two ways that any economy can be organized. One is by freedom and voluntary choice—the way of the market. The other is by force and dictation—the way of the State.

–Murray Rothbard

Money began to evolve into more complicated economic systems, particularly following the 1600s when global trade allowed economies to become more interconnected, and nation-states began to control the issuance of money and credit. With this added complexity, the need to analyze and assess the historic and current economic systems becomes more important. Therefore, as a way to judge monetary institutions and policies, it is helpful to know the underlying ideas and belief systems that frame the discussions about money.

Just as humans have continually worked to create and alter money and banking to fit their needs, the way influential thinkers throughout history have defined money has also evolved. One of the first attempted definitions of money comes from the ancient Greek philosopher Aristotle (384–322 BC) . In *Politics: A Treatise on Government*, Aristotle describes money as "employing it for the purpose it [money] was originally intended, namely exchange."[12] Aristotle sees money as a means of exchange between people or entities. In addition to *Politics*, Aristotle discusses money in the *Nicomachean Ethics*, demonstrating a comprehensive examination of the nature, purpose, and ethical implications of money within society.

Essentially, Aristotle understood money as a creation of law and social convention designed to facilitate the exchange of goods and services. He recognized that while goods have intrinsic value for fulfilling human needs, barter trade was limited because it required a double coincidence of wants. Money, therefore, emerged as a solution to this problem, acting as a medium of exchange that could be universally accepted and easily divided to match the value of various goods. This made trade more efficient, supporting the development of markets and the economy. Moreover, Aristotle distinguished between money's use as a medium of exchange, which he saw as natural and necessary for the functioning of society, and its use for accumulating wealth, which he critiqued.

Aristotle argued that the pursuit of wealth for its own sake was unnatural and morally problematic. In *Politics*, he discusses the concept of chrematistics, or the art of acquisition, distinguishing between natural acquisition, or obtaining goods necessary for life and the household, and unnatural acquisition, or accumulating money beyond what is needed for virtue and the good life. He believed that while it was natural and necessary to use money to facilitate exchange and meet needs, using money to endlessly accumulate more money through interest and speculation, for example, perverted its purpose. Yet, it is important to note that Aristotle did not have the benefit of witnessing the transformative effects of capitalism and how the proper and creative deployment of money led to significant advances in technology and the realization of human potential. Still, Aristotle likely drew inferences from observations of Greek aristocracy or similar elite classes who, over two thousand years before the beginning of capitalism, accumulated money for what he might have

---

[12] *Aristotle. A Treatise on Government,* trans by William Ellis. (London: J M Dent & Sons,1928): 1258b.

considered to be shallow reasons, such as status, power, or hedonism.

Aristotle also viewed money as a unit of account, providing a measure by which the value of goods and services could be compared, thereby enabling just transactions. In *The Ethics of Aristotle*, he discusses justice in exchange and the role of money in ensuring equality in trade, using the concept of proportionality to argue that transactions should result in equitable outcomes for all parties involved. Through these discussions, Aristotle laid the groundwork for much of Western thought on the nature and ethics of money, emphasizing its role in enabling exchange and social interaction while cautioning against its potential to undermine moral and social values when pursued as an end in itself.

Another early perspective on the definition of money comes from a religious text, *The Arthashastra*, by Kautilya (ca.350–283 BC). Kautilya, also known as Chanakya, was an ancient Indian teacher, philosopher, economist, jurist, and royal advisor. Written around the fourth century BC, the *Arthashastra* is a comprehensive treatise on statecraft, economic policy, and military strategy. In this work, Kautilya includes a definition of money, "The examiner of coins (*rúpadarsaka*) shall regulate currency both as a medium of exchange (*vyávahárikim*) and as legal tender admissible Into the treasury (*kosapravesyám*)."[13] Like Aristotle, Kautilya sees money as a useful tool for trade but also includes several recommendations on how it can be used for taxation. Furthermore, he discusses the concept of money in terms of gold and silver coins, which were the prevalent forms of monetary exchange in his time. He understood money primarily as a medium of exchange and a standard of value that facilitated trade and economic activities.

In a departure from Aristotle's ideas, Kautilya also emphasized the role of the state in regulating the economy, including the issuance and control of money. He advocated for the state's involvement in mining, minting coins, and standardizing measures to maintain economic order and enhance the treasury's wealth. Throughout the

---

[13] Kauṭalya. *The Arthashastra*. (Penguin Books India, 1992):115.

117

Arthashastra, he reflects a sophisticated understanding of economic principles, recognizing the importance of a stable and trusted medium of exchange for the health of the state's economy and the well-being of its people.

Nearly thirteen centuries later, Adam Smith (ca.1723–1790) published an entire treatise on money and its role within the government, *An Inquiry into the Nature and Causes of the Wealth of Nations*. In this 1776 work, he states that "money is the known and established instrument of commerce, for which everything is readily given in exchange, but which is not always with equal readiness to be got in exchange for everything."[14] Like Aristotle, Smith argues that it is ultimately an instrument of commerce used for the purpose of exchange, but he also adds that the basis of the value is in the labor required to get the commodity being exchanged. Smith notes:

> The value of any commodity, therefore, to the person who possesses it, and who means not to use or consume it himself, but to exchange it for other commodities, is equal to the quantity of labour which it enables him to purchase or command. Labour therefore, is the real measure of the exchangeable value of all commodities.[15]

For Smith, the value of money is set by those who labor for commodities being exchanged. This role of money helps overcome the inefficiencies of barter by eliminating the need for a double coincidence of wants, where two parties must have exactly what the other desires.

According to Smith, money serves as a standard of measurement that allows people to assign and compare values to a wide variety of goods and services. This function simplifies trade and commerce by providing a common language for valuing and pricing different items, making economic calculation easier. Smith also recognized money's function as a store of value, allowing individuals to

---

[14] Smith, Adam. *An Inquiry into the Nature and Causes of the Wealth of Nations*. (T. Nelson and Sons, 1852):335. https://www.gutenberg.org/ ebooks/3300.
[15] Smith, *Wealth of Nations*, 31.

preserve wealth over time. By holding money, people can save the value of their labor or goods to be used in the future, facilitating planning and investment.

Smith's analysis of money also focused on how these functions contribute to the efficiency and operation of markets. He argued that for money to effectively fulfill these roles, it must be durable, portable, divisible, and have a stable value. While Smith's discussion of money was grounded in the context of the eighteenth-century economy, his definitions and insights into the functions of money have endured, continuing to influence economic thought and policy to this day.

Finally, modern definitions of money reflect its evolving nature in the digital age and the complex roles it plays in the global economy. *Merriam-Webster Dictionary* defines money as "something generally accepted as a medium of exchange, a measure of value, or a means of payment."[16] This definition captures the traditional roles of money while remaining broad enough to encompass various forms of money, including digital currencies.

Furthermore, the *Oxford English Dictionary* offers a similar definition, describing money as "any circulating medium of exchange, including coins, paper money, and demand deposits."[17] The inclusion of demand deposits highlights the modern financial system's complexity, where money can exist in digital form as balances in bank accounts, not just physical currency.

The rise of digital currencies and cryptocurrencies has definitely expanded the definition of money in recent years. The Bank for International Settlements refers to digital money, or crypto assets, as a "digital representation of value…may be used as a means of exchange and store of value, or for payment, remittance and

---

[16] Merriam-Webster.com Dictionary, s.v. "money," https://www.merriamwebster.com/dictionary/money.
[17] Oxford English Dictionary (OED) Online, s.v. "money," https://www.oed.com/view/Entry/85068#eid271209335.

investment purposes."[18] These modern definitions reflect an understanding of money that goes beyond its physical manifestation, encompassing digital forms and emphasizing its functions and the trust and agreement upon which its value depends. As technology and economic practices evolve, so too does the concept of money, adapting to meet the needs of increasingly complex and interconnected global economies.

Ultimately, how money is defined and how it operates is dependent upon economic principles or the lens through which people view and set forth policies on money. The two most prominent economic schools of thought used today are the Austrian economic model and the Keynesian economic model (see table 2 at the end of this chapter for a quick comparison). Though the Keynesian model has had a far greater influence on economic thought and policy making around the world, particularly in the twentieth century, these two frameworks serve as perfect intellectual antagonists for one another. In fact, they stand in complete opposition with regard to how they answer the most fundamental questions of economics.

The Austrian School of Economic Thought was founded by the nineteenth-century economist Carl Menger (1840–1921). He provided a foundational analysis of the origins and nature of money in his work, particularly in the 1871 *Principles of Economics*. Menger's definition and theory of money emphasized its organic development from the market rather than being instituted by law or government decree. Menger argued that money emerged naturally as individuals sought a more efficient means of exchange than barter. To solve this problem, certain goods that were more widely acceptable in trade began to be used as intermediaries in exchange. Over time, these goods became recognized as money because of their liquidity or ease of being traded and their ability to facilitate transactions more efficiently than earlier barter systems.

Additionally, Menger argued that the key qualities that led to a good being adopted as money included divisibility, durability, portability,

---

[18] Financial Stability Institute (FSI). "Crypto, tokens and DeFi: navigating the regulatory landscape", FSI Insights on policy implementation, no 49.

and recognizability. These characteristics ensured that the goods could be widely accepted and used in exchange. Gold and silver, for example, came to be recognized as money because they naturally possessed these attributes to a high degree. Menger's theory of the origin of money is significant because it highlights the spontaneous order of the market, where money is the outcome of human actions. His definition underscores money's role as a medium of exchange that emerges from the interactions and needs of individuals within an economy, setting the foundation for subsequent economic thought on the nature and function of money.

Two later prevalent and influential followers of Menger, Ludwig von Mises (1881–1973) and his student, Murray Newton Rothbard (1926–1995), advanced their own definitions of money. In his seminal work, *The Theory of Money and Credit*, Mises approached the definition of money by emphasizing its function in the economy, particularly focusing on its role as a medium of exchange. According to Mises, money serves as a widely accepted medium of exchange. He argued that the essential function of money is to facilitate transactions between parties, thereby overcoming the inefficiencies of barter systems that require a double coincidence of wants.

Like Menger, Mises elaborated on how money emerges naturally in an economy as certain goods become universally accepted in trade due to their marketability, which is determined by various factors such as divisibility, durability, and transportability. Mises further developed his Regression Theorem, which seeks to explain the origin of money's value. He posited that the value of money today is based on the expectation that it will be accepted in exchange in the future, which in turn is based on its acceptance in the past. That is, one must be able to regress money back to its original use as a commodity with some kind of non-monetary value, something that it was valued for, before it was used as money. This historical continuity of acceptance gives money its current value, making it a crucial component of economic calculation and planning. His definition and analysis of money underscore the importance of understanding monetary phenomena not just in terms of physical attributes or legal designations but also as a key component of the market process and economic interaction.

Murray Rothbard emphasized the role of money as a medium of exchange that emerges naturally within the market to facilitate transactions between individuals. Rothbard defined money as a commodity that comes into general use as a medium of exchange in the free market. He stressed that for an item to become money, it must first be desired for its non-monetary uses. Then, through a process of market selection, it becomes widely accepted as a medium of exchange. This perspective aligns with the Austrian School's emphasis on the spontaneous order of the market and the subjective theory of value, asserting that the value of money, like all goods, is determined by individual preferences and utility.

Moreover, Rothbard expanded on the concept of money's origins and its function in the economy by discussing its role in enabling economic calculation, allowing individuals to compare prices and allocate resources efficiently. He also critically analyzed the effects of government intervention in the monetary system, mainly through the establishment of central banking and fiat money, arguing that such interventions distort economic signals and lead to cycles of boom and bust. Rothbard's definition and analysis of money also delve into the ethical implications of monetary policy, advocating for a return to a gold standard and a banking system based on 100% reserve requirements. He argued that such a system would prevent inflation, protect property rights, and maintain economic stability by ensuring that money retains its function as a true medium of exchange and store of value, free from manipulation by governments or central banks.

Another influential Austrian economist was Friedrich Hayek (1899–1992). Contemporaneous and in complete opposition to Keynes, Hayek was a prominent critic of central planning, articulating his opposition most famously in his 1944 book *The Road to Serfdom*. Hayek's arguments against central planning stem from his broader views on the role of knowledge in society, the function of prices in the economy, and the dangers of totalitarianism.

Hayek argued that central planning was inherently flawed due to the impossibility of aggregating all necessary information that economic actors need to make decisions. He believed that knowledge in society is dispersed among individuals and that central planners could never have access to all this localized knowledge. This dispersal of knowledge, according to Hayek, made it impossible for a central authority to make informed decisions on resource allocation as effectively as the decentralized mechanism of the market. The price system plays a crucial role in Hayek's critique. He saw prices as a mechanism for communicating information about the relative scarcity and demand for goods and services. By freely fluctuating, prices help coordinate the actions of individuals in a way that balances supply and demand, something that a centrally planned economy, with prices dictated by political demands, struggles to achieve. Without this price mechanism, central planners lack the necessary signals to allocate resources efficiently, leading to wastefulness and economic disarray.

Furthermore, Hayek warned of the sociopolitical implications of central planning. In his aforementioned book, he argued that central planning tends to lead towards totalitarianism because it consolidates too much power in the hands of the state. He contended that even the most well-intentioned plans would eventually lead to a loss of individual freedoms. This is caused as governmental control over economic life extends to political and personal realms, ultimately restricting individual liberties.

Overall, the Austrian economics perspective places a significant focus on the individual as the key driving force behind economic actions and outcomes. Unlike the opposing economic theory that relies heavily on government intervention or centralized planning, the Austrian school believes that the value of goods and services is not determined by any forces external to the personal preferences and choices of individuals in the market. As novelist and philosopher Ayn Rand put it, "Value presupposes an answer to the question: of value to whom and for what?"[19] In other words, one of the fundamental principles of Austrian economics is the concept of

[19] Rand, Ayn. *For the New Intellectual.* New York: Signet, 1961. P. 98.

"subjective value." This means that the worth of something is not an intrinsic quality but rather depends on how much people desire it and are willing to pay for it. This perspective highlights the importance of individual decision-making in shaping prices and economic activities. Austrian economists argue that understanding human behavior, entrepreneurship, and innovation is essential for comprehending economic processes and predicting market outcomes.

Austrian economic principles are often critical of government interventions in the economy, such as price controls, subsidies, or monetary policy manipulation. Austrian economists contend that these interventions can often lead to negative unintended consequences, distortions in the market, and economic imbalances. They advocate for free markets, where individuals and businesses engage in voluntary exchanges driven by their self- interest and creative innovations. The belief is that minimal government interference in markets allows for more efficient allocation of resources and fosters economic growth.

In contrast, the ideas of the British economist John Maynard Keynes, mentioned earlier as one of the contributors to the Bretton Woods monetary conference, represented a paradigm shift in economic theory. The Keynesian school emerged as a movement away from classical economics, which argued for the self-regulating nature of markets where supply and demand would naturally balance out with no need for government intervention. Instead, Keynes believed that the market was imperfect, and the government was required to fix it. Keynes argued for the idea that the total demand for goods and services, called aggregate demand, was the primary driver of economic activity. He argued that when there is not enough demand, high unemployment and economic stagnation would result. Therefore, he believed that the government needed to use tools like increased public spending, central bank and tax policy to influence and boost demand, stimulate economic growth, and stabilize the economy.

Keynes examined money primarily in terms of his liquidity preference theory. This theory attempts to explain why people prefer to hold the cash form of money, or the physical banknotes and coins that can be directly used in transactions as opposed to less liquid assets such as gold or real estate. Liquidity is defined as the characteristic of being easily converted to cash without extensive delay or affecting the broader market, therefore the most liquid asset is cash itself. According to Keynes, money is held for three main motives: the transaction motive that facilitates everyday transactions, the precautionary motive that creates a reserve in case of unexpected needs, and the speculative motive that takes advantage of future changes in the interest rates or asset prices. These motives reflect money's role as a medium of exchange and a store of value but are particularly focused on the demand for money as a liquid asset that can be easily accessed and used immediately without needing to be converted to cash first as other assets would require.

Keynes further explored how the preference for liquidity influences interest rates, investment, and economic output. He argued that money, through its interest rate, affects the level of aggregate demand in an economy, thereby influencing employment and production levels. Central to Keynesian economics is the belief that, due to what he and his followers characterized as the rigidities and imperfections in the market, adjustments to restore equilibrium can be slow and painful. As a result, Keynes advocated for active government intervention to manage economic cycles. This intervention could take the form of fiscal policy, including government spending and tax policies, as a means to influence larger-scale economic conditions and stimulate demand. Keynesians believe that during a recession, increased government spending can inject money into the economy, encouraging consumption and investment, ultimately leading to increased production and employment. Keynesian economics also emphasizes the importance of monetary policy through adjustments to interest rates and the money supply by central banks in order to manage economic stability. Lower interest rates, for example, reduce the cost of borrowing, encouraging businesses to invest and consumers to spend, thereby boosting economic activity.

Keynes's ideas have had a profound impact on modern economics and economic policy. Economists who follow his paradigm believe the notion that government intervention in the economy can play a crucial role in stabilizing economic fluctuations and achieving full employment. Keynes argued that markets do not always self-correct and that during economic downturns, individuals and businesses might not spend or invest enough to maintain healthy levels of economic activity. This can result in high unemployment and underutilization of resources. Keynes contended that governments could stimulate economic growth and employment during times of recession by increasing government spending or cutting taxes, thereby boosting aggregate demand. This approach became known as demand-side economics. He argued that an initial injection of government spending into the economy would create a chain reaction of increased consumption and investment as people and businesses respond to the initial stimulus.

The post-World War II era saw the widespread adoption of Keynesian policies over those of the Austrian economists among Western countries, with governments actively using fiscal and monetary tools to mitigate economic fluctuations. Due to the actions of policymakers, government leaders, and bankers, particularly in the twentieth and twenty-first centuries, Keynesian economics has profoundly influenced monetary policy. Therefore, there has been a belief in the consistent need for government action to ensure stability and growth. The legacy of these actions is evident in the continued use of fiscal and monetary policies to navigate economic challenges and in ongoing debates about the extent and forms of government intervention in the economy. Whereas, if Austrian views had been the dominant paradigm over the twentieth century, markets would have been free to act according to individuals and natural forces of supply and demand. In other words, there would not have been a need for so many government and central banking policies to manipulate the economic systems that impacted the world.

It should be emphasized, however, that the Keynesian economic paradigm has been the overwhelmingly dominant one for at least the last hundred years of global history. Keynesianism has an intellectual monopoly at all levels of academia, from the introductory textbooks taught in secondary and college economics classes, to the driving theoretical framework for doctoral dissertations. Its economic interventionist premises are assumed to be correct and continue on a path of being an unexamined self-evident foundation for politics, law, and finance. Most political policy discussions over the last century simply haggle over the details and the extent to which the state will manipulate money and banking. Only the Austrian economists, and those influenced by them, bothered to ask whether the state should do anything at all.

Austrian economic thought rose to prominence when Friedrich Hayek won the Nobel Prize for Economics in 1974, forcing Keynesians to at least address the non-statist alternatives that the Austrians raised. Although initially primarily limited to small think tanks like the Foundation for Economic Education (FEE), over the past half-century, Austrian thought has been given more of a public hearing. This is particularly true with the presidential campaigns of Ron Paul in 2008 and 2012, and his son Rand Paul in 2016. Even though Keynesian economic doctrine and the state interventionist policies it champions is still the driving force behind political and economic policy making today, the Austrians at least provide a compelling alternative that Keynesians are increasingly needing to answer to.

Table 2: Austrian versus Keynesian Economics		
Elements Compared	**Austrian View**	**Keynesian View**
Role of Government	Minimal; markets self-correct through individual actions.	Active; government intervention is necessary to manage economic cycles and ensure stability.
Economic Cycles	Caused by artificial manipulation of interest rates and money supply by central banks, leading to malinvestments.	Result from changes in aggregate demand; government spending can help mitigate downturns.
Monetary Policy	Advocates for a limited role of central banking and supports sound money principles, often favoring a return to the gold standard.	Supports active monetary policy, including adjusting interest rates and controlling money supply to influence economic activity.
Fiscal Policy	Generally opposes government spending and borrowing, arguing they lead to inefficiencies and distort market signals.	Encourages use of fiscal policy, including government spending and taxation, to manage demand and stimulate economic growth during downturns.

Theory of Value	Emphasizes subjective theory of value; prices are determined by individual preferences and marginal utility.	Focuses on aggregate demand in determining economic outcomes, with less emphasis on individual valuation.
Approach to Analysis	Methodological individualism; focuses on individual choices and actions.	Aggregate analysis; focuses on total economic output, employment, and demand.
View on Inflation	Inflation is seen as a result of increasing the money supply more than economic output, advocating for a stable money supply.	Inflation is often considered a necessary evil to combat unemployment; monetary policy can be used to manage inflation levels.

Source: Deanna Heikkinen

Chapter 12: The Era of Fiat

A law cannot give to bills that intrinsic value, which the universal consent of mankind has annexed to silver and gold.

— John Locke

The issues that arose from Keynesian policies, Bretton Woods, and the mid-century economic issues came to a head in the early 1970s. The system began to unravel due to various pressures, including the growing strain on the U.S. gold reserves and imbalances in international trade. The situation was compounded by foreign governments continuing to convert their USD reserves into gold, leading to an even greater lack of confidence in the USD. In addition, with the worldwide reach of the Bretton Woods Agreement, monetary decisions made in the U.S. would ultimately impact other nations around the world.

As a result, like Jekyll Island, another surreptitious meeting took place that would impact not only American but global economics. At the United States presidential retreat of Camp David in Maryland, President Richard M. Nixon, along with some of his top advisors gathered to try and fix the money system. Reminiscent of the 1910 meeting, President Nixon invited strategic allies, including the Federal Reserve Chairman Arthur Burns; soon-to-be Treasury Secretary John Connally; and future Federal Reserve Chairman Paul Volcker, as well as twelve other top members of Nixon's administration, to a secret meeting. After meeting for three days, on August 15, 1971, Nixon was ready to address the American people and reveal his new economic plan to the world. In his statement from the White House Oval Office, Nixon announced the suspension of the American dollar's convertibility into gold, effectively marking the end of the Bretton Woods system and the gold standard era.

This address and the policy that ensued was known as "Nixon Shock." It also served as the definitive move to put the U.S. and by default many other nations on a fiat money system. No longer backed by any gold, as was the case with many other nations around the globe by this time, its currency was based on an arbitrary faith that its users had in the government that printed it. Nixon's decision to suspend the convertibility of the USD into gold effectively marked the transition of major world currencies to a fiat system.

Although many countries had temporarily suspended the gold standard during World War I to finance their military efforts by printing more money, this announcement marked a transition to a long-term fiat money system. Even with a precedent for the use of fiat currency in some countries, for example, the majority of the nations involved in WWII, including Britain, France, Germany, Italy, Japan, and Russia, this change no longer allowed holders of their currency to redeem it for gold. Nations using fiat money no longer needed to keep gold on reserve to pay currency holders who wanted their gold back. This allowed the gold in the reserves to shrink compared to the amount of their currency in circulation. As a practical matter, it allowed countries to print as much currency as they wanted without a need for gold or anything else to back it up.

Unfortunately, as seen in the earlier Chinese Dynasties and their dealings with the first paper money, the uncontrolled printing of currency led to inflation. Nixon's policy in the early 1970s caused this phenomenon once again, leading to the "Great Inflation." During this time, inflation rates from the mid-1960s, which were about 1%, rose to 20% by mid 1980. Without the monetary discipline imposed by the need to keep sufficient gold reserves to ensure the currency's legitimacy, central bankers suddenly had little need for restrictions on lending. Not even the desire to maintain the solvency for the institution itself was an impediment. By abandoning the gold standard, Nixon not only removed the restraints that gold imposed on monetary policy, but he also opened the door to practically unlimited government spending. This was carried out via the mechanism of the central bank's ability to buy the bonds that would cover the difference between tax revenue and spending. As a countermeasure to combat inflation, Paul Volcker raised interest rates when he took over as Federal Reserve Chairman in 1979. Higher interest rates caused borrowing to become more expensive and reduced the amount of money and credit available in the system. This action caused economic activity to crash.

Volcker's Federal Reserve policies and leadership are widely credited with ending the inflation of the 1970s. Nevertheless, it is important to note that Nixon's ending of the dollar's ability to be redeemed in gold disconnected it from its underlying value. Instead of monetary stability being derived from the supply of a scarce and immutable metal, it was now driven by political expediency. Though inflation receded during Volcker's term as Fed Chairman, central banks were still political entities, run by human beings and subject to political whim. It is important to remember that without Nixon's decision to close the gold redemption window, there would be no inflation crisis for Volcker to fight. The true cause of the inflation of that era was the sudden removal of the limits imposed by the physical scarcity of gold, the insatiable need for more government spending, and the government's newfound ability to finance their spending without limit through their central bank.

The precedent set by Nixon opened the door for other countries to do the same. This would be the case in Europe. In the 2000s, partner nations within the European Union (EU), an economic and political alliance, created a new, collectively agreed upon fiat currency called the Euro. The Euro was designed to be managed by the European Central Bank (ECB) and countries who used it created a new coalition called the Euro Zone. The ECB's policies sought to provide stability across member states, focusing on price stability, managing inflation, and economic integration of the member countries.

However, like most central banks around the world, they were highly influenced by Keynesian economics, particularly evident in its responses to economic downturns. Policies implemented by the ECB advocate for active government intervention to stimulate demand during recessions by manipulating interest rates and implementing policies to encourage borrowing, spending, and investment.

Like Europe, Asian countries such as Japan, China, and India also operated on fiat currencies. These currencies, also managed by their central banks, were created with policies specific to their political goals. For instance, the People's Bank of China manages the Renminbi with an eye toward economic growth and stability, while the Reserve Bank of India focuses on managing inflation.

The central banks of Japan, China, and India have also been influenced by Keynesian policies to various degrees, particularly in their responses to economic downturns and efforts to stimulate growth. The Bank of Japan has long applied Keynesian-inspired measures, including near-zero or negative interest rates and buying bonds, to combat deflation and stimulate economic activity in the country's prolonged period of economic stagnation. In addition, the People's Bank of China, while operating in a more controlled economic environment, has similarly used monetary policy tools to manage demand and ensure economic stability. These tools include employing measures such as adjusting reserve requirements and using targeted lending facilities to encourage spending and investment.

Finally, the Reserve Bank of India has also shown a Keynesian influence in its monetary policy, particularly through interest rate adjustments to control inflation and stimulate or cool the economy as needed. This alongside open market operations were used to manage liquidity in the banking system. All three central banks have demonstrated a commitment to using monetary policy actively to influence economic outcomes, a core principle of Keynesian economics. Along with the specific tools and the context in which they are applied, they do all vary because each country has a unique economic and political environment.

Outside of these economically dominant areas, developing countries have also worked to transition to fiat currencies, in the attempt to gain access to global trade markets, as well as to secure development funds from the IMF and the World Bank. These organizations, after they fulfilled their original purpose in rebuilding war-torn countries at the end of WWII, now needed to find new reasons to justify their existence. However, this pivot often led to these developing countries accruing significant debt, as the conditions for loans frequently required austerity measures and structural adjustments. These policies, driven by a stated intention to stabilize economies, often resulted in confiscatory taxation and economic hardship. Additionally, currency devaluations are often a condition of IMF assistance. Although intended to make exports more competitive, the IMF programs also made imports more expensive, which only exacerbated poverty and made natural resources cheaper for foreign investors. This further entrenched economic dependence and underdevelopment on the developing nations, while not solving the problem of currency stability the IMF actions sought out to do.

As a result of the instability of the economics and politics in these unindustrialized nations, national currencies were often deemed unacceptable by the local populace, forcing their government to abandon their currency altogether and adopt another nation's currency as their own. For example, this was the case of El Salvador adopting the USD in 2001. Ultimately, this financial and monetary endgame results in the loss of economic sovereignty, making the developing countries entirely dependent and subject to the economic decisions made by someone else's central bank or the IMF.

This global reliance on fiat currency and central banking subject to Keynesian regulatory actions has exposed countries to currency volatility. Even so, there is the belief by many nations that central banks are better able to control inflation and contribute to long-term economic stability. This is sometimes done with the help of official government policies to enforce central banking regulations. In addition to the controlling monetary policies by central banks after Nixon ended the convertibility of the USD to gold, the global monetary system transitioned to what is often referred to as the "dollar standard."

Under this system, the USD continued to be the primary reserve currency used globally. Its dominance has been maintained through a combination of factors rather than formal enforcement by any single international entity, such as a signed accord like the Bretton Woods Agreement. This arrangement extended the importance of the U.S. financial markets, reestablishing the global trust in the currency, and also putting them into a more central position for economic and political endeavors. Ultimately, this steadied the significant quantities of the USD to be held by governments and institutions as part of their foreign exchange reserves.

The use of the USD as a reserve currency became even more solidified in the mid-1970s with agreements between the U.S. and Saudi Arabia. Through agreements devised between Secretary of State Henry Kissinger and the Saudi Prince, Fahd Ibn Abdel Aziz, the trade of oil by the main producers of it, notably Saudi Arabia, required payment in the US dollar. This became known as the petrodollar. Because of this dollar standard, many global transactions, including international investments, loans, and bond issuances, were and up until very recently, conducted in USD. This caused the demand for the USD to rise in order to satisfy the need for international settlements, which further strengthened its hold on the worldwide economy. In addition to the petrodollar, the USD has remained the global reserve currency without interruption for much of the twentieth and into the twenty-first centuries because of it also being backed by the U.S. military.

Another aspect of why the USD has held its dominant position around the world is that it has often been seen as a "safe haven" currency. This means that investors turn to dollar-denominated assets in times of global economic uncertainty. This perception has been demonstrated by the relative stability and strength of the U.S. economy and the trust in the U.S. government's ability to uphold the value of its currency. Since the U.S. has a powerful political and military influence, this also plays a role in maintaining the dollar's status. The network of global alliances and the country's role in international institutions contribute to the widespread use of the USD. Finally, as more transactions were conducted in USD, it became more convenient and less risky for other countries and businesses to also use the USD, creating a self-reinforcing cycle that maintained the currency's dominance.

In reality though, the use of the USD as the world reserve currency is starting to wane as the world encounters new financial issues and the U.S. Federal Reserve has printed a significant amount of money since 2019. For instance, at the 2023 meeting of a joint venture between Brazil, Russia, India, China, and South Africa (BRICS) in Johannesburg, South Africa, these nations discussed ways to get around using the USD for trade and settlements. Furthermore, Saudi Arabia and the United Arab Emirates (UAE) have expressed interest in finding alternative methods to conduct trade, particularly for oil sales, as opposed to the simple use of the USD as their preferred fiat trade currency. The decline of the USD may become even more of a reality as the BRICS alliance is becoming more attractive to nations around the world. In fact, at the 2023 BRICS meeting in South Africa, six new countries from a list of twenty-three nations who requested, were invited to join the coalition. These include Argentina, Egypt, Ethiopia, Iran, Saudi Arabia, and the UAE.

Even with some pushback on the USD as the global reserve currency, the interconnectedness of the global economic system coupled with currencies not being backed by anything, makes it possible for one country's economic downturn to have an international impact. Therefore, as one might expect with the use of fiat money, the worldwide financial crisis of 2008 demonstrated a failure in the interdependent economic system. This financial disaster, called the Great Recession, was the most severe worldwide economic crisis since the Great Depression during the 1930s. It began with the collapse of the housing market and high-risk mortgage loans in the United States. Triggered by precarious lending practices, the proliferation of complex financial products like mortgage-backed securities, and regulatory failures, the crisis led to massive bank failures and a credit crunch in the U.S., which then rippled across the global financial system. Stock markets worldwide plummeted, unemployment rates soared, and many countries fell into recession as international trade and investment sharply declined. The impact was felt across various sectors, leading to significant job losses, home foreclosures, and reduced consumer spending.

As a result of this crisis, governments and central banks around the world responded with unprecedented fiscal stimulus measures, bailouts for financial institutions, and aggressive monetary policies aimed at stabilizing the economy and restoring confidence in the financial system. Far from inspiring a reexamination of the loose monetary policies that created the risky credit environment, central banks believed that this economic disaster required even further intervention. Consequently, the Federal Reserve looked for a radical solution and found it in the policies of the Bank of Japan in the early 2000s called quantitative easing.

Low interest rates in Japan of the 1980s led to risky loans and lax lending standards, which caused the inflation and overvaluation of assets such as their stock market and real estate. As the loans began to fail in the early 1990s, so did the value of the inflated assets, leading to economic stagnation and a banking crisis. Japanese companies were burdened with enormous debt originally backed by the assets that had lost their value and now had to focus on paying off debt rather than rebuilding their companies and maximizing profit. Rather than letting market forces play out, and unable to lower interest rates further, the Bank of Japan simply created new money digitally and purchased government bonds and other securities from the banks directly. Their hopes were to flood the banks with new money far exceeding their reserve requirements that they would then lend out the money and thereby stimulate economic activity. Although the Bank of Japan was certainly successful in flooding bank reserves with new capital, the act of creating new money did not also make the new loans any less risky. Even with the injection of new cash, banks were reluctant to convert it into loans by reducing their lending standards significantly, and the economic growth was much less than expected.

Japan's inability to stimulate the economy did not stop central bankers from attempting similar measures. Following the Great

Recession, the Federal Reserve carried out their version of quantitative easing between 2008 and 2009 by purchasing $600 billion in mortgage-backed securities from commercial banks during the housing crisis. This action flooded banks with excess liquidity, placing unexpected amounts of cash in their reserve accounts. With the sudden influx of money to lend as well as lower interest rates, banks could encourage lending and spending to help build the economy back up. The Federal Reserve injected money directly into the economy, executing in reality what was only implied by Nixon's decision to close the gold redemption window.

Although the Federal Reserve quantitative easing programs may have artificially and temporarily stabilized the U.S. financial system and economy by lowering interest rates, increasing asset prices, and restoring confidence in financial markets, there were more outcomes that have not been as favorable. The influx of liquidity and low interest rates led to significant increases in stock and real estate prices far beyond their true value, driven by speculation. Historically, this would often be followed by a crash due to interest rates returning to normal, and the liquidation of what the Austrians would call "malinvestment," or the deployment of capital towards ill-conceived investment in ventures that would never have been made in a sound money environment. Those with significant holdings in these inflated assets saw their wealth increase, while the lower interest rate environment meant that people who had savings and fixed-income investors saw lower returns on their investments, losing ground against inflation with every passing day. And every political administration since the beginning of each round of quantitative easing has based their economic policy decisions around the attempt to forestall the inevitable reckoning in which the malinvestments get liquidated and the bill comes due.

Despite the Rube Goldberg complexity of the current monetary system, and the destruction of value caused by the universal adoption of arbitrary fiat money, central banks are still the driving force behind monetary policy as envisioned by Keynesian economic theory. In fact, it is fiat that allows the central banks to exert maximum control over the economy, as it is disconnected from the limitations that sound money places on banks. In order to see how fiat money works today, think about a familiar currency note or coin. Without being able to exchange it for gold, it is not worth much more than the paper or metal it is made of, failing to represent real underlying stored value. Yet, its acceptability as money arises from the collective agreement and trust of those who use it and their faith in the political leaders and central bankers controlling the money. This trust extends to the belief that it will hold up as a store of value, immutable against arbitrary changes. However, that belief is proving to be wrong as many countries around the world continue to have central banking policies that impact its value, such as printing more money or adjusting interest rates.

Even so, fiat money does meet a few of the characteristics of money discussed earlier. Fiat money serves as a unit of account and is fungible, so any note or coin of the same value can be exchanged. Modern paper or digital currency provides a standard for pricing goods and services and also helps with economic planning and accounting while its uniformity is crucial for comparing the value of diverse goods and services within an economy. Additionally, fiat money is highly portable in and of itself, though government policies are increasingly willing to restrict this through capital controls. Although paper currency and coins are easy to carry and transact with, more modern digital forms of fiat currency, like electronic transfers and credit cards have enhanced this property even further, while at the same time the long arm of the government is gaining in its ability to restrict digital transactions. Finally, fiat money is also divisible, which is essential for facilitating transactions of varying sizes. It can be easily broken down into smaller units, like dollars into cents, allowing for precise pricing and affordability of a wide range of goods and services.

However, fiat currency does not fully address all of the requirements of money. For example, as mentioned above, it emphatically does not work as a store of value, thanks to the central authority that controls it. Fiat is largely determined by central bank regulations and monetary policy due to factors like interest rates, inflation, and economic growth influencing its value. Furthermore, the scarcity of fiat money is controlled by central banks and governments, who have the ability to add and retract currency from circulation based not on economic benefit but on political expediency. As Hayek warned, even if central bank officials wanted to manipulate the monetary system to benefit the society as a whole, they would forever lack the knowledge to do so successfully. Still, regardless of central bank attempts to tighten the money supply after the worldwide Covid-19 lockdowns began to be lifted in 2022, the possibility of adding more currency, whether through actual paper currency, the digital manipulation of bank ledger accounts, or through the large-scale purchase or selling of bonds or other artificial means, has become a normalized practice that looms over the global economy.

While central banks can attempt to use tools such as monetary policy to promote stability, fiat currencies can still be subject to economic cycles, political decisions, and market perceptions. Consequently, there is a profound impact of central bank policies on individuals, problems such as the loss of money's value due to inflation, restrictions on money movement, and the erosion of financial freedom and privacy through government and banking regulations.

Chapter 13: The Precarious Path of Monetary Control

Inflation is taxation without legislation.

-Milton Friedman

The issues that have been caused by central banking and the intellectual force of Keynesian economic theory that gives central banks the justification for their existence, have led to severe consequences for individuals, businesses, and even other countries around the globe. These can be examined through the historical instances of government confiscation of wealth, as seen in the US, Australia, Cyprus, Greece, India, Venezuela, Zimbabwe, and Canada, showcasing the vulnerabilities inherent in fiat money systems. These examples illustrate the complex relationship between monetary policy, economic freedom, and the individual's ability to control their financial destiny in a world where central banks wield significant power over the economy, as well as the individual lives of the people that use the money.

Central banks and governments have the ability to manipulate markets through interest rates and money printing, and the consequences of their choices are inflicted on the individuals that hold the money. Rather than being a store of value, and an accurate measure of work accomplished, money's primary function, to be a proper means of communicating real value, is broken. When centralized authorities attempt to engineer an economy by changing the nature of the money itself, the ones hit hardest are the ones that had the most faith in the money. Ultimately, this is all a matter of freedom, for if people cannot completely control the value of the money they earn from working, an investment of their own time and energy, then they are not truly living free lives.

Many people around the world have felt the deleterious effects of the fiat money system controlled not by the free choices of economic participants, but by legislation and laws. These regulations can often restrict people from moving their money to another country or in some cases, allow them to keep the money they have. In many societies, there are controls on how people can transport their money. These laws restrict the movement of currency by individuals and are typically aimed at controlling the flow of money for the stated purpose of preventing money laundering and safeguarding a country's economic stability. Governments regulate the flow of money in and out of the country and can include limits on the amount of currency that can be taken out of the country, place restrictions on foreign investment, and regulate currency exchange, which often include caps on the amount of foreign currency that residents can buy or keep. These restrictions on how people transport money across borders inherently limits individual freedom on money that they hold.

In addition, there are also regulations that require banks to report their customers to regulators or government agencies as well. These often include large transactions, or anything deemed as suspicious activity, which is rarely clearly defined. This can include various amounts being monitored from international transfers or cash withdrawals. Although under the auspices of preventing money laundering and illegal activities, this impacts the freedom people have over the money they ostensibly own. Therefore, their value as an individual whose time and energy went into making that money is lost. Individuals and businesses may also be required to report international transactions over a certain amount to financial authorities, such as the tax agency. Although these reporting requirements are often originally put into law to prevent illegal activities, they can easily be used by governments and agencies to monitor the money owned by individuals as well. For example, in some places when one withdraws any amount of money that a bank feels is a large sum, the bank teller inquires what the money is to be used for, which may be noted on to the account. This information can then be shared with anyone the bank deems appropriate.

Finally, some countries impose taxes on foreign transactions and investments in foreign assets as a way to deter people from moving large sums of money across borders. These policies vary greatly between countries and are designed to maintain economic stability, prevent financial crimes, and comply with international financial standards. Yet, they also impact individuals and their ability to transport, use, or keep private the money they have earned or inherited when traveling or moving abroad. Furthermore, there have been government edicts and banking regulations that have led to people losing the money due to confiscation by authorities. This is a violation of individual freedoms because as mentioned before, human value is measured in the time and energy, including brain power, people spend to earn money. If they no longer can keep or keep the value of the money they earn from this expenditure, then they are slaves to a system in which they have no control.

As a stark example of government monetary control, American President Franklin D. Roosevelt confiscated gold from U.S. citizens in 1933. Although the U.S. was still on the gold standard, Executive Order 6102, essentially required every American to turn in any gold they owned in exchange for the value put forth by the government (not the market value) in USD. The order included a $10,000 fine or even imprisonment to anyone who did not comply, though it was notoriously difficult to enforce, particularly for those who held their own gold rather than storing it with a third party, such as a bank.

The stated reason for the executive order was to prevent "hoarding," which was really the practice of saving the soundest form of money in gold and spending the least valuable currency in paper cash. In the face of the Great Depression of the 1930s, Roosevelt wanted to force economic activity to occur by taking away the form of money most likely to be sequestered in return for a currency most likely to be spent. Though John Maynard Keynes's landmark book *The*

General Theory of Employment, Interest, and Money would not be published until 1936, Roosevelt's advisors were certainly aware of his ideas. Executive Order 6102 remains a precedent setting landmark for government violations of property rights justified by dubious collective economic benefit while giving the Federal Reserve more control over economic policy and adding to the national gold reserves.

Similarly, money confiscation also occurred in Australia during the twentieth century, specifically with the government's decision to demonetize and recall gold coins. This process was part of the broader effort to move away from the gold standard and control the circulation of gold within the economy. As part of the economic response to the Great Depression, the Australian government passed the Gold Standard Act of 1931. This act effectively ended the use of gold as standard money in Australia and required the surrender of gold coins to the Commonwealth Bank in exchange for paper currency. This move was aimed at consolidating gold reserves and stabilizing the currency by transitioning fully to a fiat money system, where the currency's value was not directly tied to gold. Although two years earlier than the U.S. Gold Confiscation Act in the U.S., this policy was similar in that it was hard to enforce but was a way to add to the Australian gold coffers.

In more recent times, there have been other widespread confiscations of money belonging to citizens due to banking policies or government actions. These include Cyprus in 2013, Greece in 2015, and India in 2016. During the Cypress financial crisis, a significant one-time levy, or tax, was imposed on uninsured deposits in two of the country's largest banks. This was part of a bailout agreement with the Eurogroup, European Commission, ECB, and IMF. Deposits over €100,000 were subjected to a tax of 9.9% while those under that amount were taxed at 6.75%, essentially taking €9,900 per €100,000 anyone had in the bank as a way to recapitalize the banks. In other words, people lost almost up to 1/10 of their savings just for having their money in a bank.

Another example from 2015 included banking controls that limited cash withdrawals from banks and restricted international transfers.

This effectively froze a part of the citizens' access to their bank deposits. Furthermore, in 2016 the India government agencies demonetized all ₹500 and ₹1000 banknotes as a measure against black market money and corruption. However, intended to deter criminal activity, it also hurt many honest citizens. This led to a rush to exchange old notes for new ones, with limits placed on the amount that could be exchanged, effectively making a portion of citizens' cash holdings worthless. These policies and actions by those who had authority over banks and money in the respective countries hurt the citizens who had put faith in the fiat currency and those that controlled it.

Yet, in recent years, there has been a different type of monetary confiscation which has targeted individuals for ideological reasons. Recently in Canada, during a Covid-19 policy protest in 2022, Canadian government officials froze the bank accounts of citizens who they believed had supported the protest. Since the Canadian dollar was issued by a central bank and was often held in a private bank account, the government had the ability to seize the bank account through the Emergencies Act of 1988. Originally intended as a means to provide a legal framework that would allow the Canadian government to quickly respond to emergencies such as war or natural disasters, this seizure of individual assets marked the first time it had been invoked since its creation. All of these examples of how central banks can work with the government to control the money one has already earned demonstrates that people actually do not have full authority over the money they earn through their work, investments, or inheritance.

In the end, the most widespread issue of fiat money and freedom is the inability to have any control on the long-term value of the currency. The value of fiat money depends on the public's trust in the issuing government and its monetary policies. As already discussed, political leaders and central banks control the money supply and interest rates, directly influencing inflation. Consistently, high inflation erodes the purchasing power of money, reducing its value as a store of wealth. Ultimately, printing more money, quantitative easing, and other central banking actions degrades the value of the currency over time, causing them to make even more, reactionary policies that continue to hurt those using and holding the currency.

Another tool that central banks use that impact individuals that hold money is the intentional devaluation of currency. Devaluation, or the financial strategy that deliberately creates a downward adjustment of a country's currency value, has been used as a policy to address trade imbalances by making a nation's exports more attractive by lowering the value of the currency it is denominated in. However, the procedure of intentionally devaluing currency has been used to address other economic crises.

An example of devaluation comes from the mid-1990s involving the Mexican Peso. Known as the Tequila Crisis, it was not a collapse of the currency, rather it was an intentional and severe devaluation. The crisis originated from a combination of factors, including political uncertainty, large current account deficits, and the fixed exchange rate regime that Mexico maintained at the time. When Mexico suddenly devalued the peso in December 1994, it led to a loss of investor confidence and capital flight, or the outpouring of money from a country due to negative monetary policies, both causing a sharp economic downturn. The Tequila Crisis highlights the risks associated with fiat currencies in emerging market economies, particularly when they are not supported by sound central bank fiscal and monetary policies. However, leading up to the crisis, Mexico had enjoyed a period of economic growth and investment, largely driven by the liberalization of trade and financial flows, including the North American Free Trade Agreement (NAFTA) which promised closer economic ties with Canada and the United States.

Yet, beneath this surface of growth, there were significant vulnerabilities. The Mexican government had fixed the peso to the USD to stabilize the economy and attract foreign investment. To maintain this coupling, the government relied on short-term foreign currency debt instruments, known as *Tesobonos*, to finance its deficit. This strategy made the country's financial health heavily dependent on the confidence of international investors and on maintaining large reserves of USD.

148

Furthermore in 1994, several political and economic events began to undermine investor confidence in Mexico. These included the Zapatista uprising in Chiapas, the assassination of a presidential candidate, and growing concerns about overvaluation of the peso and Mexico's large current account deficit. As confidence waned, investors started pulling out their money, leading to a rapid decline in Mexico's foreign reserves. By December 1994, the situation became unsustainable. The Mexican government, running out of reserves to support the peso's fixed exchange rate, was forced to devalue the currency through its central bank, Banco de México (Banxico). This devaluation sparked a panic, leading to a massive sell-off of pesos for USD. The peso's value plummeted, and the crisis deepened as inflation soared and Mexico faced a severe economic downturn. The crisis was eventually alleviated by a combination of strict measures within Mexico and a significant financial bailout led by the U.S., with additional support from the IMF.

The bailout was contingent on Mexico implementing economic reforms, including greater transparency in its monetary and fiscal policies, and more independence away from the government for Banxico. The multi-billion-dollar package primarily composed of loans and loan guarantees aimed at stabilizing the Mexican economy and preventing the crisis from spreading to international markets. Spearheaded by the U.S. under President Bill Clinton, the plan utilized the Exchange Stabilization Fund to extend around $20 billion to Mexico, with additional support from the IMF which contributed about $17.8 billion and the Bank for International Settlements. Along with help from other nations this brought the total aid to approximately $50 billion. This emergency financing was intended to bolster Mexico's foreign currency reserves, support the peso against speculative attacks, and restore investor confidence. Fortunately, in this case, Mexico was able to stabilize its economy; however, the crisis could have been avoided if it were not for their detrimental economic policies.

Devaluation coupled with the inflation that typically follows causes an enormous problem for nations. Inflation, unlike devaluation, which is a specific monetary strategy, is a consequence of devaluation or other central banking and regulatory monetary policies. With fiat money, governments and central banks have significant control over the money supply, such as printing more money or implementing policies that increase the amount of money in circulation. If too much money is printed or circulated without an increase in economic growth or the amount of goods and services over time, it can lead to a rise in prices, the erosion of savings, and an overall rise in the cost of living. As a result, governments and regulatory agencies often respond to higher costs with monetary policies that either continue the same problems or make them worse.

These actions often cause more inflation as seen with the U.S. and in Europe in the late 2010s and early 2020s. These impacted nations experienced significant inflation due in part to supply chain disruptions and a strong fiscal response to the COVID-19 pandemic. The inflation rate reached levels not seen in several decades, with particular increases in the prices of goods, housing, and energy. Furthermore, through a series of stimulus checks sent to citizens, the U.S. government printed money at an alarming rate. In fact, through three legislative acts passed from March 2020 through March 2021, $5.8 trillion was offered to individuals and businesses to stimulate the American economy, roughly 28% of the gross domestic product (GDP) in newly acquired national debt. Similarly, inflation rates across the EU have varied, with some member states experiencing higher rates due to energy dependency and supply chain issues. Both the U.S. Federal Reserve and the ECB have had to navigate the complex task of setting monetary policy to try and counteract rising energy prices, particularly due to geopolitical tensions, environmental policies, and supply constraints. This has significantly impacted worldwide inflation, prompting regulatory responses including monetary tightening and fiscal measures to shield the most affected sectors and populations. The Federal Reserve responded with a series of interest rate hikes aimed at controlling inflation, but also unsurprisingly causing economic activity to contract.

Another example of inflation brought on by harmful regulations and monetary policy came from Argentina. In this case, the inflation problem was and still is deeply rooted and multifaceted, presenting a persistent challenge for the country's economy over the years. The inflation issue in Argentina was a result of economic mismanagement, fiscal deficits, and monetary policy challenges. The government had historically financed its spending through the printing of money, leading to an oversupply of currency and driving up inflation. This was compounded by the lack of confidence in the national currency, the Argentine Peso, which led to a preference for the USD and created a cycle of depreciation for the peso. As the peso lost value, the cost of imports rose, further fueling inflation. Additionally, Argentina faced challenges with its fiscal policy, relying heavily on borrowing and facing difficulties in accessing international markets due to a history of defaults. This situation limited the government's ability to finance itself through means other than printing money, exacerbating inflationary pressures.

Price controls and subsidies were implemented as short-term measures to control inflation, but these often led to shortages and other distortions in the market and did not address the underlying issues. Efforts to stabilize the economy and the currency through negotiations with international organizations like the IMF have been part of the response but their actions were often aligned with more regulations and central banking controls. The impact of high inflation in Argentina continues to be widespread, affecting the cost of living, eroding purchasing power, and contributing to economic instability. It created a challenging environment for businesses, influences investment decisions, and exacerbates social and economic inequalities. The government's struggle to control inflation reflects broader challenges in achieving economic growth and stability.

In their most recent election of 2023, some Argentinians used their currency as confetti before Javier Milei, a Libertarian candidate, won the election. He ran on the promise of revolutionary reforms to help the country bounce back from this financial crisis as well as ending a lot of regulatory policies across all realms of society he felt were unnecessary. Although still new into his role as President, Milei has started implementing his reforms, some of which he argues may hurt the economy even more before it is fixed. Time will tell if and how he is able to ultimately help Argentina and its people live a freer, happier life.

Hyperinflation is another form of inflation where the rate of inflation increases so significantly over a short period of time. A notable example of currency hyperinflation from history occurred between WWI and WWII in Germany. Ruled at that time by the Weimar Republic, the nation faced an economic crisis in the early 1920s. This was primarily due to the burdensome war reparations from WWI along with the excessive printing of money that caused the German Mark to lose its value rapidly. The Weimar Republic ruled the German state from 1919 to 1933, while this period of hyperinflation occurred in 1922 and 1923. This crisis was characterized by the rapid depreciation of the German Mark, where prices for everyday goods and services increased at an astronomical rate, and the value of the currency plummeted. To meet its financial obligations, both domestically and for WWI reparations, the German government began printing more money. Initially, this was seen as a solution to pay off debts and fund government spending without raising taxes, a classic recipe for inflation.

As more money chased the same amount of goods, prices began to rise. The inflation gradually turned into hyperinflation as the government continued to print money at an accelerating rate to keep up with increasing prices and to cover its spiraling debts. This created a vicious cycle: as the value of the Mark plummeted, the cost of reparations, which were fixed in foreign currencies, and the price of imports rose dramatically, necessitating even more money printing. Another critical element in the devaluation was the loss of public and international confidence in the German Mark. As people realized that their money was rapidly losing value, they rushed to spend it on goods or foreign currencies, which could retain value. This behavior further accelerated the rise in prices and the need for more cash to be printed. The value of the German Mark against foreign currencies collapsed. At its peak, the exchange rate reached astronomical levels, where trillions of marks were equivalent to a single USD. This made imports incredibly expensive and further worsened the economic situation.

The crisis was eventually contained in late 1923 with the introduction of the Rentenmark, a new currency backed by real assets, in this case land and industrial assets rather than gold. The Reichsbank was given independent control over the currency, and the printing of money was severely restricted. The introduction of the Rentenmark restored some level of confidence in the German currency and brought an end to the hyperinflation period. More recent cases of hyperinflation occurred in Venezuela and Zimbabwe. In Venezuela, there have been numerous phases of hyperinflation causing various economic crises for years. The hyperinflation in Venezuela, which reached critical levels starting in 2014, can be attributed to a complex mix of economic mismanagement, overdependence on oil, and government spending.

The Venezuelan economy has long relied heavily on oil exports for its revenue. During times of high oil prices, the government, under Presidents Hugo Chávez and Nicolás Maduro, ramped up public spending, subsidizing a wide range of goods and services to maintain popular support. However, when global oil prices plummeted in 2014, the country's main source of income significantly decreased, leading to a severe financial crisis. To cover the resulting budget deficits and maintain social programs and subsidies, the government resorted to printing more money. This massive increase in the money supply, coupled with a lack of confidence in the government's ability to manage the economy, led to runaway inflation. Efforts to control prices through regulations further exacerbated the situation by creating shortages of basic goods, which, in turn, drove prices up even more.

The lack of diversification in Venezuela's economy, excessive reliance on oil revenues, and the government's response to the ensuing fiscal crisis have been central to the hyperinflationary spiral, severely impacting the country's economy and the daily lives of its citizens. As a result, Venezuela's currency also went through massive devaluation, which played a crucial role in making Venezuela's hyperinflation crisis worse. As the Venezuelan government resorted to printing more money to cover budget deficits amid falling oil prices, the value of the bolívar plummeted against major currencies. This devaluation made imports much more expensive, a critical issue for a country that relies heavily on imported goods for basic necessities. Consequently, the prices of food, medicine, and other essential items soared, driving domestic inflation higher as businesses passed the increased costs onto consumers.

Furthermore, the rapid devaluation fostered inflationary expectations among the populace and businesses, leading consumers and retailers to anticipate continuous price rises. This prompted them to increase prices preemptively or purchase goods in advance. Consequently, the government repeatedly redenominated, or changed the value and denomination of the currency notes in order to cope with hyperinflation. Two major devaluations occurred in 2018 and then again in 2022. The first of these introduced the Sovereign Bolivar (Bolívar Soberano), which removed five zeros from the current currency, the Bolívar Fuerte. This action worked to simplify transactions that became more complicated due to hyperinflation. The next instance in 2021, removed six zeros from the Sovereign Bolivar, and introduced the Digital Bolivar (Bolívar Digital). This caused the Sovereign Bolivar to become almost worthless. These efforts hurt citizens who held the currency the most and have largely failed to stabilize the economy as it continues to face economic challenges.

Similarly in Zimbabwe, during its hyperinflation crisis during the 2000s and 2010s, the Zimbabwean government issued new currency denominations and periodically removed zeroes off its currency. For example, a $100 Zimbabwe dollar banknote would all of a sudden be worth $10 Zimbabwe dollars. This severely reduced the value of the money held by citizens, again not only devaluing the money for people holding the currency, but also devaluing the people's net worth and savings.

Zimbabwe's hyperinflation reached its peak in 2008. The roots of the crisis can be traced back to a combination of poor economic policies, political instability, and the land reform program initiated in the early 2000s. The government's decision to forcibly redistribute land from white farm owners to black farmers. Without adequate support or training for the new landowners, this led to a dramatic decline in agricultural production, which served as the backbone of Zimbabwe's economy. As food production plummeted, Zimbabwe began to experience food shortages and a significant drop in export revenues. In response to the growing economic crisis, the Zimbabwean government, led by President Robert Mugabe, began printing money in an attempt to finance its deficit and maintain public services. This excessive printing of money, without corresponding economic growth, led to a rapid devaluation of the Zimbabwean dollar and spiraled into hyperinflation. Prices of goods and services doubled frequently, at one point reaching an astronomical annual inflation rate of 89.7 sextillion percent in November 2008.

The consequences of hyperinflation were catastrophic for the Zimbabwean population. Savings were wiped out, leaving people's wealth virtually worthless overnight. The cost of basic goods and services became astronomical, leading to widespread poverty and hunger. The government was forced to abandon the Zimbabwean Dollar in 2009, legalizing the use of foreign currencies such as the USD and South African Rand to restore stability. However, the damage to the economy and the lives of ordinary Zimbabweans was profound, and the country continues to struggle with the aftermath of its hyperinflation crisis. Zimbabwe still grapples with a large external debt burden, limiting its access to international financial markets and constraining economic growth. Political instability and governance issues, including corruption and policy inconsistencies, further deter investment and complicate economic recovery efforts. Socially, the legacy of hyperinflation has left deep scars, with many Zimbabweans still living in poverty and facing challenges in accessing basic services and goods. The combination of these factors means that despite moving past the peak of its hyperinflationary period, Zimbabwe's path to sustainable economic recovery and stability remains a difficult and ongoing process.

Although inflation is much more common, as economic policy makers in the age of central banking have favored inflationary prescriptions, occasionally deflation can occur, which is the tightening of money supply and credit. This generally leads to a collapse in asset values and a crash of economic activity. Economists influenced by the Austrian school regard deflation as a long-term benefit to an economy, as they believe they are a result of markets naturally correcting themselves after a period of risky decision-making and malinvestment, often caused by easy credit. They believe that as bad loans and weak business ventures fail, they are flushed out of the system, and capital can begin to flow into stronger and more productive investments.

Additionally, Austrians point out that as the destruction of failed ventures as well as the loss of appetite for risk leads to a tightening of credit, the money supply itself contracts, and the value of money increases. Ultimately, deflation encourages savings and capital accumulation, and leads to productive investment. As a contrast to the Austrian view, Keynesian economists try to encourage spending and consumption, as they believe that is what drives economic stability. In periods of low economic activity, they believe that spending from both the private and public sector will stimulate demand, create jobs, and propel an economy forward to recovery.

Nowhere is the conflict between these two competing visions of economics more evident in how each of them regarded the Great Depression that dominated the global economy in the 1930s. It was essentially a deflationary spiral in which the easy credit and risky monetary behavior of the previous decade led to the implosion of equity markets, the financial institutions left hanging with failed and worthless debtors, and the corresponding loss of faith by depositors who tried to retrieve their savings, causing a cascade of bank runs. Ultimately, what resulted was a severely contracted money supply. This deflation fueled the economic crisis even more, leading to widespread unemployment and business failures, as debt and malinvestment unwound around the globe.

Austrian economists viewed the Great Depression as the result of prior excessive credit expansion and artificial interest rate manipulation by central banks, which led to unsustainable booms and inevitable busts. They argued that the remedy should have been to allow the market to correct itself without government intervention. According to Austrian economic theory, this would have involved permitting bankruptcies, liquidations of bad investments, and deflation to run their course, thereby purging the economy of malinvestments and setting the stage for a sustainable recovery. Government attempts to stimulate the economy through increased spending and monetary expansion were seen as counterproductive, prolonging the depression and leading to further distortions in the economy.

The U.S. government, on the other hand, responded to this deflationary period with several strategies guided by Keynesian economic principles and their underlying belief that even more spending would be needed to stimulate demand. These included the Emergency Banking Act of 1933, the New Deal public works programs, controlling pricing and production for agricultural and industrial products, increasing the money supply, and having the government take on debt to stimulate the economy. The emergency banking act established the Federal Deposit Insurance Corporation (FDIC) to try and help restore confidence in the banking system by insuring bank deposits up to a certain amount. Those in power that artfully stabilized the banks were crucial in stopping the deflationary spiral caused by bank failures and people trying to retrieve their money from them.

In addition, through a series of programs and projects instituted during the Roosevelt administration, called the New Deal, the government aimed to provide immediate economic relief to people by providing jobs, which they believed would increase spending. The New Deal was a series of federal programs, public work projects, financial reforms, and regulations aimed to provide immediate economic relief, recovery from the depression, and reforms to prevent future economic disasters. Yet, these strategies were short cited and had long-term ramifications. One of the primary issues was the significant increase in government spending, which was financed through higher taxes and borrowing money. The government raised funds by increasing taxes, including introducing new taxes such as the Social Security tax. It also borrowed money by issuing government bonds, which were bought by American citizens, financial institutions, and even the Federal Reserve. The Federal

Reserve played a crucial role by purchasing U.S. Treasury securities, which increased the money supply and helped to keep interest rates low, thereby facilitating more government borrowing at affordable rates. This quantitative easing was favored over borrowing money in the conventional sense from foreign governments or banks.

These decisions once again had unintended consequences on both the financial health of the nation but also the regulatory environment in which its citizens now lived. The government's role in the economy expanded to an unprecedented extent, leading to an increase in the national debt but also gaining an amount of control over the economy and the monetary system that was previously unimaginable. While this spending superficially created the appearance of adding new jobs by funding programs such as the Civilian Conservation Corps, the Public Works Administration, and the Works Progress Administration, it also raised concerns about the long-term fiscal sustainability of the U.S. government.

The New Deal also led to the creation of various regulatory bodies intended to add more government oversight to the financial markets and the banking system, including the FDIC and the Securities and Exchange Commission (SEC). These reforms delegated the responsibility of due diligence away from the private individual and toward government agencies that could, as all human institutions, be captured. Though it may have restored confidence in the banking system and the stock market, it also imposed new costs on businesses in terms of compliance with regulations, and increased the risk that its oversight functions could be captured by moneyed interests.

Consequently, New Deal policies prolonged the Great Depression by interfering with natural market adjustments and creating uncertainties for businesses and investors. Programs that set minimum wages and prices prevented the market from finding its equilibrium, potentially maintaining higher unemployment rates. Regulatory changes and increased taxes to fund government programs created an environment of uncertainty, discouraging investment and slowing economic recovery. Additionally, Austrian economists argue that focusing on immediate consumption and relief through government spending diverted resources from crucial capital accumulation and investment, potentially crowding out private sector spending. By not allowing market mechanisms to facilitate recovery against the long-term consequences of increased government intervention and debt, the New Deal initiatives may have delayed necessary structural adjustments within the economy, thus extending the duration of the economic downturn.

Moreover, the New Deal had significant long-term social and economic impacts, including the establishment of a social safety net through programs like Social Security, which provided retirement benefits and unemployment insurance via a tax on the earnings of citizens. These programs represented a fundamental shift in the relationship between the federal government and American citizens, laying the groundwork for the modern welfare state. However, these programs also required significant government expenditure and the establishment of new taxes to fund them. The agricultural sector also experienced profound changes due to New Deal policies, particularly through the Agricultural Adjustment Act, which aimed to raise farm prices by controlling production. While this helped some farmers by boosting agricultural prices, it also led to the destruction of crops and livestock at a time when many were going hungry, and it disproportionately affected sharecroppers and tenant farmers.

Finally, during the recovery period following the Great Depression, the U.S. government also increased spending through budget deficits rather than through tax increases, which was designed to boost the economy. As illustrated by how the U.S. politicians and agencies regulated deflation in the 1930s, which led to short term fixes, they had to continue to create new policies to find ways of manipulating the fiat currency. They even manipulated various industries, such as agriculture and banking so that trust and faith in both the central bank and the government would continue. Due to these programs and regulations, the national debt of the U.S., which had been present since its inception funding the Revolutionary War and Civil Wars, went from $20 billion in 1933 to $49 billion in 1941. Furthermore, in 1944, after funding WWII, the national debt increased to $201 billion, demonstrating how "profitable" war could be for a nation.

As a result, just like what happened in the first two world wars, fiat currency has continued to fund numerous wars throughout the twentieth and twenty-first centuries. Although historically, funding for wars was primarily derived from a combination of direct and indirect methods that were deeply intertwined with the economic and social structures of the time. For instance, in the Middle Ages, plunder and tributes from conquered territories provided immediate resources, while taxation on land, property, and transactions served as a steady source of revenue for ongoing military expenses. This feudal system played a significant role, with vassals owing military service to their lords, thereby offsetting some costs of raising armies.

Furthermore, in the past, states and rulers also engaged in borrowing from wealthy individuals and merchant banks, and managed state treasuries and reserves, accumulated through taxation and trade surpluses. In times of need, they resorted to minting additional coins or debasing the currency, despite the risk of inflation. Additionally, the sale of titles, lands, and even government offices provided funds and transferred the burden of military service, while contributions from the church supported wars framed as crusades or religious conflicts. These methods, reflecting the governance models and economic systems before the fiat currency era, were fundamental in sustaining military campaigns and shaping the geopolitical landscape of the pre-1900 world.

Alternatively, in a fiat economy, governments often resort to printing money, a process that can be implemented relatively quickly to meet the immediate needs of financing a conflict. By increasing the money supply, governments can spend more on their military without having to immediately raise taxes or sell bonds to the public, which might be politically unpopular or impractical during wartime conditions. This ability to create money allows for rapid mobilization of resources and can provide a significant advantage in the early stages of conflict. However, the use of fiat money to fund wars also comes with significant economic risks, most notably inflation. As more money is printed and circulated without a corresponding increase in goods and services, the value of the currency can decline, leading to rising prices and erosion of purchasing power. If not managed carefully, this can lead to hyperinflation, severely disrupting the economy and potentially undermining the war effort itself.

Thereupon, the reliance on fiat money to finance wars can lead to long-term economic consequences, including increased national debt if the government issues debt instruments to absorb the excess money supply after the conflict ends. The challenge of managing this debt, along with the inflationary pressures created by the expanded money supply, can impact economic stability and growth for years or even decades after the war has concluded. Ultimately though, what commonly ensues is a greater national debt. Both inflation and deflation impact the value of money and the general price level of goods and services in an economy.

Fiat money can potentially lead to inflation or deflation issues due to various factors, primarily related to how it is managed. With that said, central banks, typically influenced by Keynesian thought, generally believe that inflation is better than deflation because it stimulates demand and spending and make policies that attempt to keep inflation around 2% per year. They argue that it is the best way to counteract higher inflation and even worse in their minds, deflation. Particularly, in countries with high levels of debt, like Britain and the U.S. Although devaluation, inflation, and deflation all impact fiat currency, they are not entirely new as seen throughout this journey of economic and banking history. These economic crises were all possible because of centralized monetary systems.

Chapter 14: Centralization versus Decentralization

No one is more of a slave than he who thinks himself free without being so.

–Johann Wolfgang von Goethe

Money has evolved through the process of human choices drawn out over time, from tiny seashells to uniform cacao beans, from beautiful glass beads to equal grains of rice, from metal coins stamped with the face of emperors to paper dollars stamped with the face of presidents. All of these examples were important and useful in their time and place, but all of these forms of money inevitably ran into limitations as their population and societies grew and became more complex. Specifically, these limitations included widespread acceptability at scale or portability at large distances.

Sometimes, solutions to these limitations emerged seemingly out of nowhere, gaining acceptance because they solved important monetary problems. Cowrie shells, for example, became an acceptable currency over a large geographic area, from the Pacific Islands to Africa, because they were an easily recognizable form and beauty that allowed for people to communicate value over great distances. There was no single king, emperor, or central authority that demanded it be accepted everywhere. But there were many kings, emperors, authorities, and also farmers, fishermen, and merchants that found it useful. So, their mutual interests converged to make it an acceptable monetary solution, or in other words, a decentralized solution.

At other times in history, these monetary solutions were made by singular forces such as government, regulatory agencies, and central bankers. The example of the Song Dynasty in China shows a government authorizing the use of paper money after the fall of the Tang Dynasty. The Song Dynasty took over to lend its prestige and power to give credibility to their new monetary system. Its existence comes into being from the decision of a central authority, rather than disparate parties that come together for mutual benefit and trade without an authority dictating the nature of the relationships, or in other words, a centralized system.

A decentralized system is characterized by the distribution of power and decision-making across multiple entities or individuals, rather than being concentrated in a single central authority. In these systems, control is spread out to various levels or nodes, allowing for a more participatory approach where different parties can operate independently while still contributing to the overall system's functionality. Decentralized systems are characterized by individual participants coming together by choice to form a network united by mutual interests.

One modern type of decentralized network can be seen with open-source software projects, such as the Linux operating system. As an open-source project, its source code is freely available for anyone to view, modify, and distribute, fostering a collaborative environment where developers from around the world contribute to its development and improvement. It operates on a meritocratic system where contributions are reviewed and accepted based on technical merit, with core developers managing various parts of the system. Decisions are made through consensus on public mailing lists and forums, ensuring transparency and community involvement. The primary goals of Linux are to provide a robust, flexible, and free operating system for various computing environments. Its philosophy emphasizes freedom, collaboration, and continuous improvement. Development and improvements are driven by a global community of developers who propose changes, which are then reviewed, discussed, and integrated by the community. This decentralized approach allows for diverse input and rapid iteration.

In contrast, Microsoft Windows is a closed, centralized operating system developed and maintained by a single company. Microsoft controls all aspects of Windows' development, from features to updates. Decisions are made internally by a hierarchical team of developers and managers, and the source code is proprietary. Users rely on Microsoft for updates and new features, which are released according to the company's schedule and priorities. The key differences between Linux and Windows highlight the advantages and disadvantages of decentralized versus centralized systems. Linux's decentralized model encourages widespread collaboration, rapid innovation, and transparency, but requires a higher degree of technical proficiency to use and does not have a single authority to go to for support. On the other hand, Windows' centralized model ensures consistency, unified direction, and the ability to scale, but can be slower to adapt to the changing needs of its users.

Community-based organizations provide another modern instance of decentralization. These organizations operate at a local level, with community members participating directly in decision-making processes. Examples include neighborhood associations, local cooperatives, and grassroots movements, where the emphasis is on local control and participation. These decentralized structures empower individuals within the community to have a direct say in the matters that affect their lives, fostering a sense of ownership and accountability.

In centralized systems, control and regulation are managed by a central authority, which oversees resources, information, and policies. This central body ensures uniformity and compliance across the entire system, often through regulations and standards. However, it is important to recognize that centralization does offer numerous benefits, particularly in terms of division of labor, domain expertise, and economies of scale. Centralization allows for the efficient division of labor, where tasks are broken down into specialized roles, enabling workers to focus on specific functions. This specialization increases productivity and efficiency as employees become more skilled and proficient in their designated tasks. For instance, in a centralized manufacturing plant, different teams might handle procurement, production, quality control, and distribution. This division of labor ensures that each aspect of the production process is managed by experts, leading to higher quality products and faster production times. The assembly line system pioneered by Henry Ford is a classic example, where centralized control allowed for the specialization of tasks, significantly reducing the time and cost of manufacturing automobiles.

Centralized organizations can also benefit from the concentration of domain expertise, where knowledge and skills are pooled together within a single entity. This concentration of expertise as well as shared resources under a single organizational structure can enhance the ability of the organization to solve problems by bringing organizational power into a sharp and focused direction. For example, in a centralized research and development department, scientists and engineers collaborate closely, sharing insights and breakthroughs that might not occur in a decentralized structure. Centralization can also create economies of scale, where the cost per unit of output decreases as the scale of production increases. This is achieved through the consolidation of resources, bulk purchasing, and streamlined operations. Large corporations, such as multinational retailers, benefit from centralized procurement processes that allow them to negotiate better prices with suppliers due to the large volumes they purchase. Walmart, for example, uses centralized buying power to keep prices low, passing on savings to consumers and maintaining a competitive edge in the market.

However, centralization also comes with significant hazards. One of the primary risks is corruption. When power and decision-making are concentrated in the hands of a few, it becomes easier for those individuals to engage in corrupt practices without oversight. A single bad actor in a trusted organization can leverage the prestige and trust built up over time by that organization to act in an untrustworthy manner, something that can happen if the organization's prestige allows it to skip or omit oversight. A concrete example of this is the Enron scandal in the early 2000s. Enron, once one of the largest energy companies in the world, had a highly centralized corporate structure. Key executives, including CEO Jeffrey Skilling and CFO Andrew Fastow, were able to manipulate financial statements and hide massive debts through complex accounting fraud. The concentration of power allowed these executives to engage in unethical practices without adequate oversight. When the fraud was eventually exposed, Enron declared bankruptcy, leading to the loss of thousands of jobs, billions in shareholder value, and a profound erosion of trust in corporate governance. This case illustrates how centralization can create an environment conducive to corruption, with devastating consequences for the organization and its stakeholders.

Authoritarianism is a further risk of centralization. When power is concentrated, it can lead to an environment where dissent is not tolerated, and decisions are made unilaterally without input from lower levels of the organization. This can stifle innovation and create a culture of fear and compliance rather than one of creativity and collaboration. For example, in a highly centralized corporate structure, a CEO or top executive team might dictate company policies and strategic directions without consulting lower-level managers or employees. This can lead to a disconnect between the leadership and the workforce. This can result in the loss of direct information that customer-facing frontline workers are privy to as well as decreased morale and reduced innovation. Employees may fear retribution for questioning decisions or suggesting alternatives, leading to a stagnation of ideas and a lack of progress.

With authoritarianism comes inflexibility, another risk of centralization. Centralized systems often struggle to adapt quickly to changing circumstances because decision-making processes are slower and less responsive to local conditions. This can be particularly detrimental in rapidly changing industries where agility is essential. A stark example of this inflexibility was seen in the response of the Federal Emergency Management Agency (FEMA) to Hurricane Katrina in 2005. FEMA's centralized structure required decisions and approvals to come from the top, which significantly delayed the deployment of resources and aid to the affected areas.

Local and state officials, who were more familiar with the immediate needs and conditions, were often left waiting for federal approval before they could act, hampering immediate relief efforts. The bureaucratic delays, lack of local knowledge, and inadequate communication resulted in a slow and ineffective response, highlighting the dangers of inflexibility in centralized systems.

The world of education provides examples of both centralized and decentralized approaches. Prior to the middle of the nineteenth century, education was largely decentralized, with each family or individual deciding on their own how to educate themselves. Communities would frequently band together and build one room schoolhouses. But just as often, families would teach their children on their own. Benjamin Franklin attended a formal school for only two years and was largely self-taught. George Washington was taught at home by his father and brother, and studied mathematics, surveying, and practical subjects intended for farm life. John Adams had a much more extensive formal education and studied law at Harvard College. Each chose the path suitable for his own life.

Modern education in America is much more centralized than the world of Franklin, Washington, and Adams. Over the past century and a half, state and local governments have taken more and more of the responsibility of education away from families by shouldering the cost of building schools and hiring and vetting teachers and administrators. This centralized school systems creates systems to ensure accountability, enforce standards, and to oversee the system as a whole. Centralized authorities offered free schools to the public, which would become more expensive and more demanding of community resources. Over time, families would relinquish more control while the system became so complex that ever more centralization was required to administer and run it. Ultimately, national policies. standards, and oversight would override local decision making, leaving individuals with little control or say in what their children were learning or who was teaching them.

As the decentralized approach is premised upon the efficacy of individual choice and agency while the centralized approach tends to restrict it in favor of hierarchical control by authority, these systems can often conflict with each other. The culture of Ancient Greece, for example, exuded confidence and self-worth, and their myths told stories of individual heroes who, though they might have had flaws, were capable of greatness and glory. The structure of the ancient Greek city-states, or poleis, operated autonomously with their own government and policies. This decentralized political organization allowed for diverse forms of governance, from democracies in Athens to oligarchies in Sparta, each tailored to the specific needs and preferences of their local populations. Culturally, they considered themselves to be Greek, connected by certain shared values, such as language and religion. Yet, the city-states remained independent and autonomous, believing themselves to be capable and deserving of self-rule.

The Persian Empire, on the other hand, contemporaneous with the ancient Greek city-states, were highly centralized, particularly under emperors such as Cyrus, Darius, and Xerxes, who wielded substantial power over the territories they controlled, including the various cities within their domain. The Persian emperor was regarded as a god with the unquestioned divine right to rule. The very structure of the Persian state guaranteed the totality of the emperor's control, and the righteous subjugation of those within the empire. Each province was governed by an official appointed by the emperor, and to whom he owed his allegiance to. The Persian state itself consisted of bureaucracies that administered everything from tax collection, to maintaining order, to the regulation of trade, and the building of infrastructure. The emperor employed a network of inspectors, known as the King's Eyes and Ears, who traveled around the empire to collect information on the conduct of each official to maintain loyalty and control.

With such diametrically opposed political systems and world views, it is no surprise that these two civilizations would inevitably engage in conflict with each other. The Greco-Persian Wars, spanning from 499 to 449 BCE, were a series of conflicts between the Greek city-states and the Persian Empire. The wars began with the Ionian Revolt, where Greek cities under Persian control rebelled but were eventually subdued. Seeking to punish mainland Greece and prevent future uprisings, Persian King Darius I launched an invasion, leading to the Battle of Marathon in 490 BCE. Despite being outnumbered, the Athenians used superior tactics and local knowledge to achieve a surprising victory, highlighting the advantages of their decentralized structure.

The Persians, who viewed the Greeks as barbaric and uncivilized, underestimated their opponents. They regarded their own way of life as organized, worldly, and touched by divinity. This cultural superiority complex contributed to their belief that the Greeks, with their small, politically fragmented city-states, posed little threat to the sophisticated and centralized Persian Empire. A decade later, Darius's successor, Xerxes I, initiated a massive invasion, resulting in famous battles such as Thermopylae, Salamis, and Plataea. At Thermopylae, a small Greek force led by Spartan King Leonidas delayed the Persians, allowing the Greeks time to prepare their defenses for the crucial battles to come. The Battle of Salamis was a crucial naval engagement where the Greek fleet, composed of ships from various city-states, used their superior maneuverability and knowledge of local waters to defeat the larger Persian navy.

However, it was the decisive Battle of Plataea in 479 BCE that saw the Greek forces achieving victory on land, effectively ending the Persian threat. The Greek success in these wars demonstrated the strength of their decentralized system, where independent city-states could unite against a common enemy. The Greek army consisted primarily of citizen-soldiers, known as hoplites, from various city-states like Sparta, Athens, and Corinth. These hoplites, heavily armed and fighting in a unified phalanx formation, were free citizens mustered to defend their land and way of life rather than serve an emperor. In contrast, the Persian army was a diverse, professional force composed of soldiers from across the vast empire, including elite units like the Immortals and conscripted troops from various regions.

This contrast in military organization mirrored the broader societal differences between the decentralized Greeks and the centralized Persians. The Greek city-states, valuing the idea of the citizen-soldier, fostered a sense of personal investment and motivation among their troops. Each soldier fought to protect his home, community, and his fellow soldier. The Persian army, while highly organized and professional, often consisted of soldiers fighting as part of a vast imperial machine with less personal stake in the outcome. The Greeks' decentralized approach ultimately proved superior at Plataea, leading to their decisive victory over the centralized Persian Empire.

Two thousand and forty-four years after the Battle of Plataea, the conflict of mindset between decentralized and centralized forces played out on another stage during the D-Day invasion on June 6, 1944. The Allied forces, largely consisting of American troops, along with soldiers from the United Kingdom and Canada, became known for their independence, flexibility, and ability to adapt quickly to the changing battlefield conditions. At Omaha and Utah beaches, American troops faced fierce resistance from the entrenched German forces. The Germans, with their highly centralized and hierarchical command structure, had fortified their positions along the Atlantic Wall, expecting to repel any Allied invasion. However, this rigid structure, which relied heavily on orders from higher command, proved to be a significant disadvantage when communication lines broke down and rapid decision-making was required.

Initially, the German defenses at Omaha Beach, manned by the 352nd Infantry Division, inflicted severe casualties on the Americans. Machine gun fire from fortified positions mowed down the first waves of U.S. soldiers, creating chaos on the beach. Despite this, American troops demonstrated remarkable resilience and improvisation. Soldiers adapted by using whatever cover they could find, using their helmets to dig trenches, reorganizing into small units, and attacking the German positions with determination and ingenuity. Meanwhile, at Utah Beach, a navigation error actually worked in the Americans' favor, landing them in a less heavily defended area. The U.S. forces quickly adapted to the unexpected circumstances, demonstrating their ability to function independently of detailed higher command instructions. This flexibility allowed them to advance rapidly and secure their objectives despite the initial disarray.

In contrast, the German response was hampered by their centralized command structure. Many senior commanders were away from their posts, and the delay in getting orders from the higher command, including Hitler himself, caused critical delays in the German counterattacks. The lack of initiative among lower-ranking officers, who were accustomed to strict adherence to orders, further exacerbated the situation. This clash of mindsets, the American decentralization and adaptability versus German centralization and rigidity, mirrored the ancient conflict between the Greeks and the Persians. Just as the Greek city-states' independence and flexibility had triumphed over the Persian Empire's centralized authority, the Americans' ability to improvise and adapt on the beaches of Normandy ultimately led to their success and marked a turning point in World War II.

Monetary history has always had a similar underlying tension between the forces of decentralization vs centralization. Like many human innovations, money often begins as a product of decentralized evolution with thousands or even millions of individual choices inching demand forward until adoption occurs, only to later coalesce into centralized control structures. The decentralized process weeds out the less broadly useful solutions through organic selection, with only the most successful solutions proving their worth by being the ones left standing over time. Once the solution becomes entrenched, centralized authorities, such as tribal chieftains, emperors, or central bank chairmen, give their approval so the monetary solution does not need to be continually validated over and over again. The paper receipts might gain acceptance as money through the private deposit houses of the Tang Dynasty, but later, the officials of the Song Dynasty would authorize its use as government approved legal tender.

Still, these monetary advancements did provide solutions for real problems, such as widespread acceptability. Even though centralization created new problems, such as corruption, authoritarianism, and inflexibility, it did provide a means by which trust in the monetary system could happen immediately through the power and prestige of the ruling authority. Centralized money systems also meant that the users of the money no longer had to be as vigilant on an individual level in validating the money's worth. In the process of granting its imprimatur, or official endorsement, the central authorities also made money more abstract and disconnected from its underlying value. In the modern day, central banks and governments have captured money and created a system so complex that only those who possessed so-called "expert knowledge," from elite universities teaching only acceptable dogma, were deemed worthy to control it. Money was no longer an instrument for the sovereign individual, but an impenetrable labyrinth in which the map and keys were held by political elites that controlled the money itself.

Today and throughout history, most of the current financial systems that have existed are centralized where someone or some authority has control over the money. Now, with the rise of digital technologies, the amount of control and surveillance that a government can exert on its citizens can be amplified to a degree previously imagined only by authors of dystopian science fiction. This is particularly true with the invention of the Central Bank Digital Currencies (CBDCs). CBDCs are a digital form of a country's fiat currency, which is issued and regulated by the nation's central bank. Unlike credit and debit cards that allow transactions to be made more conveniently and generally without restriction by linking payments directly to bank accounts or a credit line, CBDCs have a higher degree of surveillance as well as the ability to arbitrarily restrict its use by the controlling authority.

Still, it is worth noting some of the benefits that may possibly stem from the CBDC's digital nature. Again, not unique to CBDCs but rather applicable for any type of digital money, these central banks created currencies that could allow for innovation in how financial transactions are conducted and managed. These benefits might include increasing financial inclusion, especially in regions with underdeveloped banking infrastructure. Digital currencies may significantly reduce the cost of transactions, especially cross-border payments. A digital money solution may also eliminate or reduce third party intermediaries, such as private banks, making both domestic and international transfers faster and cheaper while streamlining payment systems and making them more efficient.

However, there are likely more negative impacts of the adoption of CBDCs as they significantly increase the immediate control of central banks over monetary policies and economic management. These may include even more government intervention via central banks to control the monetary system. CBDCs would make it much easier to adjust the money supply under the guise of managing inflation; but ultimately, it is allowing CBDCs direct control of the economy, particularly when it comes to individuals that is the most troubling. Since these digital fiat currencies offer central banks more precise tools for implementing monetary policy, the central banks would be able to bypass commercial banks and interact directly with citizens, potentially leading to more targeted financial interventions. Targeted financial interventions refer to specific actions taken by central banks or governments directed at particular sectors, groups, or economic activities.

These interventions are presented as a way to address specific economic challenges or objectives, such as offering stimulus or other assistance to certain sectors of society or even to collect taxes or fines. However, they can also be used for nefarious reasons, such as easily restricting funds of certain individuals. Although this has happened with the current fiat system with government officials working with private banks to freeze bank accounts, like what happened in Canada during Covid-19. With CBDCs, this process will become much easier and not involve any intermediaries that may try to protect their customers.

Furthermore, in countries with less robust legal protections or where authoritarian regimes are in power, the misuse of CBDCs for political control becomes even more of a concern. There could be scenarios where governments use financial tracking and control as a means to suppress political opposition or minority groups. To address these concerns, some propose the incorporation of privacy-protecting features in CBDC systems. This could include anonymizing transactions up to a certain limit or ensuring that transaction data can

174

only be accessed under strict legal conditions. Yet, neither of these offer real solutions for individuals as recent history has shown even those limitations can be circumnavigated through emergency powers or under the guise of law enforcement. With CBDCs, government agencies and representatives would have complete power over people's money and if they wanted, could use targeted financial interventions to promote behaviors that align with their specific agenda, or worse, punish those who do not align with their ideas.

For instance, CBDC transactions could be used to establish social or economic credit scores, similar to systems currently being developed in some countries. They might provide incentives for investment for particular business or individual practices and behaviors. Furthermore, they may offer subsidies for research and development in certain sectors for only certain causes, like medicine. In addition, corporate environment, social, and governance (ESG) scores or a social-credit score system may act as a way for governments and regulatory agencies to monitor spending by individuals or companies. Monitoring systems could result in controlling certain spending habits by individuals, such as denying a person the ability to purchase meat or how far from their home they are allowed to use their money. These scores could also be used to determine individuals' access to services like loans or insurance. A system where a person's or business's ideas or behavior directly affects social credit could lead to a scenario where citizens feel compelled to conform to certain behaviors to maintain a good score, which is essentially a form of social control. Furthermore, businesses may also be negatively impacted through fines or even shut down.

In addition to the loss of freedom to use the money someone earns, there are a lot of privacy concerns and the potential for misuse of CBDCs. The ability of CBDCs to provide a person's entire detailed transaction data in real-time gives rise to questions about individual privacy, state surveillance, and the potential for authoritarian control. CBDCs, by their digital nature, allow for the tracking and recording of all transactions. While this can be beneficial for preventing illegal activities like money laundering and tax evasion, it also means that governments could potentially have access to detailed records of individuals' spending habits and financial lives, eliminating financial privacy.

The fear for liberty-minded people and organizations is that this data could be used for extensive surveillance and erode any financial privacy. This possibility raises significant concerns about civil liberties and government overreach. As mentioned, there have already been instances, like in Canada, where authorities have frozen bank accounts for political reasons, such as during protests or civil unrest. With CBDCs, the ease and speed with which this can be done could exponentially increase. The ability to quickly freeze or restrict access to funds through a CBDC system could also be used as a tool for political suppression or to target dissenters or groups that oppose government policies. In countries with less robust legal protections or where authoritarian regimes are in power, the misuse of CBDCs for political control becomes even more of a concern as tracking and control of the money in order to suppress political opposition or minority groups.

Ultimately, the introduction and proposal of digital fiat currencies by central banks worldwide could signify a major shift in the control and management of money. While they say the intent is to offer some opportunities for greater efficiency, financial inclusion, and policy implementation, they bring far more challenges related to privacy, financial stability, and the structure of the global financial system. Furthermore, one of the arguments in favor of CBDCs concerns access to financial services by the many people around the world who do not currently use the traditional banking system, known as the unbanked. However, CBDCs do not address one of the main reasons people choose to opt out of the system, which is often a lack of trust in banks, the monetary system, or the government.

The issue of the unbanked or people who do not currently participate in the banking system where they live is widespread. The reasons for being unbanked can include poverty, lack of access to banking infrastructure, informal employment, and mistrust of the banking system. In many rural or remote areas, especially in developing countries, banking infrastructure is limited or non-existent. In addition to geography, poverty and low income can be significant barriers. Opening and maintaining a bank account may require fees that are prohibitive for low-income individuals. Lack of proper identification, financial literacy, or understanding of banking requirements can also deter people from opening bank accounts. However, with the current state of the global financial system, there is a growing lack of trust in financial institutions, central banks, and government economic policies, leaving people to opt out of the system voluntarily. Although this is more often the case in developing countries, citizens from developed nations are also looking for alternatives to the banking system.

Unfortunately, there are issues that can arise for the unbanked population, no matter the reason they are not participating in the system. Without access to traditional banking services, unbanked individuals often lack secure ways to store or save money, leading to risks of theft or loss. In addition, the unbanked usually cannot access formal credit channels, making it difficult to finance large purchases, start businesses, or manage financial emergencies. To try and combat this for those with issues of access, mobile banking and innovations in the financial technology industry (Fintech) have been instrumental in reaching the unbanked, particularly in regions with high mobile phone penetration. Microfinance institutions and community banks offer financial services tailored to the needs of unbanked populations. Even some governments, often with the help of Non-Governmental Organizations (NGOs), are working to increase banking opportunities for those who lack access through policy reforms, financial education programs, and support for banking infrastructure development. These entities see financial inclusion as key to reducing poverty and boosting prosperity through access to traditional central bank financial services, enabling people to invest in education, health, and business opportunities.

Yet, it is not just the unbanked that have a mistrust in the financial sector. Many people who would otherwise opt out feel trapped by the modern financial institutional structure. People's mistrust of the banking system extends beyond the issue of the unbanked and encompasses a variety of concerns and experiences that have eroded public confidence over time. This mistrust can stem from several factors, including historical financial crises, perceived lack of transparency, and the role of banks in economic inequality. Financial crises, such as the Great Recession of 2008, play a significant role in shaping public mistrust. The collapse of major financial institutions due to risky lending practices and the subsequent economic downturn led many to question the stability and integrity of the banking system.

The bailouts of banks by governments, often using taxpayer money, further fueled skepticism and resentment. These actions caused people to perceive that banks were being rescued from the consequences of their own risky behaviors while ordinary citizens suffered financial losses. Transparency, or rather the lack of it, also contributes to mistrust. Complex financial products, hidden fees, invasive policies, and the use of technical jargon can make customers feel misled or overburdened. When people do not fully understand how their money is being managed, why banks are gathering more and more information on their customers' use of their own money, or how certain banking products work, they are likely to be distrustful of the institutions offering these services.

Additionally, the role of banks in contributing to economic inequality can lead to mistrust. High fees for basic banking services and penalties, such as overdraft fees, disproportionately affect lower-income individuals, making it more difficult for them to access and maintain banking services. The perception that banks primarily serve the interests of the wealthy and large corporations, offering them more favorable terms and rates, while neglecting the financial needs of average or lower-income customers, exacerbates this sense of inequality and unfairness. The rise of alternative financial services, including fintech companies reflects and feeds into this mistrust. These alternatives often market themselves as being more transparent, user-friendly, and equitable than traditional banks, appealing to those who have lost faith in the conventional banking system. However, as demonstrated, this may not be the best solution as many remain a centralized solution. Fortunately, there is another option: a decentralized money invented in 2009 called Bitcoin.

Chapter 15: The Genesis of Bitcoin

We have proposed a system for electronic transactions without relying on trust.

- Satoshi Nakamoto

On October 31, 2008, a white paper, or in-depth report on a specific topic, called "Bitcoin: A Peer-to-Peer Electronic Cash System" appeared as a potential solution to the problem of money's capture by central banks. It was published by someone (or perhaps a group of people) named Satoshi Nakamoto. The real identity of the author(s) is still unknown, but the paper presented an outline for what a decentralized electronic money system might look like. As the title of the white paper suggests, it offered the possibility of electronic money that could be exchanged peer-to-peer (P2P), or one individual directly interacting with another individual, with no permission required. Like the Declaration of Independence, the Bitcoin white paper announced a new paradigm for human relationships, and a rebellion against the prevailing governmental structure. Each of these founding documents served as a critique of the centralized ruling order, and each laid the intellectual framework for a new decentralized method of autonomous self-governance.

Although revolutionary in its farsighted design, and the first successful digital currency, Bitcoin was not the first attempt at creating a computer-based money. During the 1990s, two digital currencies appeared, DigiCash created by David Chaum and E-Gold founded by Douglas Jackson and Barry Downey. DigiCash used cryptography to have secure and anonymous transactions but went bankrupt in 1998 partly due to its lack of adoption. Going back to the idea of the gold standard, E-Gold was a digital currency backed by gold, allowing its users to transact with the gold they owned digitally. However, it was shut down by U.S. authorities, who claimed that it could be used for money laundering and other illegal activities.

Other digital currencies likely inspired Nakamoto beyond the idea of using the internet for monetary transactions. Early systems like Adam Back's 1997 Hashcash, Wei Dai's 1998 B-Money, and Nick Sazabo's 2002 Bit Gold all included technology that is somewhat incorporated into the Bitcoin network. B-Money's concept, although never fully realized, circulated on the cypherpunks mailing list, the same forum where Nakamoto released his February 9 post. Like B-Money, Bit Gold was never implemented but in theory, aimed to create a decentralized digital currency, which included several key concepts later used in Bitcoin. Through these earlier attempts at creating a digital form of money, Nakamoto may have learned from and overcome their challenges, resulting in Bitcoin's successful launch and ultimate acceptance.

Bitcoin can best be described as a computer program that runs on millions of machines empowering a network of users to communicate exchanges of value using the internet. Bitcoin users do this by transmitting scarce and non-counterfeitable units of information, or "coins," within the system. For clarification, Bitcoin with a capital "B" refers to the economic system, whereas bitcoin with a lowercase "b" refers to the individual coins.

Bitcoin transactions are broadcast to the network, grouped together, and organized into blocks of data roughly equivalent in size to a small JPEG photo. Each block goes through a confirmation process by which the network of computers works to solve computational problems to verify and cryptographically secure it before it is added to the previous block. This ongoing chain of blocks, or "blockchain," operates as a transparent ledger documenting every verified transaction going back to the very beginning of Bitcoin's existence. According to the system's rules, or protocol, thousands of copies of this ledger are distributed throughout the network in machines called "nodes." A node can be run on any personal computer, or cheap hardware capable of an internet connection and a hard drive. Running a node gives one a copy of the ledger, and anyone can examine it and perform their own audit to make sure that the transactions are going through smoothly.

Bitcoin has no central controlling authority with the power to unilaterally change the protocol, and no owner to coerce or capture it. Satoshi Nakamoto, known only through email correspondence and forum posts, shepherded the Bitcoin project through its beginning phase but disappeared in April of 2011. In an email to a fellow Bitcoin developer Mike Hearn on April 23, 2011, he said, "I had a few other things on my mind (as always)...I've moved on to other things. It's in good hands with Gavin and everyone..."[20] Since, the code for the Bitcoin software is made publicly available for anyone to review for flaws or even malicious intent, Bitcoin has continued through the work of individuals around the world. The network, its transactions, and the ledger are not secured by armed guards or the good will of the government, but by software, mathematical functions, and cryptography, making it a truly decentralized system.

The technical aspects of making and confirming a Bitcoin transaction are fairly complex, but from the perspective of the participants making the transactions, it is quite simple. The person initiating the transaction owns the Bitcoin they want to send to another person, so they open a Bitcoin "wallet" app, a digital tool that allows a user to store, manage, and transact with Bitcoin. A Bitcoin wallet contains a collection of private keys, which are cryptographic signatures used to authorize transactions and access the Bitcoin associated with those keys. The sender enters the recipient's public address on their app, typically generated as a QR code from the recipient, adds the Bitcoin they want to send along with a transaction fee, then "signs" the transaction with the digital

---

[20] Nakamoto, Satoshi. Email to Mike Hearn. April 23, 2011. https://pastebin.com/syrmi3ET

signature associated with their private key, and finally broadcasts the transaction to the network. Only a private key can send Bitcoin, while a public address can only receive it. Once the transaction is confirmed by the network and added to the ledger, or blockchain, it is irreversible.

In this system, the greatest vulnerability and the biggest impediment to engendering user confidence is the question of whether its transactions can be trusted. Just as modern fiat transactions cause participants to worry about fraud, banking malfeasance, and even outright confiscation, it is important to ask if Bitcoin has similar vulnerabilities. Therefore, perhaps the most innovative and important feature of the Bitcoin ecosystem is the mechanism by which each new block is confirmed, known as Proof of Work (PoW). PoW is a system that attempts to get the machines within the network to work together and come to a consensus about the validity of a new block. This is done before the block is added to the blockchain, in order to circumvent the possibility that any individual machine might act maliciously.

In computer science, the challenge of achieving consensus in the presence of potentially faulty or malicious actors is known as the "Byzantine Generals' Problem." This thought experiment posits a group of generals who must come to an agreement on a plan for battle, but they can only communicate through messengers. Some generals may be disloyal or traitorous and may send false messages to confuse the others and keep them from reaching an agreement. This story illustrates the difficulty of having multiple parties reach a consensus when one or more participants may have incorrect information or even nefarious motives.

To solve this problem, the Bitcoin network uses a longstanding and well-known cryptographic tool called a hash function to create a computational "puzzle" that must be solved. The solution to the puzzle requires a great deal of computational energy to find because the only way to find the answer is to make iterated guesses over and over in a trial-and-error process. However, once the answer is found, it is very easy to verify. In the PoW system, the nodes act as the generals who have to come to an agreement about the state of the

182

blockchain, or the battle plan. Specialized machines called "miners" compete to solve the puzzle using their computational power, and the first to find a solution gets to add the new block to the blockchain. The successful miner is rewarded with newly minted Bitcoin and all the transaction fees for that block.

Since the puzzle requires a great deal of power to solve but is easy to verify once the solution is found, it makes it very difficult to "cheat" because it costs more energy and effort to create a bad block than it does to detect a bad block. Miners are incentivized to perform these tasks by the block reward, just as a gold miner expends energy and effort to be rewarded with the gold they discover. If the winning miner tries to submit a corrupted or invalid block, the rest of the network, including the nodes and the rest of the miners, will reject the new block and the miner will lose the potential reward, wasting the electricity and computing power they had expended. The PoW system is therefore designed to keep each block valid by rewarding miners for their work.

The metaphor of gold mining is particularly apt with regard to Bitcoin's decentralized system. Gold mining itself is a decentralized process by which gold miners hunt for gold and expend an enormous amount of energy to retrieve it. If one operation goes down, gold mining as a whole does not end, as the demand for gold and its potential reward drives new miners to keep searching. Likewise, Bitcoin miners can come from anywhere and simply connect their mining rigs, or powerful computers designed to solve the network's computational puzzle efficiently, to the Bitcoin network via the internet. Additionally, if one Bitcoin mining operation fails, there are several million other machines that will continue to provide computing power to the network.

However, there are a few crucial differences between gold mining and Bitcoin mining. The new supply of gold is added at the rate of anywhere between one to three percent annually. When demand is high, the price rises, and miners are incentivized to find more gold, which satisfies the demand by providing supply, and the price goes back down. Gold may be a scarce commodity, difficult to find, and demands a great deal of energy, but it remains inflationary because new gold is always added. Bitcoin, by contrast, is programmed to make the miner's new block reward cut in half every 210,000 blocks, or roughly once every four years. This event is known as the "halving." Starting with a block reward of fifty Bitcoin at its inception, this was cut to twenty-five in 2012, and has continued to halve approximately every four years. Ultimately, the block reward will end in the year 2140, and miners will be rewarded only with transaction fees. Thus, the supply of new Bitcoin through the block reward is becoming ever more finite, with the programmatic intention to make it more valuable by contracting the rate of new supply.

In addition, while it is possible for gold miners to attempt to retrieve larger supplies of gold by bringing even more resources and energy to the effort, such as the use of heavy earth-moving equipment or larger gold extraction machines, Bitcoin miners do not receive larger block rewards for providing more computing power to the network. That is, the amount of Bitcoin given as a reward for each new block remains constant until the next halving event. New computing power might theoretically cause the computational puzzle to be solved faster, making the interval between blocks happen at a rate faster than the standard ten minutes. However, within the PoW algorithm is a provision called the "difficulty adjustment," which recalculates the mining difficulty every 2016 blocks, or roughly every two weeks. Thus, if more computing power is added to the network, the computational puzzle is made more difficult, and vice versa. The purpose of this adjustment is to maintain a consistent block creation time, ensuring that new blocks are added approximately every ten minutes. Like a clock that ticks every ten minutes, Bitcoin's schedule has remained unchanged since its beginning, operating without a chairman, committee, or board of governors to keep it running. Rather, Bitcoin relies only on the protocol, the consensus mechanism, and its network to function.

The steadily increasing price of Bitcoin, even though its many fluctuations, continues to drive miners to bring their computational power online, Furthermore, this is incentive for manufacturers to continue making dedicated Bitcoin mining rigs with ever more power.

Moreover, it is this expenditure of energy that helps to give Bitcoin value. As with gold, if it were easy to extract, its value would be far less, as the example of the Rai stones from demonstrates. What was once a valuable stone disk to the people of Yap Island, requiring enormous amounts of effort to extract and carve, became far less valuable when greater technology made it commonplace. Bitcoin's use of energy is not a flaw, rather it is a feature and a demonstration of the difficulty required to discover new bitcoin. Proof of Work is therefore aptly named, as it represents the proof that work was expended to make new bitcoin come into existence. In a larger sense, any good that is created, discovered, or produced requires work, and the demonstration of proof for that work is the equivalent of a certificate of authenticity and the source of trust in the good and in the producer. In Bitcoin's PoW system, this authenticity becomes objective and verifiable.

Of course, Bitcoin was not conceived in its perfect and final form and had to go through many changes over its life, changes that were made by its developer community, reviewed, and then submitted for acceptance by the community. Therefore, if the Bitcoin white paper was its Declaration of Independence, the Bitcoin protocol is its Constitution. Like the Constitution of the United States, the Bitcoin protocol can be amended, but only through an arduous process of consensus by the network. This process ensures that any changes to the protocol are thoroughly vetted and agreed upon by a majority of participants, reflecting the democratic principles embedded in constitutional amendments. In the case of Bitcoin, this consensus mechanism is enforced through the network of nodes and miners who validate transactions and maintain the blockchain. Proposals for changes, often called Bitcoin Improvement Proposals (BIPs), are discussed and debated within the community. For a proposal to be accepted, it generally needs broad support and must be implemented by a significant portion of the network.

A crucial aspect of this process is the concept of game theory, which plays a significant role in maintaining the stability and integrity of the Bitcoin network. Network participants, such as miners and node operators, are incentivized to act in ways that preserve the value and security of the network. Enacting changes that would harm the network or cause it to lose value would directly affect their own interests. Therefore, they are motivated to support only those changes that are perceived to be beneficial for the long-term health and success of Bitcoin. This game-theoretic approach ensures that the network remains resilient and resistant to malicious actors. Just as constitutional amendments require careful consideration and broad support to protect the stability of a nation, changes to the Bitcoin protocol must undergo rigorous scrutiny and achieve consensus to safeguard the network's value and functionality. This system of checks and balances helps maintain trust and reliability in Bitcoin, similar to how a constitution is designed to uphold the rule of law in a country.

At the time of this writing, Bitcoin is well into its second decade of continuous operation with new blocks added to the blockchain and new coins awarded to miners every ten minutes. It has a market capitalization of over a trillion dollars,[21] calculated by taking the current value of each coin multiplied by the number of coins in circulation, which demonstrates how trading markets regard it as a commodity. This number varies greatly from day to day, as some economic analysts call it an important commodity that must be a part of anyone's portfolio, and others call it a Ponzi scheme that will ultimately be worthless. Still, since the purpose of its creation was for it to be a new form of money, it is worthwhile to consider if it succeeded and to what extent.

Of course, the viability of any form of money exists within the context of its time in history. Gold coins, for example, could not exist until metallurgical processes were developed to purify ore, minting techniques were made to stamp the coins, and the population became large and complex enough to make the coins worth producing. Similarly, Bitcoin could not exist without sophisticated digital cryptography, the widespread use of personal computers and smartphones, and the internet to connect the various and integral parts of the network together. Therefore, in order to judge the viability of Bitcoin, it is important to ask how it is able to

---

[21] The market value of Bitcoin stated here is from June 2024.

fulfill the properties of money within its own time and compare it to what it aims to replace.

» Acceptability: Bitcoin is nowhere close to being universally accepted, in large part because the USD has been the most widely accepted currency since the end of World War II, and the standard by which everything else is measured. The U.S. government places huge regulatory and tax burdens on businesses and individuals wanting to use Bitcoin, with many of those regulations contradicting each other. However, it is important to note that Bitcoin adoption since its inception in 2009 has continually increased as a growing number of merchants, online platforms and brick and mortar shops have begun to accept Bitcoin as a method of payment.

Small communities have also started to form around the world for the purpose of creating goods and services that accept Bitcoin as payment. These "circular economies" come together with the intention of promoting Bitcoin, but also to incentivize the community to acquire and use it as a substitute for their inflationary native fiat currency. On a larger scale, payment systems such as Cash App, PayPal, and Square have begun to integrate Bitcoin into their services. Measured by market capitalization, it is clear that global trading markets take Bitcoin seriously and while it is an unanswered question as to whether Bitcoin will actually supplant the USD, the rate of Bitcoin adoption is a story of exponential growth.

» Divisibility and fungibility: Most people think about Bitcoin in terms of its essential base unit, bitcoin with a lower case "b," in much the same way that the essential base unit of the U.S. currency is the dollar. Yet, while everything that can be bought and sold in dollars is priced in dollar units, the value of each individual bitcoin is so high that it is difficult to price anything in whole bitcoins. What many do not realize is that while the USD can only be subdivided into a hundred smaller units, bitcoins can be subdivided into fractions, and the smallest unit of bitcoin is one hundred millionth of a whole bitcoin, also known colloquially as a "satoshi," or "sat" for short. Furthermore, each unit of bitcoin is uniform and can be substituted for any other unit, making it both divisible and fungible.

» Durability: The idea of a durable form of money is generally applied to a physical currency like gold, which allows it to retain its future value over time without being worn, corroded, or destroyed. But Bitcoin's durability comes not from its physical hardness, but from the power of its network. As a decentralized network, it has the benefit of having copies of its ledger distributed to its nodes and miners worldwide. Even physical attacks that disable individual machines, or even the internet itself, will not destroy the network fully. As long as the ledger and its software exist on one machine, the Bitcoin network can be restarted.

» Portability: Throughout history, money was limited in portability by its physical tangibility. In order to satisfy the other monetary requirements such as durability and scarcity, money had to be embodied in a physical form. The large-scale banking revolution advanced by the Medici family opened the door to the potential of an intangible form of money through its branch network and shared bookkeeping ledger, allowing for the possibility of far greater portability through space and time, but with the added need for trust in the institutions that administered the money. With the steady capture of money by centralized institutions over the past several centuries came the corruption and consolidation of power by central banks and their enablers. But Bitcoin offers a decentralized solution to the problem of intangible money, fulfilling the promise of near instantaneous portability, transmitting monetary value across borders at large scale and low cost, but without the perversion of trust that inevitably comes with state-enforced centralization.

» Scarcity: As a "designed" monetary system, Bitcoin was built with scarcity as a core principle, with the intention of mimicking the mining of gold from the outset. But unlike gold, no amount of effort and energy can cause the Bitcoin network to release more than its scheduled allotment of new coins through the block reward. Bitcoin will continue to cut the block reward's release of new coins in half until the final reward is mined in the year 2140. At this point, the total supply of Bitcoin will be twenty-one million coins, and nothing can change that. Bitcoin is not only a scarce asset, but also programmed to be scarce, with all of the network participants that run and propagate the protocol incentivized to make sure this foundational principle never changes.

» Immutability: The trustworthiness of Bitcoin is ultimately derived from a new property of money that emerged as a meaningful idea only in the age of digital forms of money. This seventh property of money asks the question of whether transactions are irreversible or if they can be altered after the fact. The property of immutability therefore answers the question of whether economic participants can trust the permanence of their transactions. When money is a physical bearer instrument, the question of immutability is nonsensical because possession of the money is all that is required to confirm ownership. When money is a series of entries in a ledger maintained by people, there are no systemic protocols that prohibit the ledger from changing. Certainly, laws against theft and fraud may impose stiff penalties against such actions. But the system itself does not and cannot physically restrict theft and fraud. In fact, in the case of central banks working under a politically protected framework, they are legally authorized to make additions to their balance sheet for which an ordinary corporation would be prosecuted.

Bitcoin is the first form of money to achieve this seventh property of immutability, and the only one to do so at scale. Bitcoin's immutability is one of its most essential and defining characteristics, as transactions that have been confirmed by the network and recorded in the blockchain cannot be altered afterwards. Each block is cryptographically linked to the previous block, creating a chain of linked blocks that go back to the very beginning of Bitcoin's history. Its immutability is not only programmatically built into the Bitcoin protocol, but the ledger also itself is an open and public record that allows anyone to search through it and confirm the validity of any transaction. And, as the ledger is propagated throughout the network's nodes and miners, it is the very growth of the network that hardens it.

Now, after looking at Bitcoin's monetary properties, it is worthwhile to see how well it fulfills the three functions of money: medium of exchange store of value, and unit of account.

» Medium of Exchange: Bitcoin also faces numerous challenges as a medium of exchange. Transactions on the main Bitcoin network still take a minimum of ten minutes to be confirmed, making so-called "on-chain" interactions difficult for small and fast exchanges. However, new technologies such as the Lightning Network have emerged, allowing for "off- chain" transactions to be processed almost instantaneously.

These "off-chain" technologies enable a small amount of Bitcoin to be reserved and taken offline, facilitating quick transactions. This is similar to opening a bar tab, where multiple orders can be made throughout an evening and settled with one bill at the end of the night. These off-chain, or "layer two," solutions are examples of how developers are addressing Bitcoin's scalability and speed issues to enhance its utility as a medium of exchange.

Bitcoin does serve as a medium of exchange, officially in regions like El Salvador, where it is considered legal tender, and unofficially in regions like China, where its use has been declared illegal. However, even in areas where it is not illegal, Bitcoin faces regulatory hurdles that make the legal framework of its usage uncertain. For example, in the United States, the government classifies Bitcoin as a tradeable asset. As a result, Bitcoin users are required to track their cost basis, or the price at which they purchased Bitcoin, against the realized value, or the price when it was used in exchange for something else. The difference is considered a capital gain and generates a taxable event. The cumbersome requirement to track every Bitcoin transaction for tax reporting makes using Bitcoin as a medium of exchange extremely difficult. But despite these challenges, Bitcoin's growing acceptance and technological advancements, such as the Lightning Network, are working towards making transactions faster and more efficient, which could help mitigate these issues over time.

» Store of Value: Bitcoin is often touted as "digital gold" due to its properties that resemble those of a traditional store of value like gold. Bitcoin's limited supply of twenty-one million coins creates a scarcity that underpins its value. Additionally, its decentralized nature and security through the PoW consensus mechanism prevent tampering and make it resistant to inflation. Certainly, when measured against the USD, Bitcoin looks like an extremely volatile asset, at times experiencing drawdowns of 80%. However, Bitcoin has generally experienced positive gains when held over any four-year period, as each halving cycle tends to bring new participants to the network. This of course, is based on past performance as of the publication of this book and is no guarantee of future results.

» Unit of Account: By contrast, Bitcoin is not used as a unit of account for anything except a measurement against other cryptocurrencies. The USD is still the preeminent unit of account for goods and services, with various other fiat currencies serving as regional pricing standards. Furthermore, the dollar is used to price securities relied upon to store value in the modern age, such as stocks and bonds. While on the one hand, Bitcoin's extreme volatility measured against the USD shows why it is not used as a unit of account, it is also true that the exponential growth in money and credit since the U.S. left the gold standard makes the purchasing power of the dollar substantially less valuable. Ultimately, while it is uncertain when or if Bitcoin ever serves as a unit of account, it will continue to add new blocks to its ledger and reward its miners every ten minutes using a predictable schedule that cannot be changed. Therefore, unlike the fiat dollar, its supply will always be fixed, based on the reliable standard determined by an unchanging protocol.

When examined against the properties of money, Bitcoin holds up as good if not better than all forms of money throughout history. Yet, even as its popularity continues to grow as an economic system, it still has a long way to go to be considered money by most people around the world. In the early days of Bitcoin, it began as an experiment with no guarantee of successful adoption. The first version of the Bitcoin software was released in January 2009 as the genesis block, or the first entry into the ledger known as Block 0 (zero). This first block included a reference to a newspaper headline of that time, intended to prove the date of its creation, but also highlighting the instability of the prevailing financial system: "The Times 03/Jan/2009 Chancellor on brink of second bailout for banks." [22] This message, embedded in Bitcoin's very first block, was widely interpreted as a critique of the traditional financial system and a declaration of Bitcoin's foundational principles.

Bitcoin's beginning was marked by a community of enthusiastic developers and cryptographers, people who write or decipher the encryption code used for online data security. They immediately understood the potential for creating electronic transactions that could be secured with cryptographic functions that would make them impervious to alteration without detection. This is done while at the same time allowing for the quick transmission of value across space with no geographic borders. The first Bitcoin transaction took place between Nakamoto and computer programmer Hal Finney in January 2009. For the first few years, Bitcoin was primarily a niche project, circulating within a small group of early adopters and cryptography enthusiasts.

Addressing this audience on February 11, 2009, Nakamoto wrote a post on the online forum for those interested in freedom and privacy called Cypherpunks that stated, "I've developed a new open source P2P e-cash system called Bitcoin. It's completely decentralized, with no central server or trusted parties, because everything is based on crypto proof instead of trust."[23] He went on to explain issues of trust in the financial system in this same post, "The root problem with conventional currency is all the trust that's required to make it work. The central bank must be trusted not to debase the currency, but the history of fiat currencies is full of breaches of that trust. Banks must be trusted to hold our money and transfer it electronically, but they lend it out in waves of credit bubbles with barely a fraction in reserve. We have to trust them with our privacy, trust them not to let identity thieves drain our accounts."[24] Nakamoto had distinct goals in mind for Bitcoin relating to trust and privacy. One of the main

[22] Elliott, Francis. "Chancellor on brink of second bailout for banks." The Financial Times. January 3, 2009.

[23] Nakamoto, Satoshi. 2009. "Cypherpunks online forum post." https://p2pfoundation.ning.com/forum/topics/bitcoin-open-source.

[24] *Ibid.*

principles, unlike fiat money, was that he did not want a system based on trust or to be dependent upon a central authority.

Just as previous examples in the history of money have shown, any system that required an unearned trust, from depositors relying on banks to keep their money safe, to Roman citizens expecting their coins to be kept free from debasement, money would always become corrupted and betray the trust given to it. Instead, he focused on building something that could be programmatically verified by anyone, using the rules established in the system, rather than relying on trust. This has since been used as the basis for a phrase popular in the Bitcoin space, "Don't trust. Verify."[25] It is these three words that has set the philosophical foundation for Bitcoin that continues today.

With its ability to transport immaterial value across space and time over a network whose immutable rules provide the trust that previous intermediaries could not give, Bitcoin can provide an important service in the modern globalized economy. Physical cash has become cumbersome and sometimes dangerous to carry and store, not to mention difficult to use for large transactions. While it does have the benefit of being a bearer instrument, and is generally trusted, the exchange must occur in physical proximity to both parties. Electronic exchanges allow more flexible transactions to take place, adding convenience and speed, but also requiring trusted intermediaries to handle the transaction behind opaque systems that are difficult to trust fully. Checks, credit cards, debit cards, and even services like Venmo and PayPal provide convenience but at a cost. These intermediaries verify the transaction, ensuring that there is enough money to cover it, or in the case of credit cards that are essentially a loan, they also provide a guarantee that payment is sent to the correct entity. Yet even though they provide the veneer of

---

[25] This adopted phrase "Don't trust, verify" is reminiscent of the Russian proverb "Doveryai, no proveryai" (Доверяй, но проверяй), which translates to "Trust, but verify." This proverb was popularized in the West by U.S. President Ronald Reagan during the 1980s in the context of nuclear disarmament discussions with the Soviet Union. The Bitcoin community adapted this idea to emphasize not trusting at all, but rather always verifying through code and cryptographic proof. (Massie, Suzanne. *Trust but Verify: Reagan, Russia, and Me.* Rockland, ME: Maine Authors Publishing, 2013.)

helpful and courteous service, they remain third party administrators of money that cannot be instantly and publicly audited.

Furthermore, these entities are subject to banking laws, government regulations, and even outright confiscation. Even those used for Bitcoin can be regulated as they are centralized apps or exchanges. However, Bitcoin itself, as a decentralized network with no single point of capture, cannot be. In addition, as the modern world becomes more intertwined with technology, there is even more of a push towards having central bank digital currencies, which could possibly result in countries completely abandoning physical currency in favor of a digital one. This transition would eliminate physical currency and the ability for people to have even simple P2P, or a simple person to person exchange without third parties for cash transactions. This makes the need for a decentralized, digital P2P solution even more important.

Yet, Bitcoin has not been without its challenges. In its early days, Bitcoin primarily attracted enthusiasts who were interested in its potential for providing financial privacy and freedom from governmental control. This led to one of the notorious early uses of Bitcoin, the online market platform called the Silk Road, named after the ancient trade route, that ran from Europe through Asia. Launched in 2011 by Ross Ulbricht, known online as Dread Pirate Roberts, the Silk Road operated as a hidden service on the Tor network, a free and open-source software that allows for anonymous communication. This allowed users to buy and sell goods and services anonymously, with Bitcoin being the primary means of payment. Neither Ulbricht nor Nakamoto created Bitcoin for illegal purposes; however, just like fiat money and even gold, it can be used by people for illicit activities.

Another attribute of Bitcoin is the pseudonymity, or not requiring personal identification details for Bitcoin transactions, which provides users with a sense of security and privacy, although transactions can still be tracked using wallet addresses. This made the Silk Road a hub for various illegal activities, including the sale of drugs and other illicit goods. The platform rapidly grew into a vast underground marketplace, demonstrating the practical utility of

194

Bitcoin in providing a degree of anonymity in online transactions. However, this also brought significant attention to Bitcoin from law enforcement. In 2013, the FBI shut down the Silk Road, and Ulbricht was arrested, and sentenced to life in prison without parole. This event marked a pivotal moment in the history of Bitcoin, bringing it into mainstream awareness but also creating an ongoing narrative in which its use would be associated with illegal activities. This shaped public and regulatory perceptions, thus skewing the view of Bitcoin that still exists and is reinforced through many media outlets and government policies.

Ironically, this perception of Bitcoin is misguided as there are far more illicit activities that occur in the fiat system than in Bitcoin. For example, the online marketplace, Craigslist, while being a popular platform for classified ads that facilitates the buying, selling, and exchanging of goods and services, has also faced challenges related to its use for illegal activities. Over the years, there have been instances where the platform was misused for activities such as illegal drug sales, human trafficking, prostitution, and scams. Due to its decentralized nature and the anonymity, it offers users, tracking precise statistics on these illegal activities can be challenging. However, law enforcement agencies and researchers have periodically highlighted concerns. For example, there have been reported cases of the "Craigslist killer," where individuals used the platform to commit violent crimes. Additionally, scams, ranging from fraudulent rental listings to fake job postings, have been a persistent problem, causing financial losses for unsuspecting users. The platform has taken steps to mitigate these issues, such as removing certain sections of the website and implementing more rigorous monitoring and reporting mechanisms. However, despite these efforts, the sheer volume of transactions facilitated by Craigslist means that it remains a target for those looking to exploit online anonymity for illegal purposes. The exact scale of these activities is hard to quantify due to underreporting and the transient nature of online ads, but they serve as a reminder of the potential dark side of digital marketplaces, one that exists regardless of the currency used to make transactions.

Additionally, the United Nations Office on Drugs and Crime periodically publishes reports on the global drug trade, including estimates of its financial scale. For example, the UNODC's 2021 World Drug Report noted that the global drug trade is worth an estimated 1.4% of global GDP, equivalent to about $426 billion in 2014. In contrast, the FBI seized 144,000 bitcoins from Ulbricht's personal holdings and approximately 30,000 bitcoins from Silk Road's servers when Bitcoin was about $204 per coin, making the confiscated Silk Road Bitcoin worth $35,496,000 at the time. This was a fraction of the amount of fiat money involved in the drug trafficking, yet government officials and media do not question the ethical value of fiat.

Overall, there is a distorted public perception of how Bitcoin is synonymous with illegal activities compared to the perception that the fiat monetary system is incorruptible. Another example of this spurious reasoning comes from the fiat banking industry itself. In 2012, HSBC, one of the world's largest banks, was involved in a major money laundering scandal. It broke when a U.S. Senate report accused the bank of failing to prevent the laundering of billions of USD. The investigation revealed that HSBC's lax anti-money laundering controls allowed drug cartels, terrorists, and sanctioned countries like Iran to move money through its U.S. operations. As a result, HSBC agreed to a record $1.92 billion settlement with U.S. authorities, admitting to violations of anti-money laundering laws and sanctions. However, unlike Bitcoin which is viewed negatively by the media, government, and global elites because of a few bad actors, HSBC was able to bounce back from the scandal thanks to the widely accepted belief that fiat currency and the banking industry are honorable. These misleading narratives are reinforced through the media and politicians around the world.

Even with the misconception of Bitcoin being used for criminal purposes, the liquidity is becoming easier as more platforms that facilitate the buying and selling of Bitcoin are coming online. Bitcoin can be readily converted to and from various fiat currencies, such as the USD, Euro, and Japanese Yen. In fact, there is a worldwide growing acceptance of Bitcoin by merchants, businesses, and individuals, particularly in places like Latin America and Europe. These areas are seeing more and more Bitcoin circular economies spring up. Examples from Latin America include El Salvador's Bitcoin Beach, which was the first of these communities and more recently, the mountain town of Berlin serve as an example of a growing circular economy. In addition, the region has developed Bitcoin Lake in Guatemala, Bitcoin Jungle in Costa Rica, as well as Brazil's Praia Bitcoin and Montanha Bitcoin. In Europe, places like Bitcoin City in the Netherlands, Plan B in Switzerland, and Bitcoin Valley in Italy are inspiring other places in Europe, the Americas, Africa, and Asia to also develop pockets of Bitcoin communities.

In general, more and more entities are accepting Bitcoin for goods and services around the globe. All of this adds to its acceptability and liquidity. As illustrated, Bitcoin holds up quite well when examining the properties of money. When the added value of privacy and trust as well as being immune to centralized monetary policies, it really does live up to the dream Nakamoto had back in 2008. Yet, because it is still relatively new, and for many of the reasons it was created, Bitcoin still has its critics. One of the biggest intellectual attack vectors against Bitcoin, often held by those who were influenced with Austrian economic ideas, is the belief that Bitcoin does not have "intrinsic value."

The argument that Bitcoin has no intrinsic value is based on the idea that, unlike physical commodities or traditional currencies, Bitcoin is not backed by any tangible asset. Critics argue that Bitcoin's value is purely speculative and derived solely from the belief that others will continue to find it valuable. They point out that Bitcoin does not have inherent utility, like gold, which can be used in jewelry and electronics. Yet, neither is fiat currency, which requires trust in a centralized authority, the government, and central banking system. Defenders of fiat money argue that government backing confers intrinsic value in a currency. However, this is based on the notion that the government will protect the value of the money it backs through its prestige and power, and that they ultimately have the best interests of the holders of their money in mind. This, of course, is demonstrably false in any country whose central bank engaged in quantitative easing and inflated their own currency, but also in countries such as Cypress and Mexico where government policies actually took away fiat value, as described earlier. On the other hand, Bitcoin is not centralized. Rather it is a system based on a decentralized network that validates it with a transparent accounting system. Unlike government actions, the Bitcoin network is incapable of devaluing its currency by the nature of its protocol.

Still, Ludwig von Mises' Regression Theorem is another way to restate the question of intrinsic value. If money, according to Mises, must be able to be traced back to its original non-monetary commodity value, Bitcoin must also be able to be traced back to its non-monetary source of value. But while Bitcoin is traded in various forms on the same securities exchanges as the most valuable public companies in the world, it is easy to forget that in its early days, it had no defined price whatsoever. Not until May 22nd, 2010, a day that would come to be known as Bitcoin's "Pizza Day," when developer Laszlo Hanyecz purchased two pizzas from a nearby Papa John's pizzeria at the cost of ten thousand bitcoins, that a price would be discovered for Bitcoin. As the two pizzas had the dollar value of $41, the first recognized price of Bitcoin would be .0041 bitcoin per dollar. Prior to Pizza Day, there was no universally accepted monetary value attached to Bitcoin, Therefore, in order to establish whether Mises' Regression Theorem applies to Bitcoin, it is important to ask if Bitcoin had any non-monetary value prior to Pizza Day.

Clearly, the small group of early adopters, and cryptography enthusiasts were fascinated by the novelty of the burgeoning new Bitcoin network. Bitcoin did have some worth as a collectible item, no different at this early stage than digital trading cards, apart from the immutable scarcity built into the Bitcoin network, which digital trading cards do not have. Early Bitcoin adopters would also use Bitcoin for tipping, sending bitcoins as a way to show approval for interesting and well-written posts on online forums. Some would enjoy and take pride in participating in the network in various ways, by setting up a machine for mining for example, or writing documentation to make the network easier to understand for future participants, or even debugging the early code and submitting changes for consensus approval. Participation in the Bitcoin network fostered a sense of belonging to a unique and forward-thinking community. This social aspect added a layer of non-monetary value.

Regardless of the small scale of Bitcoin's early non-monetary usage, it is important to remember that if it had no non-monetary usage before it could have its economic utility proven by Pizza Day, it would simply have disappeared from lack of use, an interesting but failed experiment. But as it survived this early stage and flourished, it is clear that Mises' Regression Theorem does, in fact, reveal Bitcoin's early non-monetary value. Additionally, as more people adopt Bitcoin, as more circular economies are formed, and as more countries adopt Bitcoin as legal tender, then the intrinsic value argument becomes less relevant. Bitcoin demonstrates its value by continuously operating nonstop, adding new blocks of transactions to the blockchain, and remaining impervious to attacks. Multiple trading markets continuously discover Bitcoin's price, and those who hold it, from individuals, to corporations, to asset managers, to nation states, prove its value by holding onto it and not selling. For holders of Bitcoin, the network is its intrinsic value. Like all things that have been used as money, it is the users that determine its value, just as past users of shells, beads, and even cacao.

The origins of Bitcoin and its fundamental structure demonstrate that it is truly a decentralized form of currency that in of itself cannot be co-opted by any central authority. Bitcoin's utility has grown as more people and institutions have adopted it. It is not run through banks, it is not beholden to government or central banking authority, it does not care about national borders, nor can it be controlled by one person. Therefore, its decentralized network becomes more robust and secure as participation increases, demonstrating that the whole is greater than the sum of its parts.

Chapter 16: Navigating the Bitcoin Ecosystem

Bitcoin can be best understood as distributed software that allows for transfer of value using a currency protected from unexpected inflation without relying on trusted third parties.

-Saifedean Ammous

With an understanding of how Bitcoin works, it is important to learn how to acquire and use it. Once difficult, the acquisition of Bitcoin has significantly evolved since its inception in 2009. As the Bitcoin network has grown and matured, changes in technology, market dynamics, and regulatory environments have influenced how people acquire Bitcoin. When Bitcoin was first introduced and until about 2012, Bitcoin mining was accessible to individuals using personal computers. Yet, over time and with the growth of the mining network, the computational power required to win the block rewards became more difficult, requiring specialized machines beyond the capability of personal computers. Early adopters could also acquire Bitcoin through websites called Bitcoin faucets that gave away free bitcoins to promote adoption. For example, the Gavin Andresen faucet initially gave away five bitcoins per visit. Furthermore, these early enthusiasts could also acquire bitcoins through direct peer-to-peer transactions or in online forums.

From 2013 until 2016, there was a transition in how people mined Bitcoin and a growth of currency exchanges dealing in Bitcoin that allowed individuals to buy Bitcoin more easily. As individual mining became less profitable due to increased difficulty, the introduction of dedicated computer chips called Application Specific Integrated Circuits, also known as ASICs, began. Miners started joining mining pools to combine computational resources, and share the rewards based on the amount of computing power contributed to the pool. Furthermore, exchanges that allowed for the purchase and sale of Bitcoin similar to fiat currency exchanges, became more prominent and user-friendly offering easier access for more people to purchase Bitcoin using fiat currencies. Finally, during this phase, some businesses, including individuals, small businesses, and even some corporations started accepting Bitcoin as payment, allowing for them to accumulate Bitcoin.

Since 2017, there has been more institutional involvement. The entry of institutional investors and large-scale traders has led to the development of more sophisticated ways to gain exposure to Bitcoin, including Exchange Traded Funds (ETFs), futures, and options markets. However, with these came regulatory developments. Consequently, with governments and financial authorities paying more attention to Bitcoin, there has been an increase in regulatory oversight, affecting how exchanges operate and how users acquire Bitcoin. In some places, such as the U.S. and Europe, these exchanges are required to comply with "Know Your Customer" (KYC) regulations in which anyone buying or selling Bitcoin has to register with government approved identification. This requirement takes away the sovereignty feature of Bitcoin, or the ability to hold Bitcoin without permission or limitations as an individual. Ultimately, KYC allows governments to monitor, tax, and in some cases, even confiscate Bitcoin that is held by third-party exchanges. Even popular third-party payment applications such as services like Venmo, PayPal and Square now allow users to buy, hold, and/or sell Bitcoin, although KYC is still required. Furthermore, Venmo and PayPal do not currently allow users to withdraw their Bitcoin, rather users who acquire it on their platform can only to sell it for fiat currency as opposed to being able to transfer it off of their platform.

Another way to acquire Bitcoin is through Bitcoin ATMs, especially for those preferring to use cash for their purchase. However, these ATMs will still require KYC if used in a location where that is a legal requirement. In fact, the only way to ensure that one is truly having a pseudonymous exchange of something for Bitcoin is to use a P2P network. Luckily, as more people use Bitcoin there are also occasions where people want to exchange it for fiat currency, possibly from being paid in Bitcoin but needing local currency for living expenses or from people who have been given Bitcoin but are not ready to adopt it fully.

Once acquired, one has to have a place to store or use it, which is done using wallets. However, the term "wallet," used in the context of Bitcoin, was intended to provide a metaphor to help describe the conditions that allow bitcoins to be stored. It conjures the image of storing paper cash in a folded leather wallet that can be placed in your pocket or purse for easy access. In practical use, a Bitcoin "wallet" is a digital tool that can create, store, and sign private keys, as well as making public keys available for receiving bitcoin in transactions. The word "wallet" makes it easy to think that your bitcoins are stored on the digital tool you run through your smartphone or personal computer, which might make you panic if you lose your phone or your computer crashes. In reality, the bitcoins are present on the Bitcoin network ledger, and the private keys held by your wallet software allow you to access and move it. As an essential component of Bitcoin, they provide a way for people to use Bitcoin and transact within the distributed ledger.

There are three types of Bitcoin wallets: software, hardware, and paper. Unlike fiat wallets that are often chosen for their aesthetic value, there are different uses and needs for each type of Bitcoin wallet. Note that it is important to distinguish between wallets that allow transactions to be made on the Bitcoin network that a user secures and controls with their private keys, as opposed to a "wallet" whose private keys are controlled by a service provider, or worse, something that appears to be making Bitcoin transactions but is really making transactions within an internal network that is not transparent and cannot be audited. The distinguishing difference is whether or not the wallet provides a transaction ID and if someone can search for that ID using any Bitcoin block explorer and confirm that the transaction has been made.

Software wallets, also known as hot storage, are easily accessible for frequent transactions, making them suitable for daily use. Similar to checking accounts in a traditional bank, they are designed to be used often, rather than to hold Bitcoin for long-term savings. However convenient they are, software wallets are generally less secure than hardware wallets because they are typically connected to the internet, as in the case of smartphone wallet apps. This makes them more susceptible to online threats like hacking or malware. In many places, they are also subject to KYC regulations. Because of this, some companies that provide software wallets may not be available everywhere as they take a stand against these regulations. Even so, software wallets are ideal for small amounts of Bitcoin and for users who transact more frequently. Many software wallets can be downloaded for free as an app on a smartphone. As discussed earlier, there are also wallets that allow fast and easy transactions to be made on the layer two solutions such as the Lightning Network. These can also be considered as the equivalent of easy and frequently used checking accounts. Some wallets even allow both base layer as well as layer two transactions to be used.

In contrast, hardware wallets, or cold-storage wallets, are specifically designed to store Bitcoin securely. They offer enhanced security as they store private keys offline, making them unavailable to online hacking attempts because they are never exposed to an online connection. Hardware wallets are typically small, allowing them to be portable and secured easily in a safe. Overall, they are also easy to use after the initial tutorial. Hardware wallets do not require connecting to a computer or smartphone to digitally sign a transaction. The technology allows one to take the digitally signed transaction file and copy it to a software wallet, which will transmit it to the Bitcoin network for inclusion into the next possible block. Hardware wallets are important for storing larger amounts of Bitcoin, especially for long-term holding, much like a savings account.

Finally, paper wallets are physical documents that contain a Bitcoin public address and private key, often in QR code format for ease of use. Although far less common now than they were in the early days of Bitcoin, paper wallets can be used for long-term storage or are used to give Bitcoin as a gift. Prior to the development of sophisticated hardware wallets, these paper wallets, a simple printout of the private keys, were considered to be a more secure form of private key storage because their physical form allowed them to not need exposure to the internet to be used. But today, with the advent of offline hardware wallets, the physical nature of paper wallets actually is its biggest risk, as they can be destroyed or lost very easily.

Once Bitcoin funds have been secured using a wallet, it is important to recognize that the onus is on the user to spend time, effort, and care into safeguarding the private keys. As a decentralized network, Bitcoin does not have a customer support line that can recover funds or cancel transactions by temporarily overriding the system protocol. Many wallets, of which nearly all modern wallets, generate a recovery phrase, also called a "seed" phrase. The seed phrase is either twelve or twenty-four words when it is first set up and can be used to recover a wallet if the device is lost or damaged. Some wallets can be encrypted with a password for additional security, but this is a function of the wallet app software and not the Bitcoin protocol itself.

Like many monetary services, there are fees when transacting in Bitcoin. These fees are accumulated, then are sent to the miners as incentive to continue to process transactions onto the ledger. The system works like an auction, with users bidding on the priority for their transaction to be added to the next block, as miners will grant higher priority to the transactions with the highest fees. Therefore, Bitcoin transaction times and fees can vary, based on the amount of the fees, and the volume of transactions waiting to be added to the ledger.

A Bitcoin transaction is considered confirmed when it is included in a block. The time it takes for a transaction to be confirmed can vary significantly. A new block is created approximately every ten minutes. However, this time can fluctuate due to the network's mining power and the inherent randomness of the mining process. If the network is busy with a high volume of transactions, a transaction might not get included in the next block, leading to delays for those who are waiting for their transaction. These transactions remain in a holding area until a miner picks them up and includes them in a block. Different services and wallets require a varying number of confirmations for a transaction to be considered secure. There is a tradeoff with time and security though as more confirmations generally mean a longer waiting time but increased security.

Transaction fees in Bitcoin are determined by a free market system. Users can include whatever fee they prefer with their transactions, but miners usually prioritize transactions with higher fees. Fees are typically calculated based on the transaction's size in computing power required, not the amount of Bitcoin being sent. So, complex transactions that require more information to be added to the blockchain will likely require higher fees. Most modern Bitcoin wallets will suggest a transaction fee based on current network conditions and required confirmation times. Users can often choose between faster confirmation with higher fees or lower fees with slower confirmation.

Transactions that do not make it to a block go into a waiting area called the mempool, short for "memory pool." This is a critical component of the Bitcoin network. It is essentially a holding area for Bitcoin transactions that have been broadcast to the network but not yet included in a block. The mempool is visible to all participating nodes in the Bitcoin network. Each node maintains its own version of this holding area and its size can fluctuate based on the volume of transactions. Nodes have limits on how much memory they allocate to the mempool and use various strategies to manage this space. Miners select transactions from the pool of transactions to include in the next block they mine. Due to this selection process, the transaction fees can fluctuate greatly. In times of high demand, users might pay higher fees to have their transactions prioritized. If the mempool is crowded, transactions with lower fees might have to wait longer to be included in a block, leading to delayed confirmations.

The size of the mempool can indicate the current demand for block space on the network. A large one suggests high transaction volume or network congestion. Wallets and users can use the data to estimate appropriate transaction fees for timely confirmations. When the network is less congested, miners will eventually clear even low-fee transactions from it. If a node's mempool becomes full, it may drop transactions from the pool, especially those with lower fees. If a transaction is dropped from a mempool, it may be rebroadcast by the originating wallet.

Block size is also an important component to the Bitcoin infrastructure. Originally, the size of each block was limited to one megabyte, comparable to a low-resolution JPEG photo, or 500 pages of plain text. In 2017, changes were made to the Bitcoin protocol that allowed for roughly twice as much data to be added to each block. Because the growth in popularity of the network could lead to congestion, the growing adoption of Bitcoin caused transactions to take longer to process and made them more expensive. However, with a limited block size, only so many transactions can fit inside each block, which means that users either have to pay more fees to get their transactions settled first, or they have to wait longer.

One of the biggest questions in Bitcoin development is how to handle the scaling of the network as it grows in popularity. Some argue for the expansion of the block size, suggesting that larger blocks would allow for more transactions per block, and ease the congestion. But as simple as this sounds, larger blocks create new problems, including network security, scalability, and decentralization, all fundamental principles in keeping Bitcoin secure and a relevant monetary system. For example, a smaller block size limit makes it more difficult for attackers to flood the network by creating large amounts of transactions with low or insignificant value. Without a block size limit, it is easy to imagine a Denial-of-Service (DoS) attack, or an attack meant to shut down servers with useless data, so it becomes unusable. These could make a block so large that it could not be added to the ledger at all.

Furthermore, larger blocks are simply more difficult to process, and the larger the network of users, the less able it is to scale. Bitcoin currently processes a new block approximately every ten minutes, but larger block sizes would disrupt that timing, making the turnaround time longer, and triggering a new difficulty adjustment, which would make the mining computations require more energy and power, and make mining more expensive. Ultimately, this would make the size of the ledger more difficult to distribute over the internet, particularly in remote locations with slower bandwidth resulting in fewer nodes and causing centralization towards parties that have more and powerful resources to devote. This is not optimal for the decentralization and consensus model Bitcoin was designed for as it would limit the number of nodes, thus the ability to ensure more users participated in the verification of the ledger.

Bitcoin was designed so anyone could participate in the consensus network. In fact, for the price of a used or small computer like a Raspberry Pi and a 2TB hard drive, anyone can run a Bitcoin node. This is possible only because the block size limit makes the size of the ledger manageable allowing it to be copied to an individual computer even without high-speed internet. Large blocks would mean that eventually the nodes could only be run on computers in large data centers with the fastest internet connections and the biggest hard drives. As such, if the nodes can only be run on these centralized machines, it means that they can be controlled and shut down. Small blocks allow nodes to be run by thousands of individuals using small, low-cost machines and in any location regardless of internet speed. The sheer number of individuals running their Bitcoin nodes ensures the integrity and resilience of the network. This is the power of decentralization as Bitcoin remains a system that distributes its control so one or many can fail without bringing the entire system down.

With all the benefits that small block limits bring, the problem of network congestion from an increasing number of transactions still remains. As discussed earlier, this was solved by another revolutionary idea that distinguishes on-chain and off-chain transactions. On-chain transactions are those that occur and are recorded directly on the ledger. They become part of the permanent public record after they are verified and added to a block. These transactions are verified by miners and are included in a block of the ledger. Once a transaction is added to a block and this block is appended to the ledger, it is considered irreversible. This makes on-chain transactions secure and resistant to fraud. Being on the ledger, these are publicly visible to anyone who accesses the ledger. On-chain transactions can be slower, especially during times of high network congestion and they also incur fees, which can vary based on network activity and the data size. On-chain is ideal for significant transactions requiring high security, transparency, and permanent record-keeping.

As previously mentioned, off-chain transactions occur outside of the ledger. They are not recorded directly on the ledger and can be executed in various ways, being faster and more efficient since they avoid the sometimes-time-consuming process of block confirmation. They often have lower or no transaction fees and can offer more privacy as they are not immediately publicly recorded on the ledger. Off-chain transactions are eventually settled on-chain, with only the net result like the final balance being recorded on the ledger. Off-chain is suited for smaller, frequent transactions, or situations where speed and lower fees are priorities.

One example of an off-chain solution is the previously mentioned Lightning Network. This off-chain system is designed to enable faster and more cost-effective transactions than Bitcoin's primary network. Bitcoin Lightning addresses the scalability issues of the Bitcoin network by creating a network of payment channels between users. Once a channel is established, transactions can occur off the main ledger. These transactions are nearly instant and can be very low cost. Users can open these channels by committing a certain amount of Bitcoin to it. Lightning payments are very common within Bitcoin users and circular economies. They can transact multiple times without needing to record each transaction on the ledger. When users are ready to close the channel, the final state of its balance is settled and recorded on the Bitcoin ledger. The Lightning Network allows for increased transaction speed, reduced costs, and improved scalability for the Bitcoin network.

But the Lightning Network is not the only layer two solution. The Liquid Network is another example of a system that can complement the Bitcoin network by taking smaller and more frequent transactions offline. The Liquid Network operates as a "sidechain" to Bitcoin, in which a certain amount of on-chain Bitcoin is locked on the main chain and is unlocked for use within the Liquid Network. This provides a separate blockchain that is pegged to Bitcoin to enable faster and more confidential transactions. It is managed by a federation of members who oversee the network and maintain its security, rather than a network of payment channels like the Lightning Network. This setup allows for the issuance and transfer of various assets and ensures quick transaction settlement times and increased privacy. As the Lightning Network was the first layer two solution, it is currently seeing more usage, which could lead to congestion and liquidity issues. Ultimately, Lightning, Liquid, and a number of other layer two networks, offer a variety of ease of use, speed, and acceptability features that make them useful. In the end, it is still Bitcoin that is being transacted on these solutions.

Fundamentally, Bitcoin represents a revolutionary leap in the concept of currency, underpinned by the innovative use of consensus, a decentralized ledger, and a fixed supply, fundamentally challenging traditional financial paradigms. It operates on the principle of mutual agreement among its users, similar to historical practices with commodities like grain or Rai Stones, ensuring its value through collective trust rather than physical backing or governmental decree. Bitcoin also fosters trust within a vast network where transactions are validated by consensus, thereby preventing any single point of failure or manipulation. The interplay between miners, who secure the network and add transactions, and nodes, which ensure the ledger's accuracy and integrity, exemplifies a robust model of decentralization.

Bitcoin's core mechanisms, including its PoW and the immutable nature of its ledger, not only safeguard against external tampering but also herald a new era of financial transparency, security, and user empowerment. Essentially, Bitcoin marks a significant departure from centralized financial systems and lays the groundwork for future innovations in digital currency. As more people become aware of how Bitcoin works and how to acquire it, the number of uses and places where it is accepted as currency can only continue to grow.

Epilogue: Bitcoin's Beacon for Freedom

*Imagine a world where everyone used something fair
and equitable to settle their economic differences.*

-Michael Saylor

The journey of money, from its inception to the digital age, mirrors the evolution of human societies, economies, and the quest for individual freedom. Initially, the concept of value exchange began with barter, where goods and services were directly exchanged. This system, while straightforward, was limited by the need for a mutual desire for what the other had to offer, often restricting the freedom of individuals to acquire what they needed.

As societies advanced, more universal mediums of exchange were sought, leading to the use of items like metal nuggets or shells, which were among the earliest forms of something akin to money. These were tangible, relatively scarce, and widely accepted, marking a significant step towards a more liberated trading system where value could be more easily quantified and exchanged.

The introduction of coins crafted from precious metals was a pivotal evolution, as it offered a standardized value that was recognized across vast regions. This uniformity in value allowed for the expansion of trade networks, significantly enhancing individual freedom by broadening access to goods and services far beyond local communities. Paper money represented another leap forward, initially as IOUs or promissory notes that could be traded for a specified amount of gold or silver. Over time, these evolved into fiat currencies, backed not by physical commodities but by the trust in the issuing government's stability and ability to maintain value. This transition to fiat currency further detached the concept of money from physical constraints, enabling unprecedented economic growth and individual financial mobility, though it also introduced new vulnerabilities like inflation and government manipulation.

The advent of Bitcoin marks the latest phase in the evolution of money, emphasizing decentralization and digital technology. Unlike its monetary predecessors, Bitcoin operates on a decentralized ledger, offering a level of transparency, security, and independence from centralized authorities. This represents a significant shift towards individual freedom, providing people with the option to transact directly with one another across the globe without the need for intermediaries or the fear of censorship. Moreover, the finite supply of Bitcoin contrasts with the potentially limitless printing of fiat currencies, appealing to those concerned about inflation and the devaluation of money by governments.

For many, Bitcoin is a gateway to individual freedom. By breaking free of the fiat system that is controlled by policies that tend to favor the elite or wealthy, people are finding ways to use Bitcoin as a store of value and to use P2P and circular economies to ensure a sovereign future for their retirement or children. There are several ways that Bitcoin is becoming more widespread. One is through the adoption of Bitcoin within a region or town or even through a community of users, creating Bitcoin circular economies. These economies aim to create a closed loop of economic activity, minimizing reliance on traditional fiat currencies and external financial systems. Central to Bitcoin's philosophy, these economies operate independently of centralized financial institutions, fostering a P2P financial network. Businesses and individuals within these economies earn, spend, and invest Bitcoin in a closed loop, aiming to create a self-sufficient economy less affected by external economic policies. The communities are often driven by individuals or groups who strongly believe in the principles of Bitcoin, such as financial sovereignty, privacy, and reduced reliance on traditional banking systems.

Circular economies work because individuals and businesses earn Bitcoin by providing goods or services within the community. This can include traditional business transactions, freelance services, or even digital content creation. Instead of converting Bitcoin to fiat currency, participants spend Bitcoin directly on goods and services within the community. This includes daily essentials, professional services, and restaurants. Participants are encouraged to save or invest their Bitcoin within the community, further strengthening the economy. Investments can be in Bitcoin-based businesses or community projects. Some Bitcoin circular economies include charitable giving, where donations are made in Bitcoin to support community projects or members in need. By reducing dependence on fiat currencies, these economies aim to protect themselves from inflation, currency devaluation, and financial crises. These communities and wider Bitcoin adoption provide an alternative for individuals who are unbanked or underbanked, offering greater access to financial services. They foster innovation in Bitcoin-based technologies and services, encouraging new business models and financial practices.

In addition to these areas where circular economies are flourishing, El Salvador became the first country to adopt Bitcoin as legal tender in June 2021. President Nayib Bukele has led the country through a series of positive changes both economically and culturally. This bold move, a first by any country, aimed to boost economic growth, attract foreign investment, and facilitate remittances, which are a significant part of the country's economy. By adopting Bitcoin and retaining the country's reserves in the currency, Bukele has been able to refuse any more IMF funding as well as to work independently outside of the fiat-controlled system that worked to enforce their political and economic policies upon his small nation. Furthermore, since its initial investment of Bitcoin, El Salvador is up eighty-three million USD. That is a significantly larger return than any fiat currency in the world. Bukele's administration has invested in infrastructure to support Bitcoin transactions, including the launch of the digital wallet Chivo, ATMs for Bitcoin transactions, and incentives for using Bitcoin. The response to Bitcoin's adoption has positioned El Salvador as a pioneer in the Bitcoin space, attracting attention from investors, enthusiasts, and tech companies interested in blockchain technology and mining. Furthermore, more and more Bitcoin advocates are moving to El Salvador, bringing their skills and entrepreneurial skills to this up-and-coming country.

Culturally, Bukele has created a positive reimagining of his once crime-laden country. Through his no-tolerance policy on gangs, the country has gone from one of the most dangerous countries in the world, touting the label of "murder capital of the world," to the one of the safest in the Americas. Domestically, Bukele and his ministers are creating a positive and optimistic place for both Bitcoin expats and Salvadorans. In fact, many Salvadorans who left the country due to the Civil War and later gang problems in the 1980s and beyond are now returning to their home country.

Furthermore, with a safer place where more and more opportunities for work and economic freedom are flourishing, El Salvador had one of the highest rates of tourists in Latin America for 2023. It is expected that the number of people moving to and visiting El Salvador in 2024 will continue to increase. One reason for this is the government's passport program that provides citizenship in exchange for a Bitcoin investment in the country. Bitcoin also has potential implications for financial inclusion, given that a significant portion of the Salvadoran population does not have access to traditional banking services. Although Bukele did provide an initial sum in Bitcoin for all citizens, the local adoption is not without issues. Like any major change within a society, time and education can make a major difference for people to accept it.

Ultimately, helping people to adopt Bitcoin involves educating them about its benefits and functionalities, providing easy-to-use tools, and addressing common concerns and misconceptions. This education is key to Bitcoin adoption and has become a mission of many individuals that see the value of Bitcoin as a medium of exchange and store of value. In fact, a way that is becoming more and more popular to create a network of users is through the idea of a circular economy. However, in order for these economies to continue and flourish, not only do tourists and visitors need to use Bitcoin, but it also has to be adopted by the local people. For this, there needs to be a way to break down complex ideas like ledger, mining, and digital wallets into easily understandable terms. This can be done by organizing community events aimed to teach people about Bitcoin and answer their questions is also extremely helpful. One can also help to provide access to articles, videos, and tutorials that explain Bitcoin's principles, usage, and advantages, preferably in the local languages. As more people become familiar and start using Bitcoin, not only to hold on to their savings or to invest their money in like a stock or retirement account, but as a regular currency to transact with, more countries will likely take the lead from Bukele and El Salvador and adopt it for their own coffers as well to be used by its citizens.

The advent of Bitcoin can be seen as a direct response to these vulnerabilities, emphasizing decentralization, limited supply, and resistance to censorship and inflation. This shift highlights a growing awareness and skepticism regarding traditional economic policies and the institutions that implement them. It underscores a desire for greater autonomy in financial affairs and a system that is less susceptible to the whims of policymakers and more anchored in immutable rules and transparency. Ultimately, as the only truly incorruptible decentralized currency ever created, Bitcoin serves as a beacon of hope for a freer future.

Glossary of Terms

51% Attack: In Bitcoin, a 51% attack occurs when a single miner or group of miners controls more than 50% of the network's mining power. This level of control can potentially allow them to manipulate transactions, double-spend coins, or disrupt the network's normal operation.

Acceptability: In economics, acceptability refers to the willingness of individuals in an economy to accept a particular form of money or currency in exchange for goods and services. Bitcoin's acceptability has grown as more people and businesses have adopted it.

Accounting System: An accounting system is a ledger that records all transactions. For Bitcoin, it is the distributed ledger and is a transparent and immutable system that maintains a public record of all Bitcoin transactions.

Barter System: Barter is an economic system where goods and services are exchanged directly for other goods and services without the use of money.

Bitcoin and bitcoin: "Bitcoin" with a capital "B" refers to the decentralized digital currency and network as a whole, while "bitcoin" with a lowercase "b" refers to the individual units of the currency.

Bitcoin Wallet: A Bitcoin wallet is a digital tool that allows users to store, send, and receive bitcoins. It consists of a public key (for receiving funds) and a private key (for authorizing transactions) .

Block: A block in the Bitcoin distributed ledger is a collection of transactions. These blocks are inked together chronologically to form a continuous chain.

Blockchain: A decentralized record of transactions that is maintained across computers through a peer-to-peer network.

Block Reward: The block reward is the amount of newly created bitcoins given to miners as a reward for adding a new block to the ledger.

Boom and Bust Cycles: These are economic cycles characterized by periods of rapid expansion (booms) followed by contractions (busts). Austrian economics often emphasizes the role of monetary policy in these cycles.

Bretton Woods Agreement: An international monetary agreement established in 1944 that fixed exchange rates to the U.S. dollar and tied the dollar to gold. It played a significant role in the global monetary system.

Bullion: Precious metals like gold and silver in their pure, bulk form, often used as a store of value.

Byzantine Generals Problem: A theoretical problem in distributed computing where multiple parties need to reach consensus, even if some participants are unreliable or adversarial. Bitcoin's proof-of-work system addresses this problem.

Central Bank Digital Currencies (CBDCs): A Central Bank Digital Currency (CBDC) is a digital form of a country's official currency issued and regulated by the central bank, designed for digital transactions and financial inclusion.

Checks: Traditional paper or digital documents used to transfer funds from one bank account to another.

Circular Economies: Economic systems that focus on using Bitcoin for transactions. These economies help promote the spread of Bitcoin and its use as currency.

City-state: A city-state is an independent political entity that consists of a single city and sometimes its surrounding territory.

Cold Storage: A method of storing bitcoins offline, typically on a hardware wallet or paper wallet, to protect them from online threats.

Commodity: A tangible good or product that has intrinsic value.

Commodity Money: Money that is backed by a tangible commodity with intrinsic value, such as grain or gold.

Consensus: In the context of Bitcoin, consensus is the agreement among network participants (nodes and miners) on the validity of transactions and the state of the ledger.

Counterfeiting: The act of producing fake or fraudulent currency or assets to deceive others.

Credit: In banking and economics, "credit" refers to the trust which allows one party to provide money or resources to another party wherein the second party does not reimburse the first party immediately but promises either to repay or return those resources at a later date.

Cryptocurrency: Digital or virtual currencies that use cryptography for security.

Currency Volatility: The degree to which the value of a currency, such as bitcoin, fluctuates in relation to other currencies or assets.

Debasement: The intentional reduction in the value or purity of a currency, often achieved by adding less valuable materials to it.

Deflation: A decrease in the general price level of goods and services in an economy, often accompanied by an increase in the value of money.

Denomination: The face value or unit of measurement of a currency, such as the dollar.

Devaluation: A deliberate reduction in the official exchange rate of a country's currency relative to other currencies.

Distributed Ledger: A decentralized digital record-keeping system for Bitcoin where multiple copies of a ledger are maintained across a network of computers.

Divisibility: The property of being easily divisible into smaller units, allowing for flexibility in transactions.

Dollar Standard: A monetary system where the U.S. dollar serves as the primary reserve currency used in international trade and finance.

Double-entry Accounting Method: A method of accounting that records every financial transaction with a column for both debits and credits.

Exchange of Value: The process of transferring one form of value, such as money or goods, for another.

Fiat Money: Currency that has value because a government declares it to be legal tender, even though it is not backed by a physical commodity.

Finite: Having a limited or fixed quantity. Bitcoin has a finite supply capped at twenty-one million coins.

Fixed Exchange Rates: A system in which the value of a country's currency is tied to the value of another single currency, a basket of other currencies, or another measure of value, such as gold, and is maintained at a constant level by the country's central bank which actively intervenes in the foreign exchange market to maintain the currency's value within a narrow band.

Floating Exchange Rates: Exchange rates that fluctuate based on supply and demand in the foreign exchange market, as opposed to fixed exchange rates.

Fractional Reserve System: A banking system where banks only hold a fraction of their customers' deposits in reserve, lending out the rest.

Fungible: Interchangeable and mutually interchangeable.

Gold Standard: A monetary system where a country's currency is backed by and can be exchanged for a specific amount of gold.

Hash: A cryptographic function that converts input data into a fixed-length string of characters, used extensively in Bitcoin technology for security.

High Time Preference: A preference for immediate consumption over saving or investing for the future.

Hot Storage: Storing Bitcoin in a digital wallet that is connected to the internet, making it more susceptible to hacking.

Hyperinflation: Hyperinflation is an extremely rapid and out-of-control price inflation, typically exceeding 50% per month, where a country's currency loses its value at an accelerated rate, leading to a severe decline in purchasing power and often resulting in economic instability and societal challenges. This phenomenon is usually caused by excessive money supply growth, and it often occurs during times of significant political or economic upheaval.

Immutability: Immutability refers to the stability and consistency of economic policies and rules over time, promoting trust, predictability, and long-term planning among economic participants, which is crucial for fostering economic growth and stability. In Bitcoin, immutability refers to the idea that once a transaction is recorded on the ledger, it cannot be altered or deleted.

Inflation: An increase in the general price level of goods and services in an economy, often accompanied by a decrease in the purchasing power of money.

Interest: The cost of borrowing money or the return on investment for lending or investing money.

Lender of Last Resort: A central bank or institution that provides emergency loans to financial institutions in times of crisis to prevent systemic collapse.

Lightning Network: A second-layer scaling solution for Bitcoin that enables faster and cheaper transactions by conducting most transactions off-chain. Eventually transactions are put onto the chain.

Liquidity: The ease with which an asset can be quickly converted into cash without significantly affecting its price.

Low Time Preference: A preference for saving and investing for the future over immediate consumption.

Managed exchange rate: Exchange rates that are generally allowed to float but the government will step in to enact policy to avoid sudden fluctuations.

Medium of Exchange: Something that is widely accepted as a means of payment in transactions, like money.

Mempool: The memory pool of pending transactions in the Bitcoin network waiting to be confirmed by miners.

Miners: Individuals or entities that use computational power to validate transactions and add them to the distributed ledger in exchange for rewards.

Nodes: Computers or devices on the Bitcoin network that maintain a copy of the distributed ledger and validate transactions.

Nonce: A number used in proof-of-work mining algorithms to try to find a hash value that meets certain criteria.

Off-chain: Off-chain transactions in Bitcoin occur outside of the blockchain network, where the transfer of Bitcoin or Bitcoin data is executed through secondary channels and are not immediately recorded on the blockchain. They offer faster and potentially more private transfers without directly impacting the main blockchain ledger such as the Lightning Network.

On-chain: On-chain transactions in Bitcoin refer to transactions that are recorded and verified on the Bitcoin blockchain, involving the transfer of Bitcoin between wallets, which become irreversible once they are confirmed and added to the blockchain after being validated by network participants, known as miners. These transactions are publicly visible and a part of the permanent, decentralized ledger, providing transparency and security inherent to the blockchain technology.

Opportunity Cost: The value of the next best alternative that must be forgone when a decision is made to allocate resources to one option rather than another.

Portability: The ease with which a currency or asset can be carried and transferred.

Proof of Work (PoW): A consensus mechanism in the Bitcoin infrastructure where miners must perform computational work (guessing random numbers) to validate transactions and add blocks to the ledger.

Precious Metals: Rare and valuable metals, such as gold and silver, often used as stores of value.

Private Key: A secret cryptographic key that allows the owner to access and control their Bitcoin holdings.

Public Key: A cryptographic key that is publicly shared and used to receive Bitcoin.

Quantitative Easing: A monetary policy where a central bank increases the money supply by purchasing financial assets, often government bonds, to stimulate economic growth.

Representative Money: Money that is backed by a promise to exchange it for a commodity, such as gold or silver, upon demand.

Reserve Currency: A widely accepted currency that is held in significant quantities by governments and institutions as part of their foreign exchange reserves.

Reserves: Assets held by banks or financial institutions to meet potential future liabilities.

Risk: The uncertainty associated with the potential for loss or gain in an investment or decision.

Safe Haven Currency: A currency that is considered a relatively stable and secure store of value during times of economic uncertainty or crisis.

Scarcity: The limited availability of a resource or asset relative to the demand for it.

Sound Money: Money that maintains its value over time and is not subject to significant inflation or devaluation.

Speculative Investments: Investments made with the expectation of significant returns, often accompanied by higher risk.

Stability: The quality of being resistant to sudden and unpredictable changes.

Standard of Value: A function of money that allows it to be used as a common measure of the value of goods and services.

Store of Value: A function of money that allows it to maintain its value over time and serve as a repository of wealth.

Time Preference: An individual's preference for consuming resources and goods either in the present (high time preference) or in the future (low time preference).

Transaction: An exchange of goods, services, or assets between two or more parties.

Transaction Fees: Fees paid by users of the Bitcoin network to miners for processing transactions.

Unbacked loans: Loans that are not backed by a physical asset or collateral.

Unintended Consequences: Unexpected and often negative outcomes of a particular action, policy, or decision.

Unit of Account: A function of money that allows it to serve as a standard measure for pricing and comparing goods and services.

Value: The perceived worth or utility of a good, service, or asset in an economic context.

Volatility: The degree of variation in the price or value of an asset over time, often used to describe the price fluctuations of cryptocurrencies like bitcoin.

Bibliography

Aitken, Rob. "'All Data Is Credit Data': Constituting the Unbanked." *Competition & Change* 21, no. 4, (2017): 274–300.

Alden, Lyn. *Broken Money: Why Our Financial System is Failing Us and How We Can Make It Better.* Timestamp Press, 2023.

Allen, Lindsay. *The Persian Empire.* London: British Museum Press, 2005.

Alonso, Sergio Luis Nanez, Miguel Angel Echarte Fernandez, DAVID Samz Bas, and Cristina Perez Rico. "El Salvador: An Analysis of the Monetary Integration Law and the Bitcoin Law." *Brazilian Journal of Political Economy* 44, no. 1 (2024): 189–209.

Ambrose, Stephen E, *D-Day, June 6, 1944: The Climactic Battle of World War II.* New York, Simon & Schuster, 1994.

Ammous, Saifedean. *The Bitcoin Standard: Sound Money in a Digital Age.* Hoboken: John Wiley & Sons, 2018.

Anderson, E. N. "An Anthropology of Chocolate." *American Anthropologist* 110, no. 1, (2008): 71–73.

Aristotle. *Politics: A Treatise on Government.* Translated by William Ellis. London: J M Dent & Sons,1928. http://www.gutenberg.org/ebooks/6762.

Aristotle. *The Ethics of Aristotle.* Translated by D.P. Chase. Boston: E.P. Dutton & Co., 1950. http://www.gutenberg.org/ebooks/8438.

Balaji, K. C., and K. Balaji. "A Study on Demonetization and Its Impact on Cashless Transactions." *International Journal of Advanced Scientific Research and Development* 4, no.3, (2017): 58-64.

Bardhan, Pranab. 2002. "Decentralization of Governance and Development." *Journal of Economic Perspectives* 16 (4): 185–205.

Barlow, Charles. "The Roman Government and the Roman Economy, 92-80 B.C." *The American Journal of Philology* 101, No. 2 (1980): 202-219.

Baron, J.P. "Making Money in Mesoamerica: Currency Production and Procurement in the Classic Maya Financial System." *Economic Anthropology* 5, (2018): 210-223.

Bellinger, Alfred R. "The Coins and Byzantine Imperial Policy." *Speculum* 31, no. 1, (1956): 70–81.

Bennyhoff James A. and Hughes Richard E. "Shell Bead and Ornament Exchange Between California and the Western Great Basin." *Anthropological Papers of the American Museum of Natural History* 64, no. 2, (1987).

Bhutta, Muhammad Nasir Mumtaz, Amir A. Khwaja, Adnan Nadeem, Hafiz Farooq Ahmad, Muhammad Khurram Khan, Moataz A. Hanif, Houbing Song, Majed Alshamari, and Yue Cao. 2021. "A Survey on Blockchain Technology: Evolution, Architecture and Security." *IEEE* Access 9.

"Bitcoin adoption raises multiple risks." *Country Report: El Salvador*, September 10, 2021, NA. Gale Business: Insights.

Bloomfield,A. "Monetary Policy Under the International Gold Standard," Federal Reserve Bank of New York, 1959.

Bojanic, Antonio N. "The Impact of Fiscal Decentralization on Accountability, Economic Freedom, and Political and Civil Liberties in the Americas." *Economies* 6, no. 1 (2018): 8-28.

Bongomin, George Okello Candiya, et al. "Agent Liquidity: A Catalyst for Mobile Money Banking among the Unbanked Poor Population in Rural Sub-Saharan Africa." *Cogent Economics & Finance* 11, no. 1, (2023).

Boomgaard, Peter. "Early Globalization: Cowries as Currency, 600 BCE-1900." *Linking Destinies*. Brill, (2008): 13-27.

Bordo, Michael D. "The Bretton Woods International Monetary System: A Historical Overview " *A Retrospective on the Bretton Woods System: Lessons for International Monetary Reform*, edited by Michael D. Bordo and Barry Eichengreen, University of Chicago Press, 1993.

Boyd, William Kenneth. *The Ecclesiastical Edicts of the Theodosian Code.* New York: Columbia University Press, 1905.

Boyle, David, ed. *The Money Changers: Currency Reform from Aristotle to E-Cash*. New York: Routledge, 2015.

Bretton Woods Agreement. Avalon Project, Yale University. https://avalon.law.yale.edu/20th_century/decad047.asp.

BRICS Information Center. University of Toronto, http://www. brics.utoronto.ca/.

British Parliamentary Papers. "The Gold Standard Act." https:// www.gold.org/sites/default/files /documents/1819may21.pdf.

Bromberg, Benjamin. "The Origin of Banking: Religious Finance in Babylonia." *The Journal of Economic History* 2 , no. 1, (1942): 77-88.

Brosius, Maria. *A History of Ancient Persia. The Achaemenid Empire.* Hoboken: Wiley-Blackwell, 2021.

Brown, Scott, Demetra Demetriou, and Panayiotis Theodossiou. "Banking crisis in Cyprus: Causes, consequences and recent developments." *Multinational Finance Journal* 22, no. 1, (2018): 63-118.

Bruner, Robert F., and Scott C. Miller. "The First Modern Financial Crises: The South Sea and Mississippi Bubbles in Historical Perspective." *Journal of Applied Corporate Finance* 32, no. 4, (2020): 17-33.

Brunton, Bruce . "The East India Company: Agent of Empire in the Early Modern Capitalist Era." *Social Education* 77 no. 2, (2013): 78–81.

Buriak, A., Vozňáková, I., Sułkowska, J., & Kryvych, Y. "Social Trust and Institutional (Bank) Trust: Empirical Evidence of Interaction." *Economics and Sociology* 12, no. 4 (2019): 116-129.

Butcher, Kevin. "Debasement and the Decline of Rome." *Studies in Ancient Coinage in Honor of Andrew Burnett* (2015): 181-205.

Cassis, Youssef, Richard S. Grossman and Catherine R. Schenk, eds. "Private banks and private banking." In *The Oxford Handbook of Banking and Financial History*, Oxford: Oxford University Press, 2016.

Chernow, Ron. *Washington: A Life*. New York: Penguin Press, 2010.

Chodorow-Reich, Gabriel, et al. "Cash and the economy: Evidence from India's demonetization." *The Quarterly Journal of Economics* 135, no.1, (2020): 57-103.

Coe, Sophie D. and Michael D. Coe. *The True History of Chocolate*. London: Thames and Hudson, 2019.

Commonwealth Bank Act of 1929. Federal Register of Legislation. Australian Government. https://www.legislation.gov.au/1929A00031/latest/text.

Cooper, Richard N., et al. "The Gold Standard: Historical Facts and Future Prospects." *Brookings Papers on Economic Activity* 1982, no. 1, (1982): 1–56.

Coquidé, C., Lages, J. & Shepelyansky, D.L. Prospects of BRICS currency dominance in international trade. *Applied Network Science* 8 65 (2023).

Dalton, George. "Primitive Money." *American Anthropologist* 66, (1965): 44–65.

Darr, Alan P. "The Medici and the Legacy of Michelangelo in Late Renaissance Florence: An Introduction." In *The Medici, Michelangelo, and the Art of Late Renaissance Florence*, New Haven: Yale University Press 2002.

David-West, Olayinka, et al. "Diffusion of Innovations: Mobile Money Utility and Financial Inclusion in Nigeria. Insights from Agents and Unbanked Poor End Users." *Information Systems Frontiers : A Journal of Research and Innovation* 24 no. 6, (2021): 1753–1773.

Davies, Glyn. *A History of Money: From Ancient Times to the Present Day.* Cardiff: University of Wales Press, 2002.

Davis James T. "Trade Routes and Economic Exchange Among the Indians of California." *University of California Archaeological Survey Reports* 54, (1961).

De Roover, Raymond. *The Rise and Decline of the Medici Bank, 1397-1494.* Cambridge: Harvard University Press, 1963.

Devereux, Michael B, et al. "Oil Currency and the Dollar Standard: A Simple Analytical Model of an International Trade Currency." *Journal of Money, Credit, and Banking* 42, no. 4, (2010): 521–550.

Diocletian. "Diocletian's Edict of Maximum Prices." Forum Ancient Coins. https://www.forumancientcoins.com/ Numiswiki/view.asp?key=Edict%20of%20Diocletian%20 Edict%20on%20Prices.

Edvinsson, Rodney, Tor Jacobson, Daniel Waldenström, eds. *Sveriges Riksbank and the History of Central Banking.* Cambridge: Cambridge University Press, 2018.

Eibl-Eibesfeldt, R.K. Hitchcock. "On Subsistence and Social Relations in the Kalahari." *Current Anthropology* 32, (1991): 55-57.

Eichengreen, Barry. "Global imbalances and the Lessons of Bretton Woods." *Economy International* 4, no. 100, (2004): 39-50.

Ellen, Roy F. "The Trade in Spices." *Indonesia Circle* 5 no. 12, (1977): 21-25.

Elliott, Colin P. "The Acceptance and Value of Roman Silver Coinage in the Second and Third Centuries AD." *The Numismatic Chronicle* 174, (2014): 129-152.

Elliott, Francis. "Chancellor on brink of second bailout for banks." *The Financial Times,* January 3, 2009.

Eusebius of Caesarea. *Life of Constantine.* Oxford: Oxford University Press, 1999.

Fauvelle, Mikael. *Shell Money: A Comparative Study.* Cambridge: Cambridge University Press, 2024.

Fazzini, Marco, Luigi Fici, Alessandro Montrone, and Simone Terzani. "A Modern Look At The Banco De' Medici: Governance And Accountability Systems In Europe's First Bank Group." *International Business & Economics Research Journal* 15, no. 6, (2016): 271-286.

Ferguson, Niall. *The Ascent of Money: A Financial History of the World.* London: Penguin Books, 2008.

Financial Stability Institute (FSI) (2023): "Crypto, tokens and DeFi: Navigating the Regulatory Landscape" *FSI Insights on policy implementation*, no 49, May.

Finley, Moses. *The Ancient Economy.* Berkeley: University of California Press, 1974.

Fitzpatrick, S. "Banking on Stone Money." *Archaeology* 57, no.2, (2004): 18-23.

Fitzpatrick, Scott M., and Quetta Kaye. "Rai Stones: The Social Value of a 20th Century Micronesian Stone Money." *Economic Anthropology* 4, no. 1, (2017): 98-115.

Flood, J. *The Moth Hunters: Aboriginal Prehistory of the Australian Alps.* Canberra: Australian Institute of Aboriginal Studies, 1980.

Forbes, BC "Men Who Are Making America." *Leslie's Weekly*, Oct. 19, 1916. https://archive.org/downloadmenwhoaremakinga00for/menwhoaremakinga00for.pdf

Forbes, Kristin J. "Strengthening Banking Systems: Lessons from Around the World and Across the Ages." *Trabajo presentado en la Conferencia sobre Reforma Estructural de la APEC*, 2004.

Franco, Pedro. *Understanding Bitcoin: Cryptography, Engineering and Economics.* New York: Wiley & Sons, 2014.

Franklin, Benjamin. *The Autobiography of Benjamin Franklin.* New York: Simon & Schuster, 2004.

Friedman, Milton. "Bimetallism Revisited." *Journal of Economic Perspectives* 4 no. 4, (1990): 85-104.

Fritzner, Yan. *Inventing Bitcoin.* Self-published, 2019.

Fuller, Bruce. *Organizing Locally: How the New Decentralists Improve Education, Health Care, and Trade.* Chicago: The University of Chicago Press, 2015.

Furness III, William Henry. *The Island of Stone Money: Yap of the Carolines.* Philadelphia: J.B. Lippincott Company, 1910.

Galbraith, John Kenneth. *Money: Whence It Came, Where It Went.* Princeton: Princeton University Press, 1975.

Gensheimer, Thomas R. "The role of Shell in Mesopotamia: Evidence for Trade Exchange with Oman and the Indus Valley." *Paléorient* 1984, pp. 65-73.

Gentle, Paul F. "Stone money of Yap as an Early Rorm of Money in the Economic Sense." *Financial Markets Institutions and Risks* 5 no. 2, (2021): 114-119.

Goetzmann, William N. *Money Changes Everything: How Finance Made Civilization Possible.* Princeton: Princeton University Press, 2016.

Goldberg, Linda, and Cedric Tille. "Macroeconomic Interdependence and the International Role of the Dollar." *Journal of Monetary Economics* 56, no. 7, (2009): 990-1003.

Goldthwaite, Richard A. "The Medici Bank and the World of Florentine Capitalism." *Past and Present* 114: 3-31, February 1987.

Goodwin, Frederick. *The XII Tables.* London: Stevens & Sons, 1886. https://avalon.law.yale.edu/ancient/twelve_tables.asp.

Gordon, Robert J. "The !Kung in the Kalahari exchange: An Ethnohistorical Perspective," 195-224. *Past and Present in Hunter Gatherer Studies.* London: Routledge, 2016.

Gortsos, Christos V. "On the Cypriot 2012-2013 Banking Crisis and the 2013 Banking Resolution." *Banking & Finance Law Review* 38, (2022): 271-284.

Gowa, Joanne. *Closing the Gold Window: Domestic Politics and the End of Bretton Woods*. Ithaca: Cornell University Press, 2019.

Goyal, P., Chakrabarti, A. "Banking the Unbanked: The Fintech Revolution." *Intelligent Engineering and Management for Industry 4.0* edited by Y.H. Kuo, et al. Springer, 2021, pp. 91-105.

Grable, J., Kwak, E.J. and Archuleta, K. "Distrust of Banks Among the Unbanked and Banked." *International Journal of Bank Marketing* 41, No. 6, (2023): 1498-1520.

Graeber, David. *Towards an Anthropological Theory of Value*. London: Palgrave, 2001.

Greene, Claire, and Oz Shy. "Unbanked Consumers and How They Pay." Journal of Economics and Finance 48, (2024): 186-195.

Griffin, Edward. The Creature from Jekyll Island: A Second Look at the Federal Reserve. 3rd ed. Appleton, WI: American Media, 1998.

Gwertzman, Bernard "'Milestone' Pact Is Signed By U.S. and Saudi Arabia," *New York Times*, last modified June 9, 1974. https://www.nytimes.com/1974/06/09/.

Hage, Per, et al. "Wealth and Hierarchy in the Kula Ring." *American Anthropologist* 88, no. 1, (1986): 108–15.

Hall, John Whitney. *Government and Local Power in Japan, 500 to 1700: A Study Based on Bizen Province*. Princeton: Princeton University Press, 1966.

Hamilton, Alexander. "Final Version of the Second Report on the Further Provision Necessary for Establishing Public Credit (Report on a National bank)." National Archives. https://founders.archives.gov/documents/Hamilton/01-07-02- 0229-0003.

Hanson, Victor David. *The Second World Wars: How the First Global Conflict Was Fought and Won*. New York : Basic Books, 2020.

Harl, K.W. *Coinage in the Roman Economy: 300 BC to AD 700*. Baltimore: Johns Hopkins University Press, 1996.

Hayek, Friedrich A. von. *The Road to Serfdom*. London: Taylor and Francis, 2006.

Hayek, Friedrich A. von. *Individualism and Economic Order*. Chicago: University of Chicago Press, 1966.

Hazlitt, Henry. *Economics in One Lesson: The Shortest and Surest Way to Understand Basic Economics*. New York: Crown Currency, 2010.

Head, Barclay Vincent. *The Coinage of Lydia and Persia; from the Earliest Times to the Fall of the Dynasty of the Achaemenidae*. London: Trübner, 1877.

Herodotus. *Herodotus: the Histories*. New York: Penguin Books, 1996. Hetzel. Robert L. *The Monetary Policy of the Federal Reserve: A History*. Cambridge: Cambridge University Press, 2008.

Heizer Robert F. "Trade and Trails," 690–693. In *Handbook of North American Indians 8, California,* Washington, DC: Smithsonian Institution, 1978.

Helleiner, Eric. *States and the Reemergence of Global Finance: from Bretton Woods to the 1990s*. Ithaca: Cornell University Press, 1996.

Hénaff, Marcel. "Is There Such a Thing as a Gift Economy?", 71-84. In Gift Giving and the 'Embedded' In *Economy in the Ancient World,* edited by Filippo Carlà and Maja Gori. Heidelberg: Universitätsverlag, 2014.

Hetzel, Robert L. *The Monetary Policy of the Federal Reserve: A History.* Cambridge: Cambridge University Press, 2008.

Holland, Tom. *Persian Fire: The First World Empire and the Battle for the West.* New York: Doubleday, 2006.

Hollingsworth, Mary. *The Family Medici: The Hidden History of the Medici Dynasty.* London: Pegasus Books, 2018.

Horesh, Niv. "Cannot Be Fed On When Starving: An Analysis Of The Economic Thought Surrounding China's Earlier Use Of Paper Money." *Journal of the History of Economic Thought* 35, no 3, (2013): 373-395.

Horwitz, Stephen. *Austrian Economics: An Introduction.* Washington, DC: Cato Institute, 2010.

Jackson, Andrew. President Jackson's Veto Message Regarding the Bank of the United States, July 10, 1832. https://avalon. law.yale.edu/19th_century/ajveto01.asp.

Jarrett, J.A. "Small Change and Big Changes: minting and money after the Fall of Rome." Unpublished, (2015). https:// eprints.whiterose.ac.uk/90089/.

Jefferson, Thomas. "Opinion on the Constitutionality of the Bill for Establishing a National Bank, 15 February 1791." National Archives. https://founders.archives.gov/ documents/Jefferson/01-19-02-0051.

Justinian, Caesar Flavius. *The Institutes of Justinian.* Translated by J. B. Moyle. Oxford: Oxford University Press, 1913. http:www.gutenberg.org/ebooks/5983.

Kamran, Sohail and Outi Uusitalo. "Banks' Unfairness and the Vulnerability of Low-Income Unbanked Consumers." *The Service Industries Journal* 39, no. 1, (2019): 65–85.

Kauṭalya. *The Arthashastra*. London: Penguin Books India, 1992.

Keynes, John Maynard. *The General Theory of Employment, Interest and Money*. New York: Macmillan, 1936. https://www.hetwebsite.net/het/texts/keynes/gt/gtcont.htm.

Kinney, Alexander B. "Embedding into an Emerging Money System: The Case of Bitcoin." *Sociological Focus* 54, no. 1 (n.d.): 77–92.

Kirch, Patrick Vinton. *The Wet and the Dry: Irrigation and Agricultural Intensification in Polynesia*. Chicago: University of Chicago Press, 1994.

Knafo, Samuel. "The Gold Standard and the Origins of the Modern International Monetary System." *Review of International Political Economy* 13, no. 1, (2006): 78-102.

Kroeber, A. L. "Handbook of the Indians of California." *Bureau of American Ethnology Bulletin* 78, (1925).

Lamoreaux, Naomi R, and Ian Shapiro, editors. *The Bretton Woods Agreements : Together with Scholarly Commentaries and Essential Historical Documents*. New Haven: Yale University Press, 2019.

Landa, Diego de. *Landa's Relación de las cosas de Yucatan: A Translation*. New Haven: The Peabody Museum, 1941.

Laughlin, J. Laurence. "The Gold Standard in Japan. " *Journal of Political Economy* 5, No. 3, (1897): 378-383.

Lee, Richard Borshay. "The Hunters: Scarce Resources in the Kalahari," 73-86. In *Conformity and Conflict: Readings In Cultural Anthropology*, 14th ed, edited by James Spradley, David McCurdy, and Dianna Shandy, Pearson, 2012.

Lewis, John David. *Nothing Less Than Victory: Decisive Wars and the Lessons of History*. Princeton: Princeton University Press, 2010.

Liu ZZ, Papa M. *Can BRICS De-Dollarize the Global Financial System?* Cambridge: Cambridge University Press; 2022.

Lopez, Ana. "Revenue in the travel & tourism market in El Salvador 2018-2028. *Statista Research Department*. Feb 27, 2024 https://www.statista.com/statistics/1397821/ revenue-travel-tourism-market-el-salvador/.

Madison, James. "Draft Veto of the Bank Bill," National Archives. https://founders.archives.gov/documents/ Madison/01-13-02-0295.

Madison, James. "The Bank Bill, [2 February] 1791." National Archives. https://founders.archives.gov/ documents/Madison/01-13-02-0282.

Madison, James. "Annual Message to Congress Washington December 5, 1815. Fellow Citizens of the Senate and of the House of Representatives." https://founders.archives.gov/documents/Madison/03-10-02-0061.

Markham, Jerry W. 2015. *A Financial History of Modern U.S. Corporate Scandals: From Enron to Reform*. London: Taylor and Francis.

Martin, Thomas R and John. Lescault. *Ancient Greece: From Prehistoric to Hellenistic Times*. Ashland: Blackstone Publishing, 2017.

Massie, Suzanne. *Trust but Verify: Reagan, Russia, and Me*. Rockland, ME: Maine Authors Publishing, 2013.

Matsaganis, Manos. "Making sense of the Greek Crisis, 2010–2016," 49-69. In *Europe's Crises*, edited by Manuel Castells et al. New York: Wiley & Sons, 2018.

McCullough, David. *John Adams*. London: Simon & Schuster, 2002.
Melitz, Jacques. "A Model of the Beginnings of Coinage in Antiquity." *European Review of Economic History* 21, no. 1, (2017): 83–103.

Metcalf, William E. *The Oxford Handbook of Greek and Roman Coinage.* Oxford: Oxford University Press, 2016.

Minas, Renate, Sharon Wright, and Rik van Berkel. "Decentralization and Centralization." *International Journal of Sociology and Social Policy* 32, no. 5-6 (2012): 286–98.

Minsky, Hyman P. *Stabilizing an Unstable Economy.* New York: McGraw-Hill, 2008.

Mises, Ludwig von. *The Theory of Money and Credit,* trans. H.E. Batson. Indianapolis: Liberty Fund, 1981.

"Money." *Merriam-Webster.com Dictionary*, Merriam-Webster, https://www.merriam-webster.com/dictionary/money.

Morris, John C. "Whither Fema? Hurricane Katrina and FEMA's Response to the Gulf Coast." *Public Works Management & Policy* 10, no. 4 (2006): 284–94.

Mundell, Robert A. "The Birth of Coinage." *Columbia University Department of Economics Discussion Paper Series*, 102, no. 08, (2002).

Menger, Carl. Principles of Economics. Glencoe, Ill: Free Press, 1950.

Naik, Jimuta. "Beginning of the Early Banking Industry in Mesopotamia Civilization from 8th Century BCE," *Social Science Research Network*, 2014.

Nakamoto, Satoshi. "Bitcoin: A Peer-to-Peer Electronic Cash System." Bitcoin.org, 2008. https://bitcoin.org/ bitcoin.pdf.

Nakamoto, Satoshi. "Cypherpunks online forum post." P2P Foundation, 2009. https://p2pfoundation.ning.com/forum/topics/bitcoin-open-source.

Nakamoto, Satoshi. Email to Mike Hearn. April 23, 2011. https://pastebin.com/syrmi3ET.

Newton, Isaac. Isaac Newton to the Lords Commissioners of the Treasury, October 22, 1718. The Newton Project. https://www.newtonproject.ox.ac.uk/view/texts/normalized/NATP00282.

Nixon, Richard. "Address to the Nation Outlining a New Economic Policy: The Challenge of Peace." American Presidency Project. https://www.presidency.ucsb.edu/ node/240602.

Oxford English Dictionary (OED) Online, s.v. "money." https://www.oed.com/view/Entry/85068#eid271209335.

Office of the Historian. "Memorandum of Conversation." Washington, June 6, 1974, United States-Saudi Arabian Cooperation. https://history.state.gov/historicaldocuments/frus1969-76ve09p2/d111.

Pacioli, Luca. *Ancient Double-Entry Bookkeeping: Lucas Pacioli's treatise (A.D. 1494 - The Earliest Known Writer on Bookkeeping)*. Denver: John Geijsbeek, 1914. https://archive.org/details/ancientdoubleent00geijuoft.

Patel, Pankaj C., and Marcus T. Wolfe. "Of Free Markets and a Secular Mind: The Value of Economic Decentralization and Individual Secular Values in Entrepreneurship." *Small Business Economics: An Entrepreneurship Journal* 58, no. 1 (2020): 93–119.

Payten, F. "The festival of the Bugong moth." Letter to A. S. Le Soeuf, 15 June 1949.

Pearson, Michael Naylor, ed. *Spices in the Indian Ocean World*. London: Routledge, 2017.

Pihl, Christopher. "A Bank in a Monarchy: An Early Modern Anomaly? The Swedish Bank of the Estates of the Realm." *Scandinavian Journal of History*, 49, no.1, (2024): 1-23.

Polo, Marco. *Marco Polo: The Travels,* trans. Nigel Cliff, London: Penguin, 1974. https://archive.org/details/thetravelsbymarcopolo.

Popov, Vladimir. "US Dollar Is Losing It Position of a Reserve Currency: How the BRICS Development Bank Can Ensure the Soft Landing." *Social Science Research Network*, (August 20, 2023).

Radbod, Shahrzad T. "Craigslist-A case for criminal liability for online service providers?." *Berkeley Technology Law Journal* 25, no. 1 (2010): 597-615.

Raker, Ethan J., and Tyler Woods. "Disastrous Burdens: Hurricane Katrina, Federal Housing Assistance, and Well-Being." *RSF: The Russell Sage Foundation Journal of the Social Sciences* 9, no. 5 (2023): 122–43.

Rand, Ayn. *For the New Intellectual*. New York: Signet, 1961.

Ravitch, Diane. *Left Back A Century of Battles over School Reform*. New York: Touchstone, 2000.

Redish, Angela. *Bimetallism: An Economic and Historical Analysis*. Cambridge: Cambridge University Press, 2000.

Rodney, Edvinsson, et al. "Introduction." Sveriges Riksbank and the History of Central Banking," 1–25. *Studies in Macroeconomic History,* edited by Rodney Edvinsson, et al. Cambridge: Cambridge University Press, 2018.

Rothbard, Murray. *Man, Economy, and State.* Auburn, AL: Ludwig von Mises Institute, 2009. https://mises.org/online-book/ man-economy-and-state-power-and-market.

Roosevelt, Franklin D. "Executive Order 6102." https://archive.org/details/pdfy-MHvlymfJYU05yELW/mode/2up.

Roth, Martha. *Law Collections of Ancient Mesopotamia and Asia Minor.* Atlanta: Society of Biblical Literature, 1995.

Safer, J.F. & Gill, F.M. *Spirals from the Sea: An Anthropological Look at Shells.* New York: Clarkson Potter, 2012.

Sanders, J. 1998. "Linux, Open Source, and Software's Future." *IEEE Software* 15 (5): 88–91.

"Satoshi." Bitcoin Talk Forum. December 12, 2010. https:// bitcointalk.org/index.php?topic=2228.msg29479#ms29479.

Schaps, David M. *The Invention of Coinage and the Monetization of Ancient Greece.* Ann Arbor: University of Michigan Press, 2004.

Sehgal, Kabir. *Coined: The Rich Life of Money and How Its History Has Shaped Us.* New York: Grand Central Publishing, 2015.

Sharpes, Donald K. *Education and the US Government.* London: Routledge, 2020.

Simmel, Georg. *The Philosophy of Money,* trans. Tom Bottomore and D. Frisby. London: Routledge and Kegan Paul, 1978.

Singh, Anjana. "Early Modern European Mercantilism and Indian Ocean Trade," 245–262. *Maritime Power Networks in World History,* edited by Rolf Strootman, Floris van den Eijnde, and Roy van Wijk Pages. New York: Brill, 2019.

Skaricic, Ana-Maria. "Uncharted Waters: The BRICS Expansion and Implications." *Policy Brief. European Policy Center.* (2023).

Smith, Adam. *An Inquiry into the Nature and Causes of the Wealth of Nations.* London: Nelson and Sons, 1852. https://www.gutenberg.org/ebooks/3300.

Solórzano, R. A. R. . "Money before Coinage. History of Pre-Columbian Currency." *Revista Procesos De Mercado* 13, no. 2, (2016): 411-27.

Statista Research Department. "Homicide rate in El Salvador from 2014 to 2023." May 22, 2024. https://www.statista.com/statistics/696152/homicide-rate-in-el-salvador/.

Stephenson, B., David, B., Fresløv, J. et al. "Year-old Bogong moth (Agrotis infusa) Aboriginal Food Remains, Australia." *Scientific Reports* 10, no. 22151, (2020).

Stojanović, Biljana. "Monetary Stability: The Byzantine Model" *Megatrend Review* vol. 231, 2006, pp. p. 57-88.

Stuenkel, Oliver. *The BRICS and the Future of Global Order.* Kanham, MD: Lexington Books, 2020.

Suetonius. "The Life of Augustus, Book XXIX." and "Tiberius Nero Caesar, Book XLVIII," *The Complete Works of Suetonius,* trans. Alexander Thomson. East Sussex, England: Delphi Classics, 2016. https://archive.org/details/1thecompleteworksofsuetonius.

Szopinski T. "Who Is Unbanked? Evidence from Poland." *Contemporary Economics* 13, no. 4, (2019): 417–426.

Tacitus. *Complete Works of Tacitus.* Edited by Alfred John Church and William Jackson Brodribb. New York: Random House, 1942.

Temen, Peter. "The Economy of the Early Roman Empire." *The Journal of Economic Perspectives* 20, no. 1 (2006): 133-151.

Thabang E. Mofokeng, Steven Mbeya, and Daniel K. Maduku. "Bitcoin Adoption in Online Payments: Examining Consumer Intentions and Word-of-Mouth Recommendations." *Future Business Journal* 10, no. 1 (2024): 1–30.

Thornton, M.K. and R.L. Thornton. "The Financial Crisis of A.D. 33: A Keynesian Depression?" *The Journal of Economic History* 50, no. 3 (1990): 655-662.

Totman, Conrad. *Early Modern Japan.* Berkeley: University of California Press, 1993.

Tsebelis, George. "Lessons from the Greek crisis." *Journal of European Public Policy* 23, no.1, (2016): 25-41.

Tzilla Eshel, Ayelet Gilboa, Ofir Tirosh, Yigal Erel, Naama Yahalom-Mack. "The Earliest Silver Currency Hoards in the Southern Levant: Metal trade in the Transition from the Middle to the Late Bronze Age." *Journal of Archaeological Science* 149, (2023).

United States Congress. "Specie Resumption Act," 296. *The Statutes at Large and Proclamations of the United States of America*, vol. XVIII, part 3, (1873-1875).

United States Congress. "Chap. XLIV.—Jin Jlct to incorporate the subscribers to the Bank of the United States," *Fourteenth Congress. Sess. I.* Ch. 44. 1816. https://fraser.stlouisfed.org/files/docs/historical/congressio nal/second-bank-united- states.pdf.

United States Congress. "Emergency Banking Relief Act," March 9, 1933. https://fraser.stlouisfed.org/title/1098,.

Van De Mieroop, Marc. *A History of the Ancient Near East, ca. 3000-323 BC.* London: Blackwell, 2015.

Verboven, Koenraad. "Demise and Fall of the Augustan Monetary System," 245-257. In *Crises and the Roman Empire*. New York: Brill, 2007.

Verhagen, Hendrik L. E. *Security and Credit in Roman Law: The Historical Evolution of Pignus and Hypotheca*. Oxford: Oxford University Press, 2022.

Villalonga, Joan Rosselló. 2018. "Fiscal Centralization: A Remedy for Corruption?" *SERIEs: Journal of the Spanish Economic Association* 9 no. 4 (2018): 457–74.

Von Mises, Ludwig. *Human Action: A Treatise on Economics*. Third edition. Washington, DC: Henry Regnery Company, 1966.

Walker, Francis Amasa. *International Bimetallism*. New York: Holt, 1896.

Wallace, Robert W. "The Origin of Electrum Coinage." *American Journal of Archaeology* 91, no. 3, (1987): 385–97.

Walter, Yoshija. "The Centrality of a Digital Strategy for Societal and Business Innovations." *Digital Transformation and Society* 2, no. 1 (2023): 27–41.

Warburg, Paul M. *The Federal Reserve System. Its Origin and Growth. Reflections and Recollections*. New York: Macmillan, 1930.

Ward, Susie Violet. "Bitcoin Vs. Gold And Stocks: How To Compare Bitcoin To Traditional Assets." *Forbes*, Aug 14, 2023. https://www.forbes.com/sites/digital-assets/2023/08/14/Bitcoin-vs-gold-and-stocks-how-to-compare- bitcoin-to-traditional-assets/?sh=2a5d82624d76.

Weatherford, Jack. *The History of Money*. New York: Three Rivers Press, 1997.

Williams, Jason A. *Bitcoin: Hard Money You Can't F*ck With*. Self-published, Going Parabolic Publishing, 2020.

Wong, Paul and Jesse Leigh Maniff. "Comparing Means of Payment: What Role for a Central Bank Digital Currency?" https://www.federalreserve.gov/econres/notes/feds-notes/comp Aring-means-of-payment-what-role-for-a-central-bank-digital-currency-20200813.html. *f* appendiox

Xue Ding, Wenxin Shen, and Shiai Wang. 2024. "Centralized or Decentralized? Communication Network and Collective Effectiveness of PBOs: A Task Urgency Perspective." *Buildings* 14 (2): 448.

Yang, Bin. "The Rise and Fall of Cowrie Shells: The Asian Story." *Journal of World History* 22, no. 1, (2011): 1-25.

Yang, Liansheng. *Money and Credit in China: A Short History*. Cambridge: Harvard University Press, 1952.

Yellen, John E. "The Transformation of the Kalahari !Kung." *Scientific American* 262, no. 4, (1990): 96–105.

Zapata Rotundo, Gerardo J. "Centralized Organizations and Intrinsic Rewards: A Study in Medium Business." *Contabilidad Y Negocios: Revista Del Departamento Académico de Ciencias Administrativas* 11 no. 22 (2016): 123–36.

Zhao, Linhai, and Ehsan Rasoulinezhad. "Role of Natural Resources Utilization Efficiency in Achieving Green Economic Recovery: Evidence from BRICS Countries." *Resources Policy* 80, (2023).

Index

About the Authors

Deanna Heikkinen is a writer, educator and homeschool advocate. Her profound passion for a liberty-minded, classical approach to education has guided her career and her writing. With advanced degrees in education, history, and anthropology, Deanna's educational philosophy is deeply rooted in the principles of classical education, emphasizing the importance of primary sources, classic literature, and the Great Books. Her approach is not just about imparting knowledge but nurturing free-thinking individuals who appreciate the intellectual heritage of humanity. She is

Using *Shells to Satoshi* as a foundation, Deanna is also authoring children's book as well as online courses for elementary through high school levels on the history of money and Bitcoin. Deanna first learned about Bitcoin in 2011 and has slowly fallen down the rabbit hole. Deanna and her husband, Joel, moved to El Salvador in 2023 to live on a Bitcoin standard and start a classical education tutoring and Bitcoin education company, Lyceum Tutoring. She currently co-hosts the Bitcoin Daily Show's Wednesday 101 Space on Twitter (X) .

Joel Marquez is a long-time Bitcoiner, first hearing about the technology in 2011. Although losing his coins in a fluke accident off the coast of California, he continues to advocate and educate friends and family about Bitcoin. After moving to El Salvador in 2023, Joel picked up his pen once again and has been working on a Bitcoin novel as well as collaborating on *Shells to Satoshi*. Joel has a degree in humanities where he has developed a deep understanding of storytelling and the human experience, which he puts to use in his writing. After graduating from film school, he worked on small budget films and has also written scripts and treatments for small projects.

Joel spent several decades working in technology where he helped people in the building industry transition from paper to technology on the job site. With his tech-savvy mind and his excellent teaching skills, he became a valuable asset to many businesses looking to modernize their workflow. Through it all, Joel has remained committed to his writing, continuing to create powerful stories that connect with audiences on a deep, emotional level. He is co-host for the Bitcoin Daily Show's Wednesday 101 Space on Twitter (X).

Thank You and Resources

Thank you for reading our book. You can find all the primary sources mentioned in the book on our website, https://www.shellstosatoshi.com/sources

Join our mailing list to get updates on the book, other writing projects, history of money and Bitcoin courses for elementary through high school levels, and our appearances on podcasts and conferences. https://www.shellstosatoshi.com

www.ingramcontent.com/pod-product-compliance
Lightning Source LLC
Chambersburg PA
CBHW030915090426
42737CB00007B/202